PACIFIC CONFLUENCE

AMERICAN CROSSROADS

Edited by Earl Lewis, George Lipsitz, George Sánchez, Dana Takagi, Laura Briggs, and Nikhil Pal Singh

PACIFIC CONFLUENCE

Fighting over the Nation
in Nineteenth-Century Hawaiʻi

CHRISTEN T. SASAKI

UNIVERSITY OF CALIFORNIA PRESS

University of California Press
Oakland, California

© 2022 by Christen T. Sasaki

A prior version of chapter 1 was previously published in Christen T. Sasaki, "Emerging Nations, Emerging Empires," *Pacific Historical Review* 90, no. 1 (2021): 28–56. Portions of chapter 3 were previously published in Christen T. Sasaki, "How the Portuguese Became White: The Racial Politics of Pre-Annexation Hawaiʻi," in *Pacific America: Histories of Transoceanic Crossings*, edited by Lon Kurashige (Honolulu: University of Hawaiʻi Press, 2017), 213–28.

Library of Congress Cataloging-in-Publication Data

Names: Sasaki, Christen T., 1978– author.
Title: Pacific confluence : fighting over the nation in nineteenth-century Hawaiʻi / Christen T. Sasaki.
Other titles: American crossroads ; 69.
Description: Oakland, California : University of California Press, [2022] | Series: American crossroads ; [69] | Includes bibliographical references and index.
Identifiers: LCCN 2022020915 (print) | LCCN 2022020916 (ebook) | ISBN 9780520382756 (cloth) | ISBN 9780520382763 (paperback) | ISBN 9780520382770 (epub)
Subjects: LCSH: Settler colonialism—Hawaii—19th century. | Nationalism—Hawaii—History—19th century. | Hawaii—Politics and government—19th century.
Classification: LCC DU627.2 .S37 2022 (print) | LCC DU627.2 (ebook) | DDC 996.9/02—dc23/eng/20220527
LC record available at https://lccn.loc.gov/2022020915
LC ebook record available at https://lccn.loc.gov/2022020916

31 30 29 28 27 26 25 24 23 22
10 9 8 7 6 5 4 3 2 1

For Mom and Dad

Contents

List of Illustrations ix

Acknowledgments xi

Author's Note on Hawaiian Language Usage xv

Introduction 1

1. Emerging Nations, Emerging Empires: Interimperial Intimacies and Competing Settler Colonialisms in Hawai'i 25

2. At the Borders of Nation and State: The 1894 Constitutional Convention 51

3. How the Portuguese Became White: The Search for Labor and the Cost of Indemnity 79

4. The Shinshu Maru Affair: Barred Landings and Immigration Detention 106

5. Historicizing the Homestead in Wahiawa Colony: From "American Family Farm" to Industrial Plantation Economy 132

Conclusion 163

Notes 171

Bibliography 223

Index 235

Illustrations

MAPS

1. Asia, the Pacific, and North America   3
2. Portugal, Madeira, the Azores, and the Cape Verde Islands   90
3. Wahiawa Colony, 1899   143

FIGURES

1. King David Kalākaua   15
2. Issei arriving in Honolulu, 1893   27
3. Members of Hui Aloha 'Āina o Nā Kane, ca. 1893   28
4. Members of Hui Aloha 'Āina o Nā Wāhine, ca. 1893   29
5. The Japanese cruiser *Naniwa* docked in Honolulu Harbor   39
6. Queen Lili'uokalani attending Queen Victoria's Golden Jubilee, 1887   56

7. "Lili to Grover," cover of *Judge*, February 17, 1894   59
8. Manuel and Eugenia Reis at home in Honolulu, 1936   94
9. Quarantine station as seen from a ship, ca. 1912   109
10. People on Kamokuʻākulikuli, or "Quarantine Island," ca. 1895   130
11. Hawaiian Pineapple Company field laborers   157
12. Pineapple trimmers   159

Acknowledgments

OVER THE decade that it has taken to complete this book, I have been lucky to have the support of a large community of family, friends, and colleagues. Anything that is good in this work comes from them.

I was fortunate to receive funding from a number of programs and institutions including the Terasaki Center for Japanese Studies at the University of California, Los Angeles; the UCLA Asian American Studies Center; the UCLA Department of History; and the Office of Research and Sponsored Programs at San Francisco State University.

My dissertation committee provided vital support for this project that extended well beyond my years at UCLA. I wish to thank my late advisor, Janice Reiff, for her encouragement and belief in this book. I am so lucky to have spent time with such a generous scholar. I am grateful that William Marotti took in this Americanist. I would not have completed this book were it not for the constant and continued support of Keith L. Camacho.

Numerous people improved this book through conversations and comments on chapter drafts. So much gratitude goes to Emily Anderson and Todd Honma for reading countless versions of each chapter. Your comments helped me to see the stakes of this project and articulate ideas that at times felt unmanageable. JoAnna Poblete, Simeon Man, and Erin Kahunawaikaʻala Wright provided crucial feedback that guided my revisions. Through the generous support of the Social Sciences Division at the University of California, San Diego, I was able to host a manuscript workshop and bring together the amazing minds of Augusto F. Espiritu, Noelani Goodyear-Kaʻōpua, Simeon Man, and Wendy Matsumura. Todd Honma did the hard work of facilitating the event in the midst of a pandemic. Each of these scholars generously offered detailed notes and generative conceptual thoughts that helped me turn my dissertation into a manuscript.

I was lucky to find a collective of graduate students at UCLA who quickly became family. Alexandra Lewis Carter, Roger Chung, Eurie Chung, Steve Hosik Moon, Tadashi Nakamura, and Phuong Tang made me laugh so hard I cried. I'll always cherish the hours we spent together in the grad lounge at Campbell Hall. A big thank you goes to fellow history graduate students, Stephanie Amerian, Heather Daly, Linda Frank, Revere Greist, Lisa Hsia, Jason Marshall, Sasha Nichols, Erika Perez, Rosemary Pollock, Patrick Sharma, Aaron Silverman, Precious Singson, and Karen Wilson. Juliann Anesi, JP deGuzman, Alfred P. Flores, Brandon J. Reilly, Kēhaulani Vaughn, and Joyce Pualani Warren welcomed me into their intellectual collective. I am eternally grateful for our friendship and shared vision.

My colleagues at the University of Hawaiʻi, West Oʻahu, SFSU, and UCSD have been a major source of support for this book. Special thanks to Leilani Basham, Laureen Chew, Joyce Chinen, Jayson Chun, Yến Lê Espiritu, Kei Fisher, José Fusté, Linda Furuto, Dayo Gore,

Russell Jeung, Andrew Jolivette, Ben Kobashigawa, Mai-Nhung Le, Jonathan Lee, Dawn Bohulano Mabalon, Eric Mar, Amy Nishimura, Eric J. Pido, Alan Rosenfeld, Anantha Sudhakar, Amy Sueyoshi, Erin Suzuki, Allyson Tintiangco-Cubales, Wesley Ueunten, K. Wayne Yang, and Grace J. Yoo. I am grateful to be part of a writing group at UCSD with Theresa Ambo, Ross Frank, Curtis Marez, Kiana Middleton, Shaista Patel, Roy Pérez, and Shelley Streeby. Thanks as well to the AAPI History Group for providing me with a space to share my work and gather such rich feedback.

Through the conversations that we've had over shared meals and across different conferences over the years, many people have helped to sharpen this book's arguments and have offered timely support. Special thanks to Eiichiro Azuma, Tracy Buenavista, Gordan Chang, Constance Chen, Catherine Ceniza Choy, Cati V. de los Rios, William Deverell, Candace Fujikane, Jordan Beltran Gonzales, Vernadette Vicuña Gonzalez, Michie Hirooka, Lauren Hirshberg, Madeline Hsu, Justin K. Ichida, David Igler, Mariko Iijima, Lon Kurashige, Roderick Labrador, Maxwell Leung, Valerie Matsumoto, Andrea Mendoza, MyLinh Nguyen, Franklin Odo, Mark Padoongpatt, Christine Quemuel, Jeanette Roan, Dean Saranillio, Charles Sepulveda, Laith Ulaby, Kathryn Walkiewicz, Susie Woo, Judy Tzu-Chun Wu, David Yoo, Mari Yoshihara, Henry Yu, and James Zarsadiaz. My Friday afternoon pandemic writing group partners, Dana Nakano and Todd Honma, have been an emotional and intellectual lifeline.

Research for this book would not have been possible without the support of the archivists and staff at the Bishop Museum, the Hawai'i State Archives, the Hawaiian and Pacific Collection at the Hamilton Library, the Huntington Library, and the National Archives. Adhann Iwashita was a tremendous help in the archives and made finishing this project during the pandemic possible. Thank you as well to Clara Hur at the Hawai'i State Archives and Krystal Kakimoto at the Bishop Museum for your unending patience and assistance with locating sources. Many thanks to David Kump for sharing stories and photos of his great-grandparents, Manuel and Eugenia Reis. Jo-Lin Lenchanko Kalimapau, Thomas Joseph Lenchanko, and members of the Hawaiian Civic Club of Wahiawā made this work so much stronger by sharing their knowledge of place with me.

It has been a pleasure to work with Niels Hooper, Naja Pulliam Collins, Stephanie Summerhays, and the rest of the staff at the University of California Press. I owe a debt of gratitude to Erin Kahunawaikaʻala Wright, who in addition to giving valuable feedback, also provided ʻōlelo Hawaiʻi editing. Many thanks to Megan Pugh, Caroline Knapp, and David Martinez, whose editorial insights made this a better book. Thank you as well to Michael Pesses for creating such wonderful maps.

I am thankful to have grown up in Hawaiʻi, the place that has graciously sustained myself and my family for generations. I am profoundly grateful to my most recent ancestors Grandma Mildred Tatsuko Sasaki, Grandpa Raymond Toshiaki Sasaki, Grandma Barbara Tsuyako Kameda, and Grandpa Donald Akio Kameda. The stories they shared of their experiences growing up sparked my interest in history. Aaron, you are the best little brother. Sam, what a journey this has been. Thank you for humoring me and taking Kina on her multiple daily walks. Your support has made a world of difference to me. I dedicate this book to my parents, Mark and Diane Sasaki. Thank you for making it possible for me to follow my dreams. *Okagesama de.*

Author's Note on Hawaiian Language Usage

WHILE IT is not my intent, purpose, or role to determine style, it is important for me to carefully outline the ways in which I utilize ʻōlelo Hawaiʻi (Hawaiian language) as a nonspeaker to provide the reader with clarity on ʻōlelo Hawaiʻi spelling throughout this book, especially when there are variations; be as accurate as possible when drawing from archival resources where pronounication markers are absent; and prioritize the use of ʻōlelo Hawaiʻi in ways that contribute to the perpetuation of the language. The conventions applied in this book were informed by similarly oriented resources using ʻōlelo Hawaiʻi in English-language contexts as well as in conversation with kumu ʻōlelo Hawaiʻi. Any mistakes in understanding this guidance are mine alone.

For the purposes of this book, the following conventions are used:

- Spellings in ʻōlelo Hawaiʻi using orthography and English translations were borrowed from resources such as Mary Kawena Pukui and Samuel H. Elbert's *Hawaiian Dictionary: Hawaiian-English, English-Hawaiian* (1986 edition) and Mary Kawena Pukui, Samuel H. Elbert, and Esther T. Mookini's *Place Names of Hawaiʻi* (1974 edition). For more information, readers should refer to these and other ʻōlelo Hawaiʻi resources readily available online and in print.
- ʻŌlelo Hawaiʻi from archival resources is written here as it was originally recorded.
- Unless quoting directly from archival resources, the names of Kanaka Maoli historical figures, organizations, places, and commonly known songs include pronunciation markers if applicable.

It is important to note that ʻōlelo Hawaiʻi is a living language and may shift in spelling and pronunciation.

INTRODUCTION

AT MIDNIGHT on January 7, 1895, Robert William Kalanihiapo Wilcox and a band of one hundred men quietly climbed the slopes of Lēʻahi (Diamond Head) with their rifles in hand.[1] Positioned on the sides of the 760-foot crater, they waited out the night under the light of a nearly full moon. Two years earlier an oligarchy led by haole (white/foreign) elites had staged an illegal coup with hopes of US annexation. Wilcox's group of royalists and loyalists was part of a larger force that had organized a counterrevolution, the 1895 Kaua Kūloko, in order to depose the haole-led oligarchy and reinstate Queen Liliʻuokalani.[2]

As the sun rose, Wilcox and his group spied a growing number of "republic" troops gathering a few miles away at Kapiʻolani Park. Several hours later Sanford Dole, president of the Republic of Hawaiʻi, the coup government, declared martial law over the archipelago. By three o'clock that afternoon the tugboat *Eleu*, outfitted with one of the republic's three cannons and several snipers, was steaming along Lēʻahi's coastline firing grapeshot at royalist forces. Under constant fire and with the republic militia on their tail, Wilcox and his troop retreated through Palolo Valley and headed into the lush forests of Mānoa, Pauoa, and Nuʻuanu.[3] On January 14, 1895, after a week of fighting, they surrendered to coup state forces in Kalihi Valley.

Roughly four hundred people were taken as prisoners for allegedly supporting the counterrevolution.[4] While most of those arrested were Kanaka Maoli (Native Hawaiian), the list of incarcerees also included those who came from Portugal, Macedonia, Denmark, Germany, Great Britain, China, and Japan.[5] The group's makeup reflected just how cosmopolitan Hawaiʻi's population was. In fact, the haole elites who had staged the coup were a definite minority, working to remake the islands under a white supremacy that—as the counterrevolution makes clear—was not a foregone conclusion.

One of the political prisoners taken in the aftermath of the 1895 Kaua Kūloko was Portuguese subject Manoel Gil dos Reis, known in Hawaiʻi as Manuel Reis. He was the licensed owner and driver of a carriage for hire in Honolulu. After spending five weeks in Oahu Prison, Reis was freed on February 13, 1895, never having been charged with a crime.[6] Following his release, Portugal filed an indemnity claim on Reis's behalf, which the coup state refused to meet. As a result of this political impasse, the Portuguese monarchy decided to halt all emigration to Hawaiʻi beginning in 1896. Following their failed 1893 attempt at US annexation, the coup government had hoped to recruit more Portuguese laborers to boost the islands' white population, but they were not willing to cede to the demands of the waning Portuguese empire. Without that labor supply, the oligarchs turned to other methods to shore up their own settler colonial power, and, they hoped, secure annexation by the United States.

How did the imprisonment of one carriage driver lead to the cessation of all emigration from the Portuguese empire to Hawaiʻi? This

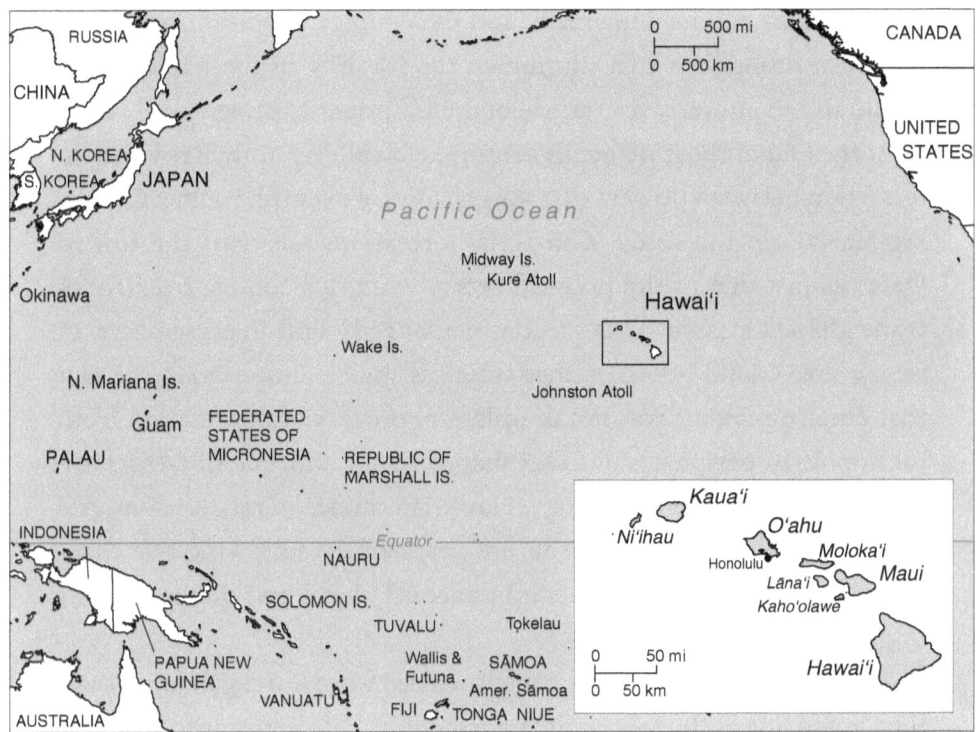

Map 1. Asia, the Pacific, and North America. Map by Michael Pesses.

question articulates the methodology driving the following historical study. By pairing the intimate and epic together in critical juxtaposition, *Pacific Confluence: Fighting over the Nation in Nineteenth-Century Hawai'i* reveals the unstable nature of both the coup state and US empire itself. The period between the illegal overthrow of the Hawaiian Kingdom and US annexation (1893–98) is often framed as an inevitable step of American expansion—but it was never a foregone conclusion. Kānaka Maoli support for restoration of the monarchy combined with their tactical use of international law, for example, exposed the haole-led oligarchy as an embodiment of countersovereignty and threw US annexation into question.[7] Rethinking Hawai'i's relevance to late nineteenth-century imperial formations demonstrates that US empire in the Pacific is not a history of unmitigated expansion. Rather, episodes such as Reis's call for indemnity and the counterrevolution constitute historical flashpoints that illuminate the fragility of the haole-led republic and the unresolved nature of the US imperial project.

At the end of the nineteenth century, Hawaiʻi lay at the crowded intersection between powers that sought control over the Pacific. Centering Hawaiʻi in the study of imperial formations positions the United States as just one of the political actors vying for control over an already global Oceania. This "decontinentalized" shift in perspective, in which the "island becomes that which is main," emphasizes the fact that empire making was not a unilateral process of domination from metropole to periphery, but was shaped by a multitude of factors, including settler colonial ideology, Hawaiian modes of relationship, and interimperial dynamics.[8] To this end, each of the following five chapters analyzes events that are simultaneously local and global in their origins and ramifications.

The stories of Oʻahu-based constituencies from Portugal, Japan, and the United States show how the intersections between transpacific imperial formations and local politics of jurisdiction revealed the nation-state to be a category of contingent and contentious practice. When Kānaka Maoli and racialized workers on the boundaries of the body politic sought to mitigate their own exploitation by the structures of colonialism and capitalism, their actions became entangled with the processes of nation-state formation and gave rise to questions that both challenged and informed ideas of state-based rights and jurisdiction. Their struggles became legible in the colonial archive as diplomatic concerns, and as such, much of the impact of their acts of dissent was erased.

Although the global significance of the Hawaiian archipelago to nineteenth-century political formations had been obscured by the ongoing US occupation, that is beginning to change thanks to the work of practitioners who are able to incorporate the large volume of historical material in ʻōlelo Hawaiʻi (Hawaiian language).[9] This book builds on their work, recovering episodes from colonial records while foregrounding Hawaiʻi-based events and communities, thereby bringing the realities of the archipelago's simultaneous colonial, interimperial, and sovereign existence into the same frame. The result is a study that extends beyond recounting world powers' actions in Hawaiʻi, to consider imperialism from the other direction. This island-based perspective illustrates not just the role that Hawaiʻi played in the political imaginary of Japan, Portugal, and the United States, but also emphasizes how Hawaiian articulations of political independence impacted the making of the modern Pacific world.[10]

The strategies and structures of late nineteenth-century empire making in Hawaiʻi, embodied in the reactive form of the coup government, were not exceptional. But pausing on each episode covered here illuminates how settler colonialism works broadly, while also emphasizing the ways it might fail. For although the calls for indemnity by a single Portuguese carriage driver may not have been deemed noteworthy by the haole-led oligarchy, reading to connect individual maneuvers with their chain of global repercussions reframes this action as a flashpoint that revealed the fiction of the coup state. Despite their attempt to create a nation-state that was recognized the world over, haole oligarchs were never able to quell the realities of Hawaiian political independence and relationship with place, or eliminate alternative rhetorics of nationhood.

As a historical form, the nation-state has been and continues to be enmeshed with empire, emerging from and depending upon the conquest of new territories.[11] From the sandalwood trade of the 1800s, to the massive industrial plantations of the twentieth century, and the tourism and military industries that currently dominate Hawaiʻi's economy, capitalism has been a driving force behind the occupation of the archipelago. Yet in late nineteenth-century Hawaiʻi, competing definitions of nation and state emerged in ways that were *incommensurate* with a capitalist nation-state. The episodes detailed in the following chapters complicate the relationship between nation and empire: the actions of poʻe aloha ʻāina (Hawaiians working to maintain their political autonomy), Meiji officials, haole oligarchs, Portuguese diplomats, and Issei (first generation Japanese) settler laborers alike challenged emerging nation-states and their increasingly pronounced forms of capitalism and imperialism, with questions over who held the power of state-based jurisdiction in places beyond territorial borders and who was "worthy" of protection. Perhaps most importantly, the histories collected here push us to think beyond the confines of "nation building as empire building" to explore how various articulations of the nation, as embodied within a people and their connection to place, were and are being used as a political and oppositional strategy against imperial state encroachments.

METHODOLOGICAL APPROACHES

I begin with my positionality as a fourth-generation Japanese settler, born and raised in Mānoa, Oʻahu, because it serves as a reminder that I must never lose sight of settler colonial conditions or the privileges I derive from them.[12] I also acknowledge the limits of *Pacific Confluence* due to my lack of command of the Hawaiian language, which means I rely primarily on translations and English-language sources. Through this work I endeavor to situate diasporic Asian and Indigenous histories in conversation with each other, and to contribute to current discussions around place-based decolonial nation-building by considering how an expansive understanding of sovereignty was, can be, and is being defined and imagined to include modalities outside of Westphalian state-based forms. For as Robert Allen Warrior so eloquently explains, if the "path of sovereignty is the path to freedom," then that freedom is not the "standard, western sort of freedom which can be immediately defined and lived. Rather, the challenge is to articulate what sort of freedom as it ʻemerge[s] through the experience of the group to exercise the sovereignty which they recognize in themselves.'"[13]

Like other recent scholarship located at the intersections of Indigenous and Asian American Studies, *Pacific Confluence* approaches the US nation-state as a product of settler colonialism.[14] It starts from the premise that the theft of Indigenous land and attempt to obscure alternative worldviews is facilitated by the settler state's self-proclaimed right to govern collective life. Extending this analysis to Hawai'i is especially relevant given the continued forms of structural violence that Kānaka Maoli persist against today, including the desecration of their sacred sites, dispossession of their land, low life expectancy, and disproportionately high rates of incarceration.

This is a work of history grounded in the perspective of those living within the whirlwind of political, social, and cultural upheaval of late nineteenth-century Hawai'i. It maintains that the subjugation and oppression of Kānaka Maoli and Asians serves as the foundation of US colonialism in the archipelago.[15] Although both communities suffered extensively under the structures of racial capitalism and white supremacy, Kānaka Maoli continue to endure the loss of the land and resources from which their very culture emanates. My intent here is not to minimize the exploitation that Asians in Hawai'i experienced or compare it to the consequences of occupation and imperialism that Kānaka Maoli persist against. Instead, I approach this history with the understanding that there is a significant difference when this violence occurs in one's homeland and that any conversation about thinking and moving together must begin with the recognition of the Kānaka Maoli right to land stewardship in Hawai'i.

While we must never sidestep the fact that Asian settler communities have often served as the agents and "brokers" of empire, we can also cultivate dialogue around overlapping histories of imperial expansion and oppression.[16] To that end, *Pacific Confluence* centers Hawai'i in the history of imperial rivalry for the "Pacific" in order to open up space to step beyond the structures of white supremacy and engage with the many intellectual and sociopolitical connections that Indigenous and

Asian communities shared. By placing these histories together in complex unity, I hope to engender opportunities for new lines of inquiry that allow, in Dean Itsuji Saranillio's formulation, different "historical and geopolitical forms of oppression to be understood as interdependent in ways that produce possibilities outside of the constrained logics of U.S. empire."[17]

In order to demonstrate that articulations of the nation-state were constructed relationally through the processes of colonization and the resultant questions of jurisdiction that arose in the imperial Pacific, I trace the global and local debates that surrounded the overthrow of the Hawaiian Kingdom through three distinct framings. Each one highlights the tensions that developed around the shifting scope of state power for the Hawaiian Kingdom, the coup government, and the Meiji, Portuguese, and US empires. The first framing reveals how each of the multiple regimes of power negotiated with the others the boundaries of state jurisdiction in the islands. The second juxtaposes the debates occurring among Kanaka Maoli, Japanese, and Portuguese communities in Hawai'i as they contested imposed definitions of citizenship and state jurisdiction. The third connects Hawai'i-based debates over racially defined national belonging to ongoing conversations in the United States.

To better understand the complexity and contingency of this era, I read across multiple archives throughout Hawai'i and the continental United States. While the bulk of my research comes from the US National Archives and the Hawai'i State Archives, understanding these sources as the "supreme technology" of late nineteenth-century empire informs my methodology of reading them as a roadmap to anxieties of the state.[18] The documents I examined reflect the ability, and lack thereof, of developing state mechanisms to monitor the boundaries of the nation. But I was more interested in how governments thought about those who challenged these imagined communities. What did it mean to the haole-led oligarchy, for example, to be called out for violating international law by Kānaka Maoli? What did it mean to Meiji oligarchs to be called on for protection by a Hawai'i-based Issei plantation laborer who would not have merited any consideration at home?

I am also interested in how those living under these conditions negotiated and navigated their lives. I turn to local and national newspaper collections, personal journals, and oral histories not merely to fill the gaps of the colonial archive, but to ascertain how these subjects understood the world and their place in it. Many of the people I track are visible for only a few moments before they slip back into illegibility. But the traces they left behind offer a glimpse of what nation-state-making looked like for those caught in the confluence of empires.

Following Epeli Hau'ofa's theoretical intervention of an interconnected Oceania, this book emphasizes Hawai'i's position as a site of confluence in order to underscore the voices of historically marginalized communities and reveal their role in shaping ideas of nation and state that circulated through networks made possible by the conditions of empire.[19] "Confluence" is used as an organizing theme in order to accentuate the plurality of social relations that those living in Hawai'i were embedded within, while also leaving room to intentionally highlight relationships that activated specific state reactions. Through the events covered here I question how competing imperial ambitions played out in the intimate scale of the body, and consider the ways in which communal ways of being in the world, such as ties to land, water, and kinship networks, were reduced to a state-based bureaucratic identity in order to be made legible and disciplined.

Within the last decade, historical scholarship has moved toward re-visioning Asian American, Pacific Islander, and US history within the context of a transpacific "oceanic turn."[20] Such studies focus primarily on diasporic communities, and the choices individuals made to move above and between the confines of bounded nation-states. One of the main arguments laid out in the chapters that follow complicates this understanding of the "transpacific" by considering how people lived *within* borders as well as across them, not just to evade the control of the state, but also to engage with it in order to remake it.

At the turn of the twentieth century, the regime of international law and diplomacy functioned to establish and reinforce a global order based on the sovereign nation-state. This was a structure that Kānaka Maoli understood well, as the monarchy had been engaging in acts of international relations for over a century.[21] In the years following the coup, Queen Liliʻuokalani and poʻe aloha ʻāina repeatedly used the theater of international diplomacy to claim the right of state-based sovereignty as a tactic of "national defense" against those who wished to usurp the Hawaiian monarchy. Although this did not result in the immediate reinstatement of the queen, it continues to work to reveal the coup state as an act of countersovereignty, or the reactionary assertion of sovereignty by the settler state.[22]

The desires, dreams, and actions of those based in ko Hawaiʻi Pae ʻāina (the Hawaiian archipelago) played a crucial role in determining a modern transpacific order that produced and reproduced forms of racial difference adherent to competing state-based regimes. For those living in this space where no one polity reigned supreme, the world was in flux. While haole oligarchs fought to convince a country still reeling from the failure of Reconstruction that annexation of an archipelago with a majority nonwhite population was in their best interest, Liliʻuokalani publicly argued for political independence through the regime of international law. As part of its imperial ambitions, the Meiji government grew increasingly interested in its growing emigrant population, while the waning Portuguese empire tried unsuccessfully to negotiate with the coup state on behalf of its subjects. The attempts to make sense out of this period of instability and rupture by those caught in the confluence of empires are often overlooked by scholars of US history and the Pacific world. Yet as the accounts explored here attest, Hawaiʻi's interimperial condition pushed nation-states, the United

States in particular, to define their boundaries in response to measures taken by communities residing on the margins.

This island-based perspective, which has yet to be fully utilized in the study of nation-state and empire making, challenges the teleological narrative of the "imperial Pacific." Rather than approaching the archipelago as a simple crossover point for migrant labor, capital, and commodities, this book issues a call to pause and examine closely a particular moment in Hawai'i's history that holds a larger story about the precarious grounds on which the modern transpacific order was created.[23] As its title suggests, this is a book about confluence. But it is also about the insidiousness of US imperialism and its collaborator, white supremacy. For while the annexation of Hawai'i was by no means a forgone conclusion in 1893–1898, *Pacific Confluence* analyzes how imperialism functioned, and continues to function, as a contingent and fluid process—one that responded, reacted, and adapted to the trials presented.

What lessons does this history hold for those currently engaged in anti-imperial struggle? Conducting research on events that occurred in a place and time where the sociopolitical future was so uncertain facilitates an engagement with the multitude of possibilities that existed and still endure today. The seeds of these alternative futures are planted throughout the era this work explores. The chapters that follow challenge us to see the nation-state as just one form of historical consciousness so that we might be free to envision nonstatist approaches to decolonization and a future that resides outside of the logics of empire.

CHANGING ARTICULATIONS OF NATION AND STATE

Navigating the intertwining histories of land loss and the path taken to access political power by white American and European elites underscores the importance of a Hawaiian concept of nationhood as grounded in the relationship between place and people.[24] Haole elite attempted to break the Hawaiian mode of relationship to place by altering the land tenure system and implementing a structure of privatized land ownership. This in turn served as the requisite for suffrage in the coup state, ensuring that it functioned to bolster the interests of the minority, haole-led oligarchy.[25]

The current academic analysis of colonization tends to privilege European and American definitions of sovereignty and the nation-state.[26] Writing from an island-centered perspective brings alternative formulations into focus. According to Jonathan Kay Kamakawiwoʻole Osorio, for Kānaka Maoli, concepts of nation and state are rooted in social, cultural, and political understandings of order under the aupuni system, which require the maintenance of pono (righteous balance) between all things: Akua (gods), aliʻi (chiefs), makaʻāinana (commoners), and the ʻāina (land) itself.[27] Osorio explains that the idea of the nation-state is complicated because of the "various ways that we might define the word . . . . For the haole that word can mean country, its government, or the people it rules. But for Hawaiians, two words are necessary to convey the meaning of nationhood: aupuni, the government established by Kamehameha, and lāhui, which means gathering, community, tribe, and people."[28]

By the late nineteenth century, Kānaka Maoli "understood how the state had come to symbolize their very survival as a people."[29] If, as Mae Ngai contends, the modern nation-state's "ultimate defense is sovereignty—the nation's self-proclaimed, absolute right to determine its own membership, a right believed to inhere in the nation-state's very existence," then, for Kānaka Maoli, in addition to kinship and genealogy, ea (political independence) is linked to the communal care of place.[30] Noelani Goodyear-Kaʻōpua explains that as an expansive principle, ea confounds the arbitrary distinction between politics and culture to encompass both independence and interdependence. She writes, "Ea refers to political independence and is often translated as 'sovereignty' (but) it also carries the meanings of 'life' and 'breath' . . . . Unlike Euro-American philosophical notions of sovereignty, ea is based on the experiences of people on the land, relationships forged through the process of remembering and caring for wahi pana, storied places."[31]

In order to strategically engage with the practices of the outside world, aliʻi often sought out knowledge of foreign nations.[32] By the 1820s, they were using this knowledge to oversee an increasingly heterogenous society that included not just makaʻāinana, but also foreign sailors, merchants, and missionaries.[33] Beginning in the 1840s, aliʻi began to selectively incorporate the Euro-American concept of state-based law in order to assert a kingdom that would enable Kānaka Maoli to be seen as rightful rulers by encroaching colonial powers and negotiate the demands of foreign communities residing in the archipelago.[34] It was not until this decade that ea became associated with state-based forms of sovereignty.[35]

In 1842 Kauikeaouli (King Kamehameha III) sent diplomats to meet with representatives from the United States, France, and Britain in order to acquire their recognition as a sovereign state. The November 28, 1843 recognition of the Hawaiian Kingdom as an independent state by both Britain and France was declared a national holiday—Lā Kūʻokoʻa (Independence Day).[36] Through this agreement, Lorenz Gonschor writes, "Hawaiʻi became the first, and for many decades, only non-Western state to be recognized as a coequal member of the Family of Nations," a status that would become even more important in the second half of the nineteenth century.[37]

Kauikeaouli also promulgated the nation's first constitution during the 1840s, which "asserted a Christian nation to protect the common people" and officially defined the terms of citizenship and naturalization.[38] The naturalization procedure was opened to all Asians living in Hawaiʻi under the first two monarchical constitutions.[39] Under pressure from American and British business interests, in 1846 the monarchy implemented a statute that recognized the category of "denizen," which allowed specially "favored aliens" to retain their foreign citizenship while also giving them access to the rights and privileges of Hawaiian citizen-subjects.

As white American and European elites increased their economic investment in Hawai'i, they intensified their efforts for the privatization of land and further inclusion in the government with little legal accountability. Although Protestant Christian missionaries advocated for privatized land ownership through claims of cultivating a "disciplined work ethic" among the Indigenous population, many also saw the potential for economic profit in the islands. With the onset of the 1848 Māhele (land division), land was made available for large-scale private ownership to Hawaiian citizen-subjects.[40] By 1850 restrictions on citizenship and other rights for foreigners had all but collapsed. In July of that year, all foreigners who were not naturalized, including Asians, were granted the right to own and sell lands in fee.[41] Just three weeks later the monarchy granted the right to vote to all men ages twenty and over who were subjects of the Hawaiian Kingdom, native-born and naturalized, as well as denizens—provided they had lived in the kingdom for at least a year, and were "neither insane nor unpardoned felons."

While a number of scholars have identified the Māhele as a form of exploitation that led to the alienation of maka'āinana from the land, societal breakdown, and later colonization, others have argued that the Hawaiian Kingdom implemented it with a different and more strategic goal: it was designed to empower Kānaka Maoli through facilitating the transition from the land tenure system to one that would allow for capitalist development. This work proceeds from the understanding that the Māhele enabled broad ownership of land and did not prevent the massive alienation of Kānaka Maoli.[42] Following the passage of the 1864 Constitution, which placed stringent property and literacy requirements on the franchise, many Kānaka Maoli lost access to the ballot box.[43] Ultimately these changes to law and access to land altered the way nation and state functioned in Hawai'i as a majority of Kānaka Maoli were stripped of their voting rights, and only a handful of the resident Chinese population met the property requirements necessary to command the right to vote.[44]

Figure 1. King David Kalākaua. Courtesy of Hawai'i State Archives.

THE HAWAIIAN KINGDOM AND THE UNITED STATES

During his seventeen-year reign from 1874 to 1891, King David Kalākaua dedicated himself to his motto, "Hoʻoulu Lāhui" (to grow/perpetuate the nation), by calling for a rise in Indigenous leadership and supporting the revitalization of traditional Hawaiian practices. As part of his strategy to assert and preserve the Hawaiian Kingdom's political independence, he skillfully used well-established diplomatic methods, such as the exchange of orders with world leaders, to set up reciprocal and symbolic relationships throughout the global arena.[45] Thanks to his intense diplomatic activity, by 1887 the Hawaiian Kingdom maintained 103 legations and consuls worldwide.⁴⁶ In 1881 Kalākaua became the first monarch to circumnavigate the world—a fact that made global headlines and brought him into contact with political leaders throughout Asia and Oceania. Using the connections he had formed on his travels, Kalākaua attempted to establish a pan-Oceanian and Asian polity as a way to harness the collective strength of the region and enhance the kingdom's global position.⁴⁷

Despite Kalākaua's efforts to fortify the Hawaiian Kingdom and calls by the Hawaiian community for leadership to remain in Indigenous hands, haole opposition to the monarchy's control grew. Haole elite agitated for the creation of a white settler state that would facilitate the installation of a new US-led transpacific order. On July 6, 1887, participants of the Hawaiian League, a group of men which included Lorrin Thurston, a third-generation American missionary descendant, and Sanford Dole, held the king at gunpoint and forced him to sign a new constitution.⁴⁸ This document, known as the "Bayonet Constitution," stripped the monarchy of its political power, solidified an oligarchy made up of a majority white American planters and businessmen, and gave control of the military to the haole-dominated legislature.⁴⁹ In essence, the 1887 Constitution solidified the connection between the development of the haole-led state and the production of racial difference adherent to competing state-based regimes.

Along with restrictive property, racial, language, and gender qualifications, the 1887 Constitution gave electoral rights to men who were residents, as opposed to citizen-subjects of the kingdom. This paved the way for US citizens to vote in Hawai'i's elections, while a large sector of the Indigenous electorate was excluded. Asians, who had formerly been included as citizen-subjects with the right to vote, were disenfranchised as "aliens."⁵⁰ In other words, after 1887, even if a Japanese or Chinese man previously had the franchise, owned property, was naturalized, or was born as a citizen-subject of the Hawaiian Kingdom, he would not have voting rights. Justice Sanford Dole summarized the situation succinctly when he explained in his 1892 Hawai'i Supreme Court opinion in the matter of *Ahlo v. Smith*, that the 1887 Constitution "substituted the race requirement for the old condition of citizenship."[51]

When Kalākaua passed away in January 1891, the Crown transferred to his sister, Lili'uokalani. Members of the Hawaiian Patriotic Leagues, which included Hui Aloha 'Āina, sister organization Hui Aloha 'Āina o Nā Wāhine, and Hui Kālai'āina (Hawaiian Political Association), launched a massive petition drive to urge the queen to promulgate a new constitution and secured the signatures of sixty-five hundred registered voters—two-thirds of the electorate.[52] In response, Lili'uokalani attempted to instate a new constitution that would restore the monarchy's power by limiting suffrage to men who had taken an oath of allegiance to the Hawaiian Kingdom. Leaders of the former Hawaiian League, now renamed the Committee of Thirteen, who included prominent American planters, merchants, and American Board of Commissioners for Foreign Missions (ABCFM) descendants, understood that if the queen were to regain political power their economic investments in the islands would be at risk.[53] With the kingdom's sugar industry already suffering from the McKinley Tariff of 1891, this group decided to take matters into their own hands and instigated the coup.[54]

On January 17, 1893, members of the Committee of Thirteen, with the aid of the Honolulu Rifles, US Marines, and US Minister to Hawai'i, John L. Stevens, overthrew Lili'uokalani and established a provisional coup government.[55] The next day, the "revolutionaries," with the backing of the US troops, took over the capital. That afternoon they announced the abrogation of the monarchy and the establishment of a provisional government until annexation by the United States could be negotiated. Within an hour of the proclamation's reading, US Minister Stevens recognized the government and extended official diplomatic recognition. Other nations, with the exception of Japan, did the same. Across the archipelago, po'e aloha 'āina immediately began organizing in protest.

The attempt to create a US-backed white settler state in Hawai'i sparked a turn-of-the-century debate over race-based nationalism, state-based sovereignty, and state-based jurisdiction that was fought on the global stage. What this book makes clear is that when approached from a Hawai'i-centered point of view, US empire in the Pacific becomes just one of a myriad of possibilities that was available at this particular historical and geographic juncture. Members of the oligarchy expected an easy incorporation into the United States, but they soon discovered that in 1893 the US government had not yet come to terms with an imperial overseas agenda.[56] In spite of overwhelming protests and petitions from Kānaka Maoli and from island-based Asian communities, leaders of the provisional government and its successor, the "Republic of Hawai'i," continued their attempt to exert sociopolitical control over the archipelago in hopes of enhancing their chance at annexation. In doing so they facilitated the reordering of state power through the production and reproduction of racial difference articulated through processes such as voting rights and access to land. One of the many ways that the queen and po'e aloha 'āina responded was by creating and circulating protest materials in both 'ōlelo Hawai'i and in the language and custom of the Western colonizer. They did this in order to counter the haole-led oligarchy's claim to moral action based on the "uncivilized nature" of Indigenous rule. Based on prior history, when faced with the coup, Lili'uokalani had reason to believe that she would be restored to power and her opposition punished.[57]

NAVIGATING THE BOOK

This book moves chronologically in five chapters, with each exploring how the trappings of the "civilized" late nineteenth-century state—international recognition, white settlement, and the incarceration of nonwhite people—played out. In March 1893, an Issei prisoner, Yosaku Imada, escaped from Oahu Prison by swimming to the *Naniwa*, a Meiji warship docked in Honolulu Harbor that had been sent there following the overthrow. This situation presented the coup government with one of its first diplomatic entanglements. At the time of Imada's escape, the newly formed provisional government had no extradition treaty with Japan. As a vessel of war, the *Naniwa* carried its national sovereignty on board. While government officials from Japan, the provisional government, and the United States debated over whether Imada should be returned to Oahu Prison, Hawaiʻi-based Issei rallied for voting rights in the islands. This movement for Issei franchise magnified the impact of Imada's escape and annexationists pointed to both situations as proof of the Meiji "menace." By placing these two events together within the same frame, chapter 1 reveals how the alignment of interimperial dynamics with competing settler colonialisms in Hawaiʻi shaped the United States' and Japan's articulations of nation-statism.

Indigenous articulations of state-based sovereignty and reactions against it were crucial to competing imperial projects in the archipelago. While diplomats debated over the return of Imada and Japanese voting rights in the provisional government, Kānaka Maoli were purposefully constructing arguments that incorporated Western understandings of state-based sovereignty into their claims for political independence. Together with the queen, the Hawaiian Patriotic Leagues used the regime of international law to disprove the haole-led oligarchy's claim to moral action.

These efforts by poʻe aloha ʻāina, combined with white anxiety over Hawaiʻi's demographics, were enough to prevent the United States from rapidly annexing the archipelago. Oligarchs in charge of the coup government hoped to change that by holding a constitutional convention in 1894 and declaring a "Republic of Hawaiʻi." But in order to legitimize the coup state, oligarchs first had to acknowledge the primacy of the Hawaiian monarchy and nation that they denounced, all but admitting the illegality of their own takeover. What's more, those at the margins of the coup state—including Kānaka Maoli, Asians, and women of both white and Indigenous descent—lobbied for voting rights in ways that exposed the oligarchy's anxious dedication not to democracy, but to white dominance. These actions compelled the haole-led oligarchy to negotiate the rights associated with national membership within an interactive transpacific community. Ultimately, chapter 2 demonstrates that the defensive discourse of the constitutional convention revealed not the sanctity and integrity of the republic, but the growing settler anxiety around the unfinished colonial project in the archipelago.

Following the creation of the republic, Lorrin Thurston, one of the haole leaders of the oligarchy, attempted to manipulate Hawai'i's demographics to align with the race-based nationalism favored in the United States. Such a change, Thurston and other oligarchs thought, would facilitate US annexation of the islands. Chapter 3 examines the efforts to racialize the islands' Portuguese community as white, as well as the simultaneous search in Portugal for an alternative white European labor source against the backdrop of the 1895 Kaua Kūloko.

As a population that hailed from a European empire, the Portuguese in Hawai'i had greater political and social freedoms than Asians, including the right to vote. Yet during the nineteenth century, the Portuguese, like other Catholic European immigrants, were far from being considered unambiguously "white," and faced an Anglo Saxon-based nativist movement focused on reducing the Pope's influence on the world. As such, they were often likened to Blacks and other ethnic minorities, and shut out of the upper echelons of US society. To add to this conundrum, a majority of Hawai'i's Portuguese community did not come from the European continent, but hailed from the islands of Madeira, Cape Verde, and the Azores—three of Portugal's colonies off the coast of Africa. Many white Americans, both on the continent and in Hawai'i, believed that these Portuguese, in particular, were "barbaric others" who constituted a threat to the sanctity of Anglo Saxon civilization.[58] Thurston, however, sought to bring the interpolating power of the emerging US empire to racialize these Portuguese laborers as white—and, in so doing, whiten the islands' population. His efforts to recruit more Portuguese labor fell apart when, in the wake of the 1895 counterrevolution and the resultant indemnity case of Manuel Reis, Portugal halted emigration to Hawai'i. By weaving together Thurston's quest for a racially malleable labor source with the history of the 1895 counterrevolution and Manuel Reis's indemnity case, chapter 3 demonstrates how white supremacy not only shaped empire, but was in turn influenced by transpacific empire building.

As chapter 4 details, by 1897, the republic was trying not just to recruit newly "white" populations, but also to deny the entrance of nonwhite others. In spring of that year, it barred the landings of three Meiji ships, the *Shinshu Maru*, *Kinai Maru*, and *Sakura Maru*, and detained a majority of those on board. In the four years since the overthrow, Japan had emerged as a power to be reckoned with. Although the Meiji state had begun its imperial formation in the 1860s, in 1895 Japan shocked the world with a military victory over China. This global development, combined with the explosive increase of Japanese "free migration" to Hawai'i, further exacerbated the fears of coup government leaders who were worried about Meiji imperial ambitions.

Republic officials attempted to wield border patrol as a method to maintain white supremacy and state power in Hawai'i by limiting the growth of the Japanese population. Their strategy also entailed prolonged detainment in order to create an inflated sense of impending racial peril that would forward their annexationist cause. Unfortunately for the haole-led oligarchy, the Meiji government turned to the regime of international law, via the 1871 Treaty of Amity and Commerce with the Hawaiian Kingdom, to fortify their argument for the release of the Japanese detainees. One of the unintended consequences of this action was the reinforcement of the Hawaiian Kingdom's state-based sovereignty and the consequent fallacy of the coup state's mode of political authority. When Japanese Foreign Minister Shigenobu Ōkuma cited the 1871 treaty in order to prove that Japanese were privy to the same privileges as the citizens or subjects of any other nation, his argument also inherently contended that treaties made and recognized through international diplomacy, like those made between the Meiji emperor and King Kamehameha V, superseded those of the republic.[59]

The final chapter carries *Pacific Confluence*'s thematic concerns forward by advancing a historicized account of "Wahiawa Colony," one of the few settlements that emerged out of Sanford Dole's 1895 island-based "homesteading" plan. Following the implementation of the coup state, Dole made major changes in Hawai'i's land policy, which he felt was undermining the likelihood of annexation by the United States. In an effort to cultivate an "American space" that demonstrated an island population suited for annexation, Dole passed the Land Act of 1895. He hoped that this law, which combined the Crown and Government Lands into the category of "Public Lands," and made them available to citizens and denizens in parcels of six hundred to one thousand acres through general leases, cash freehold, or right of purchase lease, would create a large, family-anchored, white agrarian community in the archipelago.[60]

In January 1898 Byron O. Clark, a white American agriculturalist from Altadena, California, secured the rights to a 1,350-acre plot of "homestead land" in Wahiawā, O'ahu. In August 1898, thirteen white American settler families left San Francisco for Wahiawā, bringing with them livestock, farm equipment, and plant cuttings. Contrary to Dole's hope for small family farmers working to cultivate "Anglo-Saxon ideas of family life," members of the Wahiawa Colony constituted the first systematic effort made on O'ahu by a settler association to grow a variety of crops and fruit solely for commercial purposes. The Wahiawa Colony experiment proved to be short lived—by 1939 many of the original colonists had either sold their land or simply defaulted on their payments and returned to California. But the land that was designated for colony settlement was turned over to another iteration of settler colonialism: the industrial pineapple plantation. During the first half of the twentieth century, as pineapple cultivation merged with the structures of settler colonialism already in play in the colony, Wahiawā grew to become the pineapple production capital of the world.

By placing Wahiawa Colony within the context of continental dispossession and the oligarchy's sustained effort to possess Hawai'i's Government and Crown Lands, chapter 5 underscores the coup state's connections to a larger transpacific project of racialized state violence and the structures of settler colonialism. The recreation of a particular imaginative geography in Wahiawā, that of the empty frontier primed for white settlement, helped to normalize one of the ongoing functions of the US imperial project in the islands: attempting to break the Hawaiian connection to place and, consequently, their claims to political independence.

Pacific Confluence approaches history as a critical endeavor of the present and aims to create a space in which scholars of the Pacific world, Oceania, and US empire can reflect on and see beyond current political formations that seem inevitable, necessary, and natural. Approaching Hawai'i as a site of interimperial dynamics, competing settler colonialisms, and developing nationalisms allows this work to question how the meeting—and sometimes, clash—of ideas that occurred between Kānaka Maoli, and Japanese, Euro-American, and Portuguese transients and settlers, both influenced and defied articulations of state-based sovereignty and jurisdiction—concepts that most consider inevitably commensurate with the modern nation-state. One of the arguments that this book makes when thinking about the deliberate use of state-based definitions of sovereignty as political and rhetorical strategy by Kānaka Maoli, for example, are the discursive ways that nonstatist and statist conceptualizations of the nation-state map on to each other. As an expansive idea and practice, ea has multiple meanings that include but also exceed state-based forms of sovereignty. The episodes covered in the following chapters demonstrate that engaging with Hawaiian and other ways of conceptualizing the nation-state presents the possibility of denaturalizing its fixity as a political form. This perspective opens up space to imagine alternative ways of being in relationship with each other and all that surrounds us, engage with other possibilities and futures that are rooted in Indigenous worldviews, shift from ways of life based in a capitalistic neoliberal state to one grounded in communitarian ethos, and ultimately, move from subjugation to liberation and freedom.

Most of the incidents in this book occur within a single decade, but if we think of Hawaiʻi's history in terms of the *longue durée*, Western colonial rule and occupation are not logical outcomes—they are disruptive events.[61] How might understanding the present occupation of Hawaiʻi as historical rupture open up possibilities for different sociopolitical formations and futures? This is the question that lies at the heart of this work. Since colonization relies on forced forgetting and erasure, the need to bring the past forward into our consciousness is ongoing.[62] It is my hope that by looking back to this history we will find alternative worldviews and solidarities based on relations to people and place that allow for a future beyond the settler-based nation-state.

1

EMERGING NATIONS, EMERGING EMPIRES

Interimperial Intimacies and Competing Settler Colonialisms in Hawaiʻi

ON MARCH 16, 1893, Yosaku Imada, an Issei contract laborer who was serving a prison sentence of twenty-one years hard labor, found himself assigned to work detail on Kamokuʻākulikuli, Oʻahu's reef-based "Quarantine Island."[1] As he toiled under the observation of several guards, Imada noticed a Meiji warship, the *Naniwa*, anchored offshore and decided to attempt an escape.[2] He ran the length of the bridge connecting Kamokuʻākulikuli to the *Naniwa* and swam to the ship, where he was taken onboard. Although he had no intention of creating a diplomatic crisis, Imada's early morning escapade made headlines in both Hawaiʻi and Japan.

Just four years before this incident, twenty-six-year-old Imada had boarded the *Yamashiro Maru* and crossed the Pacific Ocean. He was one of thousands of emigrants who left Japan for Hawaiʻi with dreams of economic prosperity. Imada was assigned to work as a laborer on a sugar plantation in Wahieʻe, Maui, and while there, he got married. In early April 1892, Imada returned home from a long day in the fields to find his wife in bed with a fellow Issei named Kanazawa, and proceeded to attack them with his hatchet.[3] The attack resulted in the death of Kanazawa. Although he claimed innocence, Imada was convicted and found guilty of second-degree murder under the Hawaiian Kingdom's judicial system and sent to Oahu Prison in September 1892.

Soon after Imada's escape to the *Naniwa*, Sanford Dole, who was to become the first and only president of the Republic of Hawai'i, wrote to Japan's consul general, Saburo Fujii, requesting the return of the former prisoner.[4] Fujii responded that the matter was beyond his authority and he would instead keep Imada on the warship until he received further direction from his home government.[5] Later that day the coup government placed all remaining Japanese prisoners under strict observation and removed them from work detail on the reef.

Had the *Naniwa* been a merchant ship it would have been subject to the provisional government's authority. As a vessel of war however, it carried its national sovereignty on board. Imada's act of seeking refuge onboard a Meiji warship docked in Honolulu Harbor forced developing empires to grapple with questions of race-based citizenship and state jurisdiction. Although Imada was convicted under the Hawaiian Kingdom's judicial system, by the time he swam for his freedom, the monarchy had been overthrown. In March 1893, the two-month-old coup government had yet to forge an extradition treaty with Japan and now faced one of its first diplomatic entanglements.

The toppling of the Hawaiian Kingdom activated the rivalry of American and Japanese settler colonial powers in the archipelago. To further complicate matters, the impact of Imada's escape was magnified in light of a prevailing political debate around Issei rights in Hawai'i. While the question of Imada's return to the provisional government was being negotiated, Hawai'i-based Issei and Meiji government officials were pressing for voting rights in the islands, a claim that a majority of the community would not have had access to in Japan.[6]

Figure 2. Issei arriving in Honolulu, 1893. Courtesy of Hawai'i State Archives, Hadley Collection, gift of Mrs. V. Larsen, 1972.

American imperialists and leaders of the coup state, whose goal was US annexation, used the combined threat of possible Issei franchise and Meiji involvement in the Imada case as proof of the "Japanese menace" in Hawai'i. Although much has been written about the power of the Meiji state in fostering the differential treatment of Issei as opposed to other Asians, in 1893 Japan had not yet emerged as an imperial power outside Asia.[7]

Placing Imada's escape and the Issei fight for the franchise in the context of the uncertainty that followed the coup emphasizes Hawai'i's relevance as a site where interimperial dynamics aligned with competing settler colonialisms. Writing from this perspective highlights the centrality of Indigenous articulations of state-based sovereignty to competing imperial projects in the archipelago. While Japan, the United States, and the provisional government were embroiled in the

Figure 3. Members of Hui Aloha 'Āina o Nā Kane, ca. 1893. Courtesy of Library of Congress, LC-DIG-ds-11629.

battle over Imada and Issei franchise, Kānaka Maoli were actively engaged in restoring power to their kingdom.[8] Among the many tactics that they used was the appeal to international law and Western definitions of state-based sovereignty. Immediately following the overthrow, po'e aloha 'āina, led by Joseph Kaho'oluhi Nāwahī and his wife, Emma 'A'ima A'ii Nāwahī, formed Hui Aloha 'Āina (Hawaiian Patriotic League) and its sister organization, Hui Aloha 'Āina o Nā Wāhine.[9] These two groups, together with Hui Kālai'āina (Hawaiian Political Association), organized in a recognizable "Euro-American tradition" and adopted the structural forms of the Western political system in order to dialogue with it.[10] They purposefully created protest documents in 'ōlelo Hawai'i as well as in English, a practice that further disproved the haole-led oligarchy's claim to moral action based on the "uncivilized" nature of Indigenous rule. Along with Queen Lili'uokalani's protests, in 1893 the members of the patriotic leagues presented their written objections to US Commissioner James Blount and requested

Figure 4. Members of Hui Aloha ʻĀina o Nā Wāhine, ca. 1893. Courtesy of the Hawaiian Collection, University of Hawaiʻi at Mānoa.

President Grover Cleveland's assistance in the restoration of the kingdom. Their actions, which called out the coup government as an embodiment of countersovereignty, continue to fuel the movement to restore Hawaiian independence.

Reading the state-based diplomatic record in the context of the actions taken by haole and Meiji oligarchs, the Hawaiian Patriotic Leagues, and local Issei alike demonstrates that during this time the archipelago emerged as a "contested space of modernity," and was inscribed as "Pacific" and "American," as well as "potentially Asian."[11] Ultimately, the political negotiations between the US-backed coup state and Japan mutually reinforced the status of each as an emerging imperial power. These imperial intimacies also worked to obfuscate Kanaka Maoli claims to a state-based sovereignty and mapped the Hawaiian Islands onto the US and Japan's respective colonial imaginations.

The debate over Issei voting rights and Imada's release underscored questions about who held power in the politically ambiguous archipelago. Leaders in the United States understood that with over fifty years of interest vested in the islands, the future of Hawaiʻi was of great strategic importance to an "American Pacific." Consequently, while Kānaka Maoli were purposefully constructing arguments that incorporated Western understandings of state-centric sovereignty to promote their independence, the USS *Boston*, one of the US Navy's newest warships, remained docked in Honolulu Harbor. Across the Pacific, members of the Japan-based expansionist political factions, the Association of Politics and Education (Seikyōsha) and Liberal Party (Jiyū-tō), and their like-minded compatriots of the San Francisco-based Japanese Patriotic League (Sōkō Nihonjin Aikoku Dōmei) and Expedition Society (Enseisha), expounded on Japan's "colonial destiny" and lobbied for "popular political control through democratic means" in Hawaiʻi—namely securing the right of franchise.[12] These groups viewed negotiating for the right to protect Yosaku Imada and securing the franchise for their emigrant population as opportunities to seek recognition on equal footing with Western powers.

When compared to the illegal overthrow, the case of an escaped Japanese prisoner and the Issei movement for voting rights may seem like historical footnotes. Positioning these incidents within the transnational reality that those in Hawaiʻi faced, however, reveals how seemingly inconsequential acts took on larger historical and political significance simply because of where and when they occurred. If the argument for Issei franchise had been made in the continental United States for example, the stakes would have been different, as legal restrictions aimed at Asians were already in place.[13] But as members of the haole elite called for annexation as a method of control over the "Japanese menace," they also had to contend with the fact that Hawaiʻi's population was comprised of a majority nonwhite resident community, a large portion of which were also subjects of another developing empire and of the internationally recognized Hawaiian Kingdom.

A PERIOD OF UNCERTAINTY

Questions concerning the extraterritorial reach of the developing US and Meiji empires pushed political leaders in both countries to contemplate who could claim state protection; in the case of the United States, they also fortified Asian exclusion from the body politic. Grappling with how to incorporate populations that were not welcomed in the national body but who were simultaneously ruled by the state contributed to the rebuilding of the US postbellum national identity. In other words, the annexation question pushed the white American populace not only to consider the incorporation of those outside of continental borders for the first time, but to also contemplate the specific possibility of allowing thousands of Kānaka Maoli and Asians into the nation.[14]

Only twenty-eight years before Imada decided to jump into the Pacific Ocean, the United States had faced the possibility of collapse over questions of race-based slavery, citizenship, and naturalization. Concern over the islands' demography, and its possible impact on US citizenry, had been loudly voiced in the debate over reciprocity with the Hawaiian Kingdom in 1875 and again in 1887.[15] In 1893, those who lived in the United States had to ask themselves what it would mean politically, socially, and economically for their national identity if the state were to incorporate overseas territories like Hawai'i and their resident "barbarian others."[16]

The undeniable presence of Kānaka Maoli and Asians, and particularly the Japanese, complicated the possibility of annexing Hawai'i.[17] A year before the overthrow, US Minister John L. Stevens predicted that tension would build in the archipelago from both sides of the Pacific. "Hawai'i," he wrote, "has reached the parting of the ways. She must now take the road which leads to Asia, or the other, which outlets her in America, gives her an American civilization and binds her to the care of American destiny."[18] In 1893, ousted Queen Liliʻuokalani, members of the haole-led oligarchy, and US and Meiji officials found themselves asking the same question: What state apparatus would have control over Hawaiʻi?

When the Hawaiian League overthrew Liliʻuokalani they had been under the impression that the United States would not hesitate to annex the islands. In May of the previous year, Lorrin Thurston, leader of the League, traveled to Washington, DC, after attending a planning meeting for the upcoming 1893 Chicago's World Fair. His aim was to represent the then-secret League and lobby for US support. Although Thurston was denied an audience with Republican President Benjamin Harrison, the latter had authorized B. F. Tracy, Secretary of the Navy, to tell him that if he and his compatriots successfully organized a coup, he would find an "exceedingly sympathetic administration here."[19] Thurston left Washington thinking not only that he had the US government's backing, but also that it would not hesitate to annex the Hawaiian Islands.

Immediately following the overthrow, Thurston traveled as part of a five-man commission to Washington, DC, that was tasked with securing a treaty of annexation to establish Hawaiʻi as a US territory with all debts to be assumed by the federal government.[20] Coup government leaders understood that the demographic reality of Hawaiʻi precluded its admission as a state that allowed citizenship to all existing residents, as white men of any nationality were outnumbered ten to one by Kānaka Maoli and Asians. They also recognized that they could not withhold citizenship from Kānaka Maoli or Hawaiian nationals, as the coup's own claim to legitimacy rested on the "tyranny" of Native leadership. The delegates requested that the Crown and Government Lands remain the property of the new territorial government, that the United States provide funding to improve Puʻuloa (Pearl Harbor) and lay an oceanic cable that would connect the United States to the islands, that Hawai'i-based sugar planters continue to receive the same bounty that American sugar growers were paid under the McKinley Tariff, and that the importation of Asian labor continue without restriction.[21]

Secretary of State John W. Foster understood that one of the main obstacles to annexation was white labor's fear of further competition from Hawai'i's Asian population.[22] When the commission arrived on February 3, he convinced them to abandon their request to maintain importation of contract labor from Asia. Foster also added a special article that prohibited "all future immigration from East Asia into Hawai'i and from the islands into the United States."[23] Eric T. L. Love explains that this stipulation represented a promise that the "Chinese Exclusion Act would not be undermined, [and] that the domestic racial order would be unaffected by empire."[24] Together the group worked quickly to devise a treaty that Congress would ratify before President Harrison, who was defeated for reelection by Democrat Grover Cleveland, left the office in March.[25] Foster's treaty sailed through the Republican-controlled Committee on Foreign Relations and went to the full Senate on February 17, 1893, just one month after the coup. By this time, however, Queen Lili'uokalani's royal delegates, attorney Paul Neumann and Prince David Kawānanakoa, had arrived in Washington, DC, and were busy making known their case for restoration.[26]

Lili'uokalani's goal was to ensure that an investigation into the coup would occur before the annexation treaty was ratified by the Senate.[27] To this effect, her initial letter of protest, sent to President Harrison, purposefully constructed an argument that called on Western frames of governance: she explained that the coup d'état was "against the constitutional government of my Kingdom . . . . and in direct conflict with [Hawai'i's] organic law."[28] Through this tactic the queen reaffirmed her position as rightful head of state by virtue of constitutional law, a paradigm that she knew the United States could not deny without also rejecting its own right to rule.

Unlike Harrison, President Cleveland was initially receptive to Liliʻuokalani's argument. He was wary of the provisional government's actions and US Minister Stevens's role in the overthrow.[29] As one of his first undertakings, he withdrew the treaty from the Senate on March 9th. Two days later, Secretary of State Walter Q. Gresham assigned James Blount, a former Democratic congressman from Georgia who headed the House Foreign Relations Committee and an opponent of annexation, to investigate and report to Cleveland about the "conditions of affairs in the Hawaiian Islands, the causes of the revolution by which the Queen's government was overthrown, [and] the sentiment of the people towards existing authority."[30] Gresham reminded Blount that the US government had no right to interfere in local affairs but would not tolerate domestic interference from other foreign powers.[31]

By the time Imada swam to the *Naniwa* on March 16, 1893, the United States still had not annexed Hawaiʻi as members of the haole-led oligarchy had hoped. Instead, Secretary Foster had chastised Minister Stevens for "impair[ing] . . . the independent sovereignty of the Hawaiian government by substituting the flag and power of the United States," and Cleveland had requested an independent investigation of the legality of the overthrow.[32] Having banked on a swift annexation, Thurston and his colleagues found themselves in uncharted waters. The encouragement from President Harrison, US Minister Stevens's visible support, and even the protection of the bluejackets from the USS *Boston* were now irrelevant. What had seemed so certain just a few weeks ago was now on the verge of collapse. It was no longer clear whether the coup state would maintain its authority or that Hawaiʻi, declared an American protectorate on February 1, 1893, would continue in that status.

Upon his arrival in Honolulu, Blount noted that the coup government was already working to inscribe Hawaiʻi as American space. Troops from the USS *Boston* were practicing military drills onshore and the American flag was flying over the government building. Citing concern over whether anyone could freely respond to his inquiries when the US presence was so boldly paraded about, on April 1, just two days after his arrival in the islands, Blount ordered the removal of the flag and the return of the American troops back to their ship. In her diary entry for that day, Lili'uokalani described the impact that this action had, writing that although she instructed the people to be quiet, which they did for fear of aggravating the Americans, "the men all took their hats off while tears of joy streamed down the cheeks of men as well as women."³³

Leaders of the coup state and others of the plantocracy attempted to influence Blount's view of the situation. But poʻe aloha ʻāina also made it a point to meet with the commissioner to convey their anger and concern. They informed him that Kānaka Maoli from all positions in society found the overthrow both illegal and reprehensible. Members of Hui Aloha ʻĀina presented Blount with a statement of protest addressed to President Cleveland that called on Western frames of nationhood and state-based sovereignty. They noted that they were an "association numbering over 8,000 legal voters, created for the purpose of preserving the autonomy of the country under the native Monarchy," and argued that while the queen was "simply deprived of her throne, power, and revenues . . . the people ha[d] lost their dearest liberties and civil rights . . . and were on the eve of losing even their nationality."³⁴ Members also reminded Blount that the coup government was nothing more than a "temporary *de facto* police organization" that did not have the backing of the majority of people.³⁵

Besides using diplomatic pathways of protest, poʻe aloha ʻāina also took to methods outside of official channels to object to the overthrow. They proclaimed their right to political independence through music, prayer, quilting, and storytelling. As kuʻualoha hoʻomanawanui documents, between 1860 and 1928, publications of Pele and Hiʻiaka moʻolelo (history/story) increased and provided a counternarrative to the dominant discourses of settler colonialism. These moʻolelo functioned to uphold and spread Hawaiian cultural values and language, and promote a Kānaka Maoli identity as lāhui.[36] On February 1, the day Minister Stevens declared Hawai'i a US protectorate, all but two members of the Royal Hawaiian Band, which had been funded by the kingdom since its inception in 1836, quit rather than sign an oath of loyalty to the coup state.[37] They went on to form a royalist organization called the Hawaiian National Band and in 1895 toured the United States performing songs such as the "Lili'uokalani March," "Mele Aloha 'Āina," and "Hawai'i Pono'ī" in order to gather support for Hawaiian independence.[38] Across Honolulu, Kaumakapili Church's bell could be heard each morning from four to four-thirty as it called members to pray for the restoration of their queen. Individuals voiced their discontent by sewing quilts with the design of the ka Hae Hawai'i (Hawaiian flag) or withholding their church offerings in demonstration against ministers who supported the provisional government.[39]

These actions by organizations and individuals, along with the protests of Hui Kālai'āina and the men's and women's branches of Hui Aloha 'Āina, convinced Commissioner Blount of the illegality of the overthrow and the unethical actions of the oligarchy. Despite numerous attempts at persuasion by members of the haole-led oligarchy, Blount communicated his findings in a report to President Cleveland and also made his sentiments known to Secretary of State Gresham. Just one week after his arrival in Hawai'i, he wrote to the newly appointed Gresham, and noted that when US forces were used to support the provisional government and "suppress movements on their part ... its good faith is impugned."[40]

Placed in this context, the "escapee incident" magnified the issue of political uncertainty in Hawai'i. Leaders of the provisional government and their US government accomplice, Minister Stevens, were faced with the question of how to proceed in the Imada case.[41] Stevens believed that the arrival of two Japanese warships, the *Kongo*, on January 28 and the *Naniwa* on February 23, along with the arrival of the

British cruiser *Garnet* on the same day, was more than a coincidence. Two weeks before Imada's escape, Stevens had expressed his concerns to Secretary of State Foster, claiming that British Minister Wodehouse and Japanese Consul General Fujii were planning to form a "tripartite management" between the monarchies of Japan, Great Britain, and Hawaiʻi, which would work to "squeeze out American interests" in the islands.[42] In the wake of the escape and resulting escalated concern over Japan's intentions, Stevens again wrote to the Secretary of State, this time the newly appointed Gresham, and explained that the Hawaiian Islands would be in danger of "Japanization" if the USS *Boston* troops were recalled.[43] Just five days before Blount's arrival he also advised Gresham that the American flag should not be removed from the provisional government building until the "Japanese menace" was ended.[44]

By raising the specter of "Japanization," and the possibility of a "new Japan" in Hawaiʻi, annexationists worked to push US politicians toward their goal. For example, on March 17, 1893 the *Pacific Commercial Advertiser (PCA)* which at this time served as a mouthpiece for the annexationists, ran two articles covering Imada's escape that highlighted the coup government's request for the return of the prisoner and Japan's refusal to do so.[45] One of the articles described the *Naniwa* as "a piece of Japanese territory, subject to Japanese laws, and merely temporarily set down in Honolulu harbor."[46] Three days later, the *PCA* again fueled anti-Japanese sentiment by reporting on a rumor that linked the arrival of the *Naniwa* with a possible marriage between the Hawaiian and Japanese royal families:

> There is little doubt that Japan looks upon these islands with an eye of longing, and that there has been a plan underfoot to bring them under Japanese influence by the marriage of one of the Princes of the Imperial House with Kaiulani. The young Prince now on board the Naniwa . . . is

the one whom the Japanese government have had in mind for this purpose.... So long as the United States maintains any claim to ascendency in these islands, it is safe to assume that there will be no interference from any other quarter. If that claim should be withdrawn, it is exceedingly doubtful whether Japan would withhold her hand any longer from the Hawaiian Pear.[47]

While the unnamed author of the piece admitted that the information regarding current circumstances was unverified, the truth underlying the report—that at one point in time King Kalākaua had proposed a royal marriage between the Hawaiian Kingdom and the Imperial House of Japan, drove their point home. To the *PCA* and pro-annexationists, the docked *Naniwa* represented a major threat that required a strong American presence in the islands as a countermeasure.

Throughout the next several weeks the *PCA* continued to stoke the annexationists' fire with continuous coverage of the *Naniwa*'s guest. A March 21 article entitled "Rumors of War," reported on gossip that suggested Japan's intention to take over the Hawaiian archipelago. One such story claimed that the provisional government's Executive Council would make a demand for the "Japanese murderer" and that men from Camp Boston would be directed to board the warship if the request was not met.[48] Although the *PCA* acknowledged the sensationalized nature of its coverage, its stories reinforced the idea that Hawai'i was already inscribed as Japanese space. The paper continued to report as fact that the *Naniwa* had enough small arms to "equip two to three thousand men" and that the cruiser had initially been sent to the islands to raise the Japanese flag over the government building. And where would these three thousand men come from, if they were not already on board the warship? *PCA* journalists directed their readers to consider the thousands of Issei laborers who lived in the islands and had "undoubtedly" served in the military forces at home.[49] The only

Figure 5. The Japanese cruiser *Naniwa* docked in Honolulu Harbor. Courtesy of Hawai'i State Archives, Brother Bertram Collection.

thing that was stopping the official Meiji takeover, the paper claimed, was the presence of the American flag waving in downtown Honolulu.

These rumors, together with a growing uncertainty about the support of the US government, must have weighed heavily on the minds of members of the Annexation Club as they waited for a reply from the Imperial government of Japan regarding their request to return Imada. Members of the oligarchy found themselves in a delicate position. If the earlier commitments Minister Stevens had secured from the United States remained intact, the Hawaiian Islands would soon be annexed. This was an action that the oligarchs tried to foster through underlining the presence of Japanese in Hawai'i. But having been among the group of men who pushed for the passing of the 1875 Reciprocity Treaty despite the concern voiced over the archipelago's multiracial population, Dole and Thurston understood that they first had to convince the United States that Hawai'i was compatible as an "American space" and would not threaten the country's "ideal" demography. For this maneuver, they turned to the ballot box.

JAPANESE SETTLER COLONIALISM AND THE FIGHT OVER VOTING RIGHTS

Just as the United States, Hawaiian Kingdom, and provisional government found themselves at critical junctures in the formation of the modern nation-state, so too did the newly established Meiji government. While much has been made of Japan's entrance into global expansion with the victory over China in the First Sino-Japanese War of 1894–95, Hawai'i was one of the first stages outside Asia upon which the Meiji oligarchy stood to define itself as a modern nation-state. In 1868 the 265-year reign of the Tokugawa *bafuku* had come to an end with the "restoration" of rule under the Meiji emperor. Takashi Fujitani explains that during the Tokugawa period both society and polity were "maintained by the accentuation of social, cultural, and . . . political differences . . . [which] contributed to the insularity of local communities from each other."[50] When Meiji oligarchs ushered in the "restoration" of imperial rule, they were met with a populace that had a "limited consciousness of national identity" and favored strong local rather than national ties.[51] As a result, the Meiji era opened with a flood of policy and pageantry aimed at bringing together a unified national culture.

For Meiji government leaders and Issei laborers alike, citizenship and the rights which this category entailed became relevant in the context of foreign affairs. While Meiji oligarchs were busy attempting to establish a national identity at home, they also strove for recognition in the international field.[52] Migration and colonial expansion worked in tandem to support Japanese settler colonialism, as exemplified in the occupation of Hokkaido in 1869.[53] As part of this development, officials were highly aware of how their subjects were treated in the global arena.

During the late nineteenth century the problem for the Meiji state was, "How would the individual and the nation-state be integrated?"[54] In 1893 the concept of "citizen" did not exist in Japan. Membership in the nation and the political protection which that category provided became paramount issues for Meiji leaders only when their subjects left Japan and encountered other articulations of nation and national membership in spaces like Hawai'i. Douglas Howland explains that Meiji oligarchs had hardly begun to "conceptualize the state and its integration with its constituent persons"; thus articulations of the nation-state's identity were in large part determined by encounters on the outside.[55] Consequently, both the question of Imada's return and the debate over the Issei right to vote in Hawai'i proved to be encounters that affected Japan's national and state project.

Limiting access to suffrage was one of the strategies implemented by the haole elite to maintain power amid the growing political interest in Hawai'i and the increasing Japanese population.[56] The sociopolitical instability that followed the 1893 overthrow exposed the fragility of the coup state and presented Meiji ideologues and government officials, as well as Hawai'i's Issei population—who numbered around twenty thousand—with an opening to set up the political foundation for Japanese settler colonialism in the archipelago through the ballot box. Seikyōsha and Expedition Society member Betten Nagasawa expanded on this idea in his 1894 essay "Current Circumstances in Hawai'i and Japanese Suffrage" ("Hawaii no Gensei, Nihonjin no Sanseiken") published in *Selected Essays on Yankees (Yankii Sho)*. He argued that obtaining the Issei right to vote was an integral step to facilitating the future of Japanese colonialism not just in Hawai'i, but in toto. In Nagasawa's opinion, access to the franchise would allow Japanese to take on white Americans and Europeans in Hawai'i on equal grounds and ultimately, "demonstrate their inherent racial superiority."[57]

For this Meiji ideologue, the Native claim to a state-based sovereignty was not just erased, it was deemed unworthy of recognition. Echoing the racist logic espoused by white settlers against Indigenous peoples in the "American West," Nagasawa reduced Kānaka Maoli to uncivilized beings ready for Japanese conquest and domination. According to San Francisco-based Nagasawa, the haole-led oligarchy had risen to power because Kānaka Maoli were "ignorant, idiotic people who understand neither the honor of the nation or the significance of autonomy" and would rather "dance the so-called 'hula-hula' and entertain themselves" than "devote themselves to protecting the state."[58] Elaborating on his vision of Japanese settler colonialism he wrote, "If the Japanese acquire the right of suffrage in Hawai'i and elect five or six congressmen or one or two ministers, they would not have to meet the same fate as the Chinese have met. The dominance of the Japanese will reign over the Sandwich Islands."[59] Nagasawa concluded that because Japanese people, including plantation workers and laborers, were racially superior, they would be able to topple the haole-led oligarchy, bring Hawai'i's politics and economy under their control, and lay the groundwork for a "new Japan" in the islands.[60]

Despite his fiery writings, Nagasawa did not take direct action in Hawai'i. Japanese Patriotic League member Tsutau Tsugawara, however, made the voyage from San Francisco to Honolulu at the end of January 1893 and quickly joined up with a circle of locally based Issei activists. As Eiichiro Azuma notes, the group traveled around the islands together, "hoping to affect the consciousness of common plantation workers and marshal support from them" for Japanese male suffrage.[61] As they trekked over rough dirt roads and crossed between islands in order to speak to the various Issei plantation communities, these men explained that the vote, and *their* vote in particular, was necessary not only to stop the US encroachment on Hawai'i and the Pacific, but also to expand the power of the Meiji state.

While Issei ideologues and local community leaders attempted to rally the island-based Japanese population to their expansionist cause, Hawaiian royalists also saw the potential of this large population. According to Lucien Young's testimony in the *Morgan Report*, roughly four hundred Japanese plantation workers made their way over twenty miles from rural West O'ahu into Honolulu in order to protest the overthrow.[62] With their machetes held high, they loudly demanded the restoration of the monarchy. Rumor was that this act of Japanese and Native solidarity occurred because Hawaiian royalists had informed Issei plantation workers that US annexation would result in the permanent extension of their labor contracts and that they would be "slaves [for] the rest of time."[63]

Unfortunately for ideologues like Nagasawa and rural Issei alike, after taking political power away from the monarchy, the elite haole planter class turned its full attention to the perceived threat the Japanese community presented. By 1890 Issei constituted the second largest population in the islands after Kānaka Maoli, roughly three times that of all Europeans, excluding the Portuguese, and six times that of white Americans.[64] Given this disparity in numbers, haole oligarchs, like Japanese expansionists, understood that they would lose political and economic control over Hawai'i if an Issei constituency were allowed the right to vote.[65]

The fact that access to US citizenship and voting rights rested on race was not lost on Sanford Dole. Consequently, he and his fellow annexationists attempted to put off both the Japanese and Chinese efforts at gaining equal political access within the provisional government until their desired annexation to the United States was achieved.[66] Exactly one week after the escape of Imada, Consul General Fujii wrote to Dole to remind him of the 1871 Treaty of Amity and Commerce between Japan and the Hawaiian Kingdom, which stated that Japanese subjects in the islands were entitled to "enjoying at all times the same privileges as may have been, or may hereafter be granted to the citizens or subjects of any other nation."[67] Fujii pointed out that although voting rights were accorded to Americans and Europeans, including the Portuguese, they were unlawfully withheld from the Issei.[68] To this query Dole replied that annexation negotiations between the provisional government and the United States for political union were in progress and if successful, the US federal government would become responsible in all questions concerning foreign states.[69]

One of the more immediate results of the diplomatic exchanges and everyday protests over Japanese franchise was the Issei incorporation into a national political praxis that created a conscious deterritorialized "Japanese people." In response to the continued barriers to their political participation, leaders of the Issei community attempted to inscribe Hawaiʻi as Japanese space by emphasizing both their ties to Japan and their role as colonizers. Under the guidance of members of the San Francisco-based Japanese Patriotic League, Hawaiʻi-based Issei intelligentsia and religious leaders formed the Japanese Alliance (Nihonjin Dōmei), with branches in Hilo and Honolulu. Alliance members publicly protested their denial of political rights in the coup state and submitted four separate petitions to the Japanese consulate in Honolulu. Each petition demanded that Tokyo take a proactive role in advocating for national expansion and support their struggle to obtain voting rights in Hawaiʻi.[70] Citing the development of a sustainable community which, besides providing sugar and coffee field labor, supported small merchants, small farmers, doctors, and other professionals, Alliance members framed themselves as participants in Japanese colonization and representatives of the nation who deserved the protection of the Meiji state.[71]

In this articulation of transpacific empire, the Native right to self-government, territorial integrity, and cultural autonomy did not exist. Instead, according to the over six thousand Issei who signed the petitions, the failure of the Meiji government to secure equitable political privileges disgraced and dishonored their community, and by extension, Japan. They claimed that it was not "merely because of the numerical strength that we wish political suffrage, but to maintain the dignity of 40,000,000 Japanese in Japan."[72] Evidently, residing within a space of interimperial conflict had fostered a social and political awareness that allowed the Issei community not just to place themselves within the same sociopolitical context as those in Japan, but also to feel justified in shaming the Meiji state into defending them.

REACTIONS FROM JAPAN

As the lead go-between for negotiating contract labor shipments, Commissioner of Immigration Robert Irwin had a personal financial stake in maintaining amicable relationships between the provisional and Japanese governments.[73] Writing from his office in Tokyo, he warned Dole that the Japanese Minister of Foreign Affairs, Munemitsu Mutsu, had informed him that a "strong current of public opinion in the press and among politicians and the people was showing itself in reference to the extension to Japanese residents in Hawai'i of the privilege of the electoral franchise."[74] Irwin also noted the need to balance the necessary labor source with Issei political rights, stating that if voting rights were not achieved, "some action would be taken in the next session of the Imperial Japanese Parliament which may endanger our great industrial Emigration Convention."[75]

Irwin's descriptions of the growing momentum in both political and public arenas in Japan emphasized the transnational stakes of the franchise question. Over the next three months, he sent several letters to Dole informing him of the escalating Japanese support for Issei voting rights in Hawai'i. On June 26, Irwin reported that the Liberal Party, the leaders of which were "on very intimate terms with the present Imperial Cabinet," had determined to push for the Japanese right to vote within the next diet.[76] This was followed by his report of a July 10 mass gathering at which Tōru Hoshi, an ideologue for Japanese imperial expansion in the Pacific and member of the House of Representatives, urged Meiji political leaders to press for the franchise in Hawai'i.[77]

The question of securing voting rights for Hawai'i-based Issei centered on competing settler colonialisms. In light of the fact that up until 1925, Japan imposed strict financial restrictions that limited the right to vote to elite men, the actions taken by Meiji oligarchs, Japanese alliance members in Hawai'i, and San Francisco-based ideologues demonstrate that the issue at hand was much larger than Japanese emigrants' right to vote. Azuma explains that the possibility of triumphant haole conspirators who could "relegate disenfranchised Japanese to a permanent subordinate position, thereby jeopardizing Japan's future as a dominant maritime power in the Pacific" haunted the Meiji state.[78] In truth, the rural population that comprised the majority of emigrants to Hawai'i were a great concern for the Meiji government elite and urban intelligentsia. Men like Yukichi Fukuzawa, Japan's foremost scholar in "Western studies" and a proponent of national expansionism, worried that "common people of rural origin . . . lack[ed] [the] national consciousness and modern sensibilities" needed to represent the Meiji state in the global arena and discouraged their emigration.[79] But when placed in the liminal space of late-nineteenth century Hawai'i, these rural *dekaseginin* (migrant laborers) became a proxy for Japan and as such, were a focal point of concern when mistreated by other powers.

Back in Hawai'i, Saburo Fujii gave an interview on April 3, 1893 to a *PCA* reporter regarding both the Japanese quest for franchise rights and the situation surrounding Imada. Fujii did his best to tone down the "Japanese threat" and maintain his country's request for equal treatment. He denied rumors that Japan had any interest in taking control of Hawai'i and claimed that the *Naniwa* and *Kongo* were only there to protect Japanese interest in the islands should there have been violence following the coup. He also maintained that Japanese franchise would not privilege the Issei in the islands, but only give them the same rights that citizens of European nations held. In regard to Imada, the consul general stated that the captain of the *Naniwa* could not have given the prisoner back to provisional government officials because he had "no right to return a man who claimed the protection of the Japanese flag."[80]

On April 4, one day after Fujii's defense of his country's foreign policy was printed, the *PCA* ran an editorial that, in addition to questioning the validity of his comments, reminded readers of the threat that the Issei community posed to not just the provisional government, but all of Western civilization in the Pacific: "In her new national life she

[Japan] is a young and enterprising power reaching out into the Western world, and very willing to play a leading role there. . . . Hawai'i is a convenient point at which to establish an outpost for the new Japanese power and civilization. Her great emigrating population . . . offers her a simple and easy means of conquering Hawai'i by absorption."[81] The paper also claimed that while the Japanese threat existed, it held no real danger as long as the United States maintained its presence in the islands. While annexationists used this propaganda to naturalize US claims to the archipelago despite the ongoing challenge by po'e aloha 'āina, the debate over Issei voting rights reveals how each "country's expansionism manifested self-consciousness about civilization and race."[82] Calling attention to the large Japanese presence in Hawai'i might have persuaded some in the US government of the need to speedily annex the islands, but it also forced political leaders to carefully examine who would and would not be considered members of the nation.

At 10 a.m. on April 20, 1893, Imada was expelled from the *Naniwa*. Apparently, the Meiji government did not deem his freedom relevant enough to cause a heightened political riff with the United States. According to eyewitness reports, he was brought to shore by his fellow countrymen in a small rowboat and then was set free on Dillingham Coal Wharf to make his own way.[83] Jailers from the provisional government were aware of this drop-off and were waiting to ambush Imada as he attempted to run away on the sandy beach. It was reported by the *PCA* that the Japanese sailors who dropped off Imada were disappointed that he did not have the opportunity to run the gauntlet. They were, evidently, looking forward to an entertaining escape effort and wagering on his getaway. Imada fought vigorously against the jailers as they transported him back to Oahu Prison and even attempted to escape into several Japanese-owned establishments along the way. The next day, he was spotted on work detail at Kamoku'ākulikuli, this time with a weight chained to his leg.

Roughly one year later, in May 1894, leaders of the coup state held a constitutional convention in order to solidify a permanent government in the face of the most recent failed annexation attempt. The specter of Japan's rising imperial power, articulated via Imada's escape and the Japanese fight to access franchise rights, loomed over the convention. Questions regarding the Asian right to vote were at the top of the agenda. In order to avoid the charge of open discrimination and maintain a viable labor source, the oligarchs established franchise as a function of citizenship (see chapter 2). While this barred most Issei from the ballot box, for those few who qualified, a further provision requiring the ability to read and write either in Hawaiian or English effectively shut them out. The now renamed "Republic of Hawai'i" withheld voting rights from the Issei as effectively as the coup government had in the years between 1887 and 1893.[84]

CONCLUSION: THE QUESTION OF SOVEREIGNTY AND JURISDICTION

Imada's escape and the debate over Issei franchise positioned Hawai'i between developing empires searching for ways to delineate themselves within the rapidly changing context of global and national space. As the United States defined itself as a nation through its empire, the provisional government relied on racial delineations that mirrored those of the United States to determine membership. In Japan, Meiji government officials found themselves contemplating the political rights of a class of people who did not command the same consideration at home. In Hawai'i and Washington, DC, Queen Lili'uokalani and those loyal to the Hawaiian Kingdom were purposefully constructing arguments that incorporated Western understandings of state-based sovereignty to actively promote and protect their political independence.

Placing Imada's escape within the context of the Issei movement for franchise in the coup state draws attention to the ways in which both events captured the imagination of Meiji expansionists and plantation laborers alike, seeding settler colonial visions of a "new Japan" in Hawaiʻi that countered those of haole oligarchs and American imperialists. This chapter has considered how actions taken by everyday people could sometimes challenge seemingly stable categories such as nation, state, and citizenship and bring the global into the realm of local events and individual aspirations. Imada sought only his freedom and in doing so called on the Meiji state for protection. His escape not only forced the provisional government of Hawaiʻi and the Imperial government of Japan to debate which country held access to his body, but also, like the ongoing debate over franchise rights, brought the future political configuration of Hawaiʻi and the Pacific into question.

Pausing on the case for Japanese franchise and Imada's escape also opens up space to question the relationship between sovereignty and jurisdiction, and challenge the discourse based on "legitimate" settler state governance. While Japan and the US-backed coup state each advocated for the primacy of their legal regime in the archipelago, they also fortified each other through state-based diplomatic procedure. This intersection of white American and Japanese settler colonialisms brought questions of state jurisdiction to the fore, positioning Hawaiʻi as contested space and, in the process, obfuscating Kānaka Maoli claims to political independence.

The Kānaka Maoli use of state-based sovereignty and jurisdiction in order to protect their kingdom during the nineteenth century did not preclude the fact that they also maintained an expansive understanding of both concepts based on deep connection with place. This is an understanding and relationship that was never relinquished and continues in the present. Shiri Pasternak explains that if we step outside a restrictive, state-based understanding of sovereignty, the question of jurisdiction reveals itself to be about who has the "authority to have authority" and whose "laws of belonging" apply to the land.[85] It is this mode of relationship between people and place that the coup state's anxiety was and continues to be based on. For, try as they might, leaders of the coup state were never able to extinguish the validity of ea, the Hawaiian claim to an expansive relationship, jurisdiction, and sovereignty over place. Upon their failed annexation attempt, oligarchs turned to the theater of a constitutional convention in order to allay the growing anxiety over their incomplete imperial project.

2

AT THE BORDERS OF NATION AND STATE

The 1894 Constitutional Convention

FACED WITH the failure of their annexation attempt, in 1894 the haole-led oligarchy held a constitutional convention in Honolulu. During convention proceedings, anti-Black and anti-Asian racisms continued to shape the boundaries of the coup state, as they had throughout the history of diplomatic relations between the Hawaiian Kingdom and the United States. Consider, for example, the deliberations over the 1875 Reciprocity Treaty, which would grant Hawaiian sugar duty-free access into US markets. Debates over whether the United States should develop close ties to the Hawaiian Kingdom had been occurring ever since the 1850s, when the monarchy agitated for a reciprocity treaty that would secure favorable protection and access for its sugar, molasses, wool, tallow, coffee, hides, and rice in American markets. In the years immediately leading up to the treaty's approval, arguments about the uncivilized nature of Hawaiʻi's population, such as those made by Mark Twain, who referred tongue-in-cheek to the "naked, savage, thundering barbarians," wearing only an "unnecessarily slender rag passed between the legs," were enough to hold it at bay.[1] By the end of the nineteenth century however, the United States was facing a tenuous global scenario. Freed from internal warfare, the country was now able to look outside itself and saw the slow but steady advance of European powers in the Pacific and Asia. Consequently, in 1875 imperialists secured the treaty's passing despite previous failed attempts and ongoing anxiety over incorporating a racial "other."[2]

The reciprocity treaty pitted white supremacists against one another as they jockeyed for the spoils of capitalism. While island-based sugar planters and other members of Hawaiʻi's business community were encouraged by its passing, Southern sugar interests and various members of Congress were not pleased with the outcome.[3] During Congressional debate, members of the House and Senate from the South voiced their strong opposition to the proposed treaty. Playing on the racial anxiety of a white American populace still reeling from the Civil War, Democratic Senator Thomas Norwood of Georgia declared that there was "imminent danger" of obliterating the rice and sugar interests of the South if reciprocity with the Hawaiian Kingdom were to be granted. If Southern plantations were to lose their economic viability, he warned, they would be forced to turn loose "three hundred thousand Blacks to run as savages through the wilderness" to destroy the "rich and a fruitful tract of country which has hitherto bloomed and blossomed under cultivation by the Black race managed by the White race." All of this he claimed, would be done to benefit the "heathens in the Pacific."[4]

Senator Norwood represented a state that in 1870 had voted in a "Redeemer" white-only Democratic government that was sympathetic to the former Confederacy and opposed racial equality. At the time of the Congressional debate, the United States was just beginning to exert federal control over immigration. Norwood's comments on the proposed reciprocity treaty appealed to deep-seated Southern racism by raising the fear not just of unemployed Black "savages," but also of naturalized Hawaiian and Asian others. Yet, addressing abolitionists and government officials from the North, Norwood also framed his objections as a means to protect the South's recently freed Black population, appealing to those who "have been humane to them that they shall continue their humanity . . . . They have in their wisdom made them citizens of the United States. They have taken them from a condition of mental darkness . . . and have placed them on a common platform with all other American citizens."⁵

These seemingly contradictory statements made sense to Norwood, a former Confederate soldier, in relation to the possible incorporation of the Asian and Kanaka Maoli other. In the postbellum South, the Chinese migrant was synonymous with the idea of the "coolie," a low-wage Asian laborer who existed at the border of slavery and freedom, toiling on sugar plantations formerly worked by enslaved Africans.⁶ Deploying a type of racial triangulation designed to keep Kānaka Maoli and Asians subordinated to freed Blacks, while ensuring that freed Blacks remain subordinate to whites, Norwood asked white Americans to consider "what kind of philanthropy is that which will now turn its back up on them [freed Blacks] and legislate for the heathens in the Pacific Ocean?"⁷

Just as concern over the islands' demography and its possible impact on US citizenry had been loudly voiced in the debate over reciprocity, the possibility of allowing thousands of Kānaka Maoli and Asians into the nation continued to be a problem for those agitating for annexation.⁸ By 1894, political cartoons likening Lili'uokalani to an "African savage" who was fit to rule only others like her had been circulating around the United States for some time.⁹ Such images reflected the oligarchy's concerns with upholding both patriarchal and white supremacist power, which was under threat by the ongoing call for Hawaiian autonomy and by demands for voting rights for Asians, other foreign residents, and women.

In addition to being a kingdom populated by various types of "racial others," Hawai'i's society presented oligarchs with the "problem" of women's autonomy at a time when women's suffrage was one of the most politically divisive issues in the United States. In precolonial Hawai'i, gender was not the primary consideration for determining social and political power, which was instead a category mediated by factors such as genealogical rank and lineage.[10] For a coup regime dominated by men, Native women's independence and authority, combined with their ability to skillfully use the international language of diplomacy to appeal to a global audience, posed a significant threat to the former's democratic cover.

The haole-led oligarchy's fears flared into view during the constitutional convention. Its thirty-seven delegates were charged, in essence, with devising a legal apparatus that would enable them to control populations that were simultaneously deemed outside of the national body and yet ruled by the state. Among the most pressing issues debated were the newly proclaimed republic's ability to regulate political membership and participation. Delegates pondered how to sustain a pretense of democracy while limiting the vote in order to maintain minority rule. In their attempt to quiet the discontent over the islands' demography and its possible impact on US citizenry, members of the oligarchy struggled to articulate a nation-state that would be at once an accommodation of local agitation and a reflection of the patriarchal and white supremacist power existent in the United States. They turned to emphasizing anti-Black and anti-Asian racisms in order to justify Indigenous and Asian omission from their coup state despite the Hawaiian relationship to place, and the combined Kanaka Maoli and Asian population's demographic majority.

Outside the convention, those located at the boundaries of the body politic continued to engage in acts of resistance that included organized rallies, written petitions, and skillful measures of international diplomacy. Manu Karuka explains that since settler sovereignty requires "recognition of Indigenous modes of relationship . . . in order to maintain any semblance of stability or coherence," settlers often find themselves in a constant "position of reaction."[11] Caught in this predicament of "countersovereignty," the haole-led oligarchy hoped to use the convention as a repetitive exercise designed to reaffirm their right to rule. Instead, both the convention proceedings and acts of resistance against it exposed the fragility of US imperial power rather than enforcing the sanctity of the coup state. The struggle to address the protests and concerns of Kānaka Maoli, Asians, and women of both white and Indigenous descent by the US-backed coup state compounded the growing apprehension over the incomplete imperial project in the archipelago. In short, the attempt to create a white republic emphasized the very dilemma that oligarchs found themselves struggling with: in order to legitimize the coup state, they first had to acknowledge the primacy of the Hawaiian monarchy and nation that they denounced, all but admitting the illegality of their own takeover.

COMPETING DISCOURSES OF RACE, NATION, AND SOVEREIGNTY

Following the 1893 coup, Queen Lili'uokalani wrote to President Cleveland in protest. Cleveland privately abhorred the US-backed coup, but he responded in early October 1893 with a show of impartiality, assigning himself the position of mediator and appointing Albert Willis of Louisville, Kentucky, as a replacement for US Minister to Hawai'i Stevens. Willis had no diplomatic experience and was ill-prepared to face the complicated task ahead of him. Secretary of State Gresham advised Willis that the president believed Minister Stevens had committed an international crime by aiding the coup. Gresham then charged Willis with the duty of negotiating between members of the provisional government and Lili'uokalani for her return to the throne.[12] Willis was also to make the queen understand that the United States would

Figure 6. Queen Lili'uokalani attending Queen Victoria's Golden Jubilee, 1887. Courtesy of Hawai'i State Archives.

come to her aide if, and only if, she agreed to pursue a "magnanimous" course of action and grant full amnesty to those who had conspired to overthrow her.[13]

Minister Willis arrived in Honolulu Harbor on November 4, 1893 and moved into the US legation's residence, which was some distance away from both the queen's current residence at Washington Place and ʻIolani Palace, the new home of the coup government. Instead of meeting with Liliʻuokalani in a timely fashion, Willis waited until nine days after his arrival to summon her to his office. On November 13, 1893 he met a monarch who, through her political acumen and savoir-faire, was able to not only assert her position, but also dictate the terms of negotiation in the language and rhetoric of the American colonizer. After relaying greetings from President Cleveland and his wish to "undo the wrong which had been done," the US minister asked the queen whether, if she were reinstated, she would consent to grant general amnesty to those who had led the overthrow. According to the Queen's account of the meeting, she reminded Willis that the constitution that "these very persons had forced upon the nation" declared that traitors were to suffer either banishment or death and have their property confiscated. Besides, she stated, her individual call for amnesty would hold no weight, as it was beyond her "powers as a constitutional sovereign" and required the approval of her cabinet.[14]

Willis's report back to Secretary Gresham made no note of the Queen's political savvy. Instead, his sensationalized write-up claimed that Liliʻuokalani had called for her traitors' "beheading." Her published work and private journal account of that day give no indication that she said any such thing, and she publicly denied the US Minister's allegation. However, writes Noenoe Silva, the image of the "savage pagan" who called for her oppositions' heads was promptly "deployed against the Queen and her people." Word of her desire to "behead virtually every Caucasian in Hawaiʻi" spread like wildfire throughout the United States, playing right into the racist caricatures of Liliʻuokalani that were already circulating there, which combined anti-Hawaiian sentiment with the familiar tropes of anti-Black racism.[15]

Political cartoonists, for example, often drew the queen as a barefoot woman with thick lips and unkempt hair, an "African savage" who was out for white American blood, or as another Black stereotype, the infantilized "pickaninny," who looked to the United States for support.[16] Journalists picked up on these signifiers, and some of their most infamous portrayals of Liliʻuokalani worked intertextually with the cartoon imagery.[17] Written references to "Dusky Queen Lil" symbolized the racism that was commonly found in political cartoons, which Stephanie Nohelani Teves argues "portrayed Liliʻuokalani—and by extension, Hawaiʻi—as black, savage, and female, a tactic used to denigrate all Hawaiians."[18] Writing for a series in the New York *Independent* in 1893, Reverend Sereno Bishop, a former officer of the Hawaiian Missionary Society, claimed that the queen was the child of a "mulatto" shoemaker and had a "slight African trace in the hair."[19] He asserted that "white Hawaii loathes [her] and native Hawaii has no respect for [her]," and called her uncivil and politically ignorant. Bishop's descriptions also aligned Liliʻuokalani with anti-Asian stereotypes. She was, he wrote, the "debauched Queen of a heathenish monarchy where . . . those who wish to make Honolulu a center for the manufacture and distribution of opium lie together with the lewd and drunken majority of the native race, who live largely by the lucrative prostitution of their females to the wifeless Chinese and Japanese."[20] According to such racist depictions, Hawaiʻi's monarchs were inept and immoral heathens who were unfit to govern.

In the midst of the growing public discourse against the queen and her people, on November 24, 1893 copies of the Blount Report and Secretary Gresham's recommendations for the restoration of Liliʻuokalani arrived in Honolulu. Sanford Dole and company read Gresham's recommendation for restoration as a call to arms and immediately issued sixty rifles and five thousand rounds of ammunition to the members of the Citizen Guard, a militia created to protect members of the oligarchy.[21] The oligarchs subsequently denounced the actions of Cleveland and Gresham and at a November 27, 1893 mass meeting of roughly twelve hundred coup government supporters, or just one tenth of the entire Hawaiian archipelago's population, they adopted a motion to

Figure 7. "Lili to Grover" by Frederick Victor Gillam, cover of *Judge* magazine, February 17, 1894. Courtesy of National Portrait Gallery, Smithsonian Institution.

prevent the restoration of the monarchy. Believing that they might be on trial for their lives, leaders of the coup government discussed whether the queen should be taken as a prisoner of the state. They even contemplated tearing down the existing barracks in Honolulu and using the stones to build a blockade around government buildings.[22]

On December 23, 1893, less than a week after Cleveland's message to Congress in which he referred to the overthrow as an "act of war," Sanford Dole handed US Minister Willis a letter in which the oligarchy disputed the Blount Report findings and refused to give back political control of Hawai'i to the monarchy.[23] Instead, Dole invoked the rhetoric of sovereignty, a tactic that emphasized the coup state's position as a permanent rather than interim state institution, and claimed that the United States had no right to interfere with their government.[24] Four days later, the US Senate Foreign Relations Committee on Hawai'i began to debate this very question: Was the US military's aid in the coup of an independent government justified?

These proceedings and the Morgan Report that followed were designed to validate the United States' actions in Hawai'i and neutralize Blount's conclusions.[25] While the committee conceded that US Minister Stevens had carried out unauthorized partisan activities, the 1894 report contained no recommendations for action. In the end, the Morgan Report served as nothing more than a slap on the wrist for Stevens and the coup government. It did, on the other hand, accuse the queen of an attempt to overturn the Constitution of 1887, an action the committee deemed tantamount to an "act of abdication."

The Morgan Report findings, combined with the May 1894 vote by US Congress opposing the restoration of the queen and intrusion into the affairs of the provisional government, eased the oligarchy's fears of an American-backed reinstatement of the kingdom. But it also left the question of annexation unanswered, for the May 1894 vote also opposed any American action that could lead to incorporation of the archipelago. For the time being, it seemed as if the United States were walking away from the situation in Hawai'i.[26] A little over one year after the overthrow, the haole-led oligarchy was left with the question of what to do if incorporation into the United States proved unattainable. At the same time, as the Imada incident revealed, the coup government remained susceptible to political encroachments from emerging centers of power, as well as from Old World authorities that recognized the Hawaiian Kingdom's political independence.

Following the overthrow, British and French residents in the islands, royalist supporters, and the Native press called on an 1843 Anglo-Franco proclamation that bound the two European countries to protect Hawaiʻi's position as an independent kingdom.[27] Rumor that the British minister to Hawaiʻi, James Wodehouse, was attempting to secure political backing for the restoration of the queen quickly spread around the islands. This was followed by a report that Theo H. Davies—a British subject and royalist supporter who was one of Hawaiʻi's largest sugar-factors, owner of a major mercantile firm in the islands, and guardian to Princess Kaʻiulani, heir to the Hawaiian throne—was recruiting soldiers to defend the monarchy.[28]

At the time, the British Empire was rapidly expanding, and already having laid claim to Australia, New Zealand, Fiji, and the Cook Islands, it had strong interests in Hawaiʻi. American annexationists and haole oligarchs had long claimed that Princess Kaʻiulani was under British influence.[29] Kaʻiulani's mother was Princess Likelike, sister of Kalākaua and Liliʻuokalani, and her father was Scotsman Archibald Scott Cleghorn, who had served as governor of Oʻahu under the Hawaiian monarchy. Kaʻiulani had been studying in England during the overthrow, but she arrived in Washington, DC, on March 1, 1893 and issued a statement of protest that skillfully called on the right to political independence and freedom. She declared that while young (she would turn eighteen in 1894), she was "strong in the strength of seventy million people who in this free land will hear my cry and refuse to let their flag . . . dishonor mine!"[30] As the heir to the throne, Kaʻiulani fought boldly to restore the Hawaiian Kingdom. In order to build support for her cause, the princess toured the northeastern United States before meeting with President Cleveland in Washington, DC. She also sent numerous letters to American newspapers protesting the coup and even publicly accused Lorrin Thurston of conspiring to keep her away from Hawai'i so he and his compatriots could steal the kingdom.[31]

Lili'uokalani and Ka'iulani's actions helped to remind the world that the coup state was itself an embodiment of countersovereignty. In fact, the royal women's ability to disrupt the image of unintelligent and uncivilized leadership, with one of political savvy and sophistication, proved to be a constant thorn in the side of coup government officials. In their attempts to silence both the queen and the princess, oligarchs first contemplated paying the royal women an annual sum in return for their publicly relinquishing all claims to the throne. When both Lili'uokalani and Ka'iulani refused, they considered imprisoning them in isolation on the island of Kaua'i. The goal for the coup government, as Attorney General W. O. Smith plainly stated, was to "eliminate the old lady," and her claim to the throne, from public memory and discourse. This he claimed, was imperative to fortify the coup state's political sanctity.[32] Unable to stifle the royal women or their supporters, however, oligarchs moved to solidify their hold on Hawai'i by disguising their control through the veneer of democracy.[33]

A "REPUBLIC IN NAME": THE 1894 CONSTITUTIONAL CONVENTION

Early in February 1894, Attorney General W. O. Smith wrote to Lorrin Thurston about the problem of projecting the appearance of democracy while retaining control for the oligarchy. Members of the Executive Council, Smith explained, wished to have as much of the "representative feature as possible in passing the constitution" while at the same time "guarding against [the] danger of its getting away from us."[34] With Smith's words in mind, Thurston advised Dole that "whatever else it is called," their new government "should have the word 'Republic' in the name," as the term gave it more character, distinctness, and possibly greater appeal to the United States.[35] The form of a republic, he argued, would provide the democratized control and cover for running a government that needed to dispose of its opposition, namely the monarchical rule that both Liliʻuokalani and Kaʻiulani embodied. Thurston also urged Dole to make sure "that those who are drafting the constitution will not allow fine theories of free government to predominate over the necessities of the present situation."[36]

On March 15, 1894, the provisional government passed an act which provided for a constitutional convention. Automatic membership to the convention was granted to Sanford Dole, as well as to the members of the current executive and advisory councils, which amounted to nineteen men in all—a guaranteed majority. Eighteen other delegates would be elected, but—anxious that their strategic number of seats might not be a sufficient safeguard of their power—the oligarchs mandated that those who were to be eligible to vote for the eighteen remaining delegates had to first take a loyalty oath and "swear to oppose monarchical government in any form in the Hawaiian Islands."[37]

Although the constitutional convention was meant to strengthen the integrity of the coup state and reaffirm the oligarchy's right to rule, the continued effort by poʻe aloha ʻāina to fight for political independence revealed the republic's precarity. As part of their campaign against the convention, members of Hui Aloha ʻĀina o Nā Wāhine used the same tactics that Liliʻuokalani had deployed in her communications with then President Cleveland: they sent a written statement of protest composed in the language and style of the colonizer, documenting the "uncivilized" and "despotic" nature of the haole-led oligarchy to the foreign ministers of the United States, France, England, Germany, Portugal, and Japan. The women noted that despite their own patience and trust in the United States to deliver a just and impartial decision, the leaders of the coup government, "without even the courtesy of waiting for America's final decision, [have] been straining every effort to transform themselves into a permanent government, based on the support of the alien bayonets, and are now preparing . . .

to proclaim an assumed Republic, through a constitution which is acknowledged as the most illiberal and despotic ever published in civilized countries."[38] By using the rhetoric of "liberty" and "civility," Hui Aloha ʻĀina o Nā Wāhine was able to strategically deploy terms set by others and underscore the hypocrisy of the coup government to their global audience.

While many poʻe aloha ʻāina chose to express their outrage over the constitutional convention and loyalty oath through the written word and mass gatherings, others chose to voice their protest through silence: a great majority of the population boycotted the convention by simply refusing to sign the oath. Although this may seem counterproductive, as it gave Dole and his compatriots greater control of the electorate, it also worked to delegitimize the convention: The fact that a large majority of Kānaka Maoli refused to participate in the affair exposed the staged nature of the "democratic process," and highlighted the reality of oligarchical control.

The royalist paper, *Holomua,* ran headlines declaring the registration and oath a "Mammoth Fraud," and argued that any Hawaiian should be able to register as a "P.G. (provisional government) voter."[39] The language of the loyalty oath also caused concern for foreign populations in the islands, including the Portuguese and white American communities. Both Portuguese subjects and US citizens questioned whether the oath's requirement, that the taker was to "bear true allegiance" to the coup government, would curtail their membership in the Kingdom of Portugal and the United States, respectively. To counter this apprehension, the oligarchy reminded residents of the 1887 Constitution's race-based stipulations: not only could white settlers in the islands be citizens of other countries, they did not need to be citizens of Hawaiʻi in order to vote in the upcoming election. The Chinese and Japanese populations however, were again restricted from the right of franchise.

Voter registration numbers provide a sense of how deeply the public distrusted both the coup government and the loyalty oath. In 1890, there had been roughly 13,500 registered voters in the Hawaiian Kingdom, but in 1894, the electorate pool was down to 4,477. The provisional government organized a voter registration drive but the Honolulu electorate comprised just 1,500 persons, half its size in 1890 when the last election for representatives was held.[40] Despite the low voter registration and ongoing protests from various communities in the archipelago, the oligarchs pushed forward and held the election for convention delegates on May 2, 1894. The entire membership of the convention, including both elected and self-appointed members, included six Kānaka Maoli, fourteen Hawai'i-born American citizens, four US citizens, six British subjects, two Germans, and three Portuguese subjects.[41]

As the haole-led oligarchy created a new constitution, they worked, again, to maintain the appearance of democracy while continuing to disenfranchise the majority of the population. Members of the coup state advanced a racist teleology that positioned the republic as the "logical" end to an archaic monarchical system run by "heathens," and "primitive natives," while they themselves, they suggested, were "revolutionaries," styled after those who declared the United States independent from Great Britain. In his opening speech, Dole claimed that "the monarchy, after a period of decadence which was threatening and prejudicial to all public and private interests, came to a logical end—through its own plot to turn back the movement of public progress and to subjugate all national energies and aspirations in the interest of despotism."[42] The annexationist press, both locally and internationally, followed suit, portraying the republic as an institution that granted extended liberties and freedom.

But while the newly proclaimed republic attempted to paint itself as an institution that fought against the "tyranny of monarchy," the oligarchy could not escape the reality of their situation: they had staged a coup of such questionable character that US imperialists could not sway the vote toward annexation. In addition to this moral dilemma, the populace the haole-led oligarchy now governed was comprised mainly of Kānaka Maoli and Asians. US imperialists knew they had to convince white Americans that annexing Hawaiʻi would not threaten the country's racial order. It soon became clear that the main issues to be decided in writing a constitution were the intertwined questions of franchise and naturalization for Kānaka Maoli, Asians, and women. A May 18, 1894 article in the pro-annexationist newspaper the *Hawaiian Star* portrayed the oligarchy's dilemma, asking, "How . . . shall the franchise be bestowed consistently with fairness and yet retain the power in the hands of those most justly entitled?"[43]

In addition to painting the haole-led oligarchy as "revolutionaries," Dole addressed the problem of franchise in direct relation to the continued attempt at annexation. After reiterating the forming republic's policy of negotiating a political union with the United States, he reminded his audience that "franchise is a duty or function of citizenship conferred by the State, rather than a right."[44] By claiming that the ability to vote was a duty and not a right of citizenship, Dole and his colleagues used the creation of the republic, modeled after an understanding of the United States, as a way to permanently disenfranchise Asians in the archipelago. This argument also turned the focus of the convention from voting rights to the question of naturalization for Asians.

ASIANS AT THE BOUNDARIES OF NATION AND STATE

As a sizeable proportion of the Chinese population in the islands were either born as subjects of the Hawaiian Kingdom or had naturalized under the monarchy, haole oligarchs had to face the fact that, prior to 1887, Hawaiian nationals of Chinese descent had access to voting rights.[45] To add to this conundrum, the large Hawaiʻi-based Japanese community also sought membership in the republic as citizens. Because the debate regarding franchise for the Japanese and Chinese populations in the coup state was entangled with the naturalization question, architects of the constitution were careful to maintain the pretense of a democracy while working to disconnect citizenship status from the right to vote.

The debates over franchise at and around the constitutional convention were shaped in part by growing concern in the United States over race-based jurisdiction for an "other" that eluded the black-white binary. During the postbellum years, Asian migration to the South and the West Coast rose, as did anti-Asian sentiment.[46] In 1882, the United States passed the Chinese Exclusion Act, and by the time of the coup, it had been renewed for another decade. Convention delegates understood that Hawai'i's racial demographics had been enough to quell American annexation in 1893, and so they attempted to hold the Chinese and Japanese communities outside the political arena through their constitution. But whether they could, or even should, do this while maintaining a façade of democracy was a matter of debate.

Two weeks into the convention, the former attorney general and royal commissioner of immigration for the Hawaiian Kingdom, William N. Armstrong, published an editorial in the *PCA* titled "The Effect of the Alien: Their Effect on the Constitution." In this piece he asked readers to consider securing a white American-based nation in the Hawaiian Islands.[47] For Armstrong, fear of the "Asiatic," who was "not inferior . . . but [a] strong and developing race," was enough to promote giving up the cloak of democratic rule in order to embrace and uphold white supremacy. He suggested that the oligarchs create "two distinct forms of government made up into one form: one for ourselves [whites] and one for aliens, who outnumber us . . . . It must be distinctly understood that besides ruling themselves, the whites must create a form of government through which they can rule natives, Chinese, Japanese and Portuguese, in order to prevent being 'snowed under.'"[48] Armstrong argued that the republic's "dominance" of the roughly "80,000 'aliens' in blood," would do much more than simply calm the fears of the white American populace. Surely, he mused, the ability of "about a thousand Anglo-Saxons and Teutons" to govern while so greatly outnumbered would be "one of the most remarkable achievements . . . in modern times" and justified eschewing democracy for a "government adapted to the situation."[49] While members of the convention readily agreed with Armstrong's determination to control Hawai'i's Asian population, his open call for a transparent dictatorship through two distinct forms of government proved to be too much for even the oligarchs to swallow. They continued designing their "republic in name," opting for more indirect tactics to limit access to voting rights, such as subjective literacy tests and stiff property requirements.

Perhaps emboldened by the coup government's seeming desire for democratic rule, members of Hawai'i's Chinese community viewed the creation of the republic as an opportunity to regain some small measure of political and social equity, which they had held under the Hawaiian Kingdom prior to the constitution of 1887. On May 9, 1894, three weeks before the start of the convention, Chinese merchants and planters sent a petition addressed to Dole and members of the executive and advisory councils of the coup state asking for "some greater respect from the Government," as they did not think that they should be "regarded in the same light as our fellow countrymen in the United States."[50] They sought, among other things, the right to vote and a treaty of friendship and commerce between the Republic of Hawai'i and Imperial China. The petition highlighted the important role that the Chinese population played in Hawai'i's business economy as importers and consumers: "We have been associated with you so long commercially, financially, and socially, have learned your language, manners, and customs . . . in the matter of trade we are not selfish for we purchase many of our goods from importers of your own race." They also took the opportunity to remind members of the coup government, many of whom held interests in the sugar industry, of the importance of Chinese labor, claiming that "plantations . . . are the life of the land . . . and Chinese labor is the only one perfectly adapted to that work.[51] The petition was signed by hundreds of Chinese merchants and laborers who designated how long they had lived in the islands, whether they had naturalized into the Hawaiian Kingdom and were thus subjects of the monarchy, where their children had been educated, and lastly, whether their wives were of Hawaiian or Chinese descent.

Regulating the access of Hawai'i's Chinese community to political rights proved especially challenging for the haole-led oligarchy and revealed the limits of countersovereignty as a political mode of authority. On the fourth day of convention proceedings, when the voting members turned their attention to approving Article 17 on citizenship and naturalization, the conversation focused on the question of Hawai'i's naturalized Chinese population. In its draft form, Article 17 stipulated that citizenship would be granted to a person who "has been or shall hereafter become naturalized according to law."[52] This policy raised questions about the several hundred Chinese who had naturalized under the Hawaiian Kingdom: Would their status continue under the new republic? As naturalized citizens, would they have the right to vote?

At least one delegate suggested disregarding any naturalization status prior to the creation of the republic. Yet, as others pointed out, this would cause the loss of citizenship for European and American residents who had naturalized under the provisional government and diminish the seeming political power and stability of the oligarchy. Provisional President Dole advised the delegates that under the most recent constitution of 1887, not all Asians who naturalized received the right of franchise.[53] With this restriction in mind, he cautioned against revoking past rights of citizenship because it would "be a precedent which would forever characterize" their government, "which is bound to protect its citizens ... at home and abroad."[54]

In order to block the right to vote for Asians who had naturalized into the Hawaiian Kingdom before 1887 or who were born as Hawai'i citizen-subjects, oligarchs turned to recognizing treaty rights: the 1894 constitution stated that if a man had naturalized under the Hawaiian monarchy, and had originated from a country that currently possessed treaty relations with Hawaiʻi, he had the right to vote. As of 1894, Imperial China and the Hawaiian Kingdom had yet to establish a treaty of friendship and commerce, which meant Chinese residents were barred from voting. And while the Meiji government had been pushing for its subjects' voting rights by using the equal-rights clause of the Japanese-Hawaiian Treaty of Amity and Commerce of 1871, Minister of Foreign Affairs Francis Hatch assured the group that he found "upon inquiry at the interior office that no Japanese had been naturalized prior to January 17, 1893," so they would not be voting either.[55]

With Hawaiʻi's Asian population effectively disenfranchised, convention delegates turned their attention to the larger, ever-present dilemma: creating a national body suited for annexation to the United States in a place with a majority Indigenous and Asian population. While oligarchs would not rescind the political status of any Chinese resident who had naturalized under the Hawaiian Kingdom, they could bar the large Japanese population from attaining citizenship in the republic through a law borrowed from the United States. In early March 1894, Thurston had suggested, in a revealing letter to Dole, that they use the Mississippi Constitution of 1891 as a model for voting restriction.[56] The so-called "Mississippi Plan" required prospective voters to explain any and all sections of the constitution in English, effectively serving as a selectively enforced literacy test to keep Black citizens from the ballot box.

Leaders of the coup government adopted a similar method when setting the conditions for naturalization: they turned to indirect stipulations such as the language requirement to place Asians outside of the political arena.[57] Included among the prerequisites for naturalization in the initial draft of the constitution was the ability to understand, read, and write in the English language. When committee members proposed allowing prospective voters to demonstrate literacy in certain European languages as an alternative to English, Mr. Vivas, a Portuguese subject and elected convention delegate, cautioned that "most of the Japanese learn more French than English." The insinuation was that while the "English only" rule might prove difficult to some Europeans, it would nevertheless be an effective method to bar Japanese naturalization. As Mr. Vivas's comments demonstrate, although members of the oligarchy did not explicitly prohibit Japanese residents from naturalizing in the Constitution of 1894, the need to create a white body politic while maintaining the facade of social equity was tacitly understood.

Perhaps the greatest challenge to the coup state's invocations of countersovereignty were Kānaka Maoli themselves, who embodied the Hawaiian nation. Language requirements and treaty relations effectively disqualified the Chinese and Japanese community from national membership and political participation, but they could not be used against the Native population. Despite the haole regime's attempts to depict Kānaka Maoli as incapable of self-governance, the latter's very existence belied the attempt to erase the primacy of the Hawaiian Kingdom and prompted a deep anxiety in the oligarchy around the incomplete colonial project in the islands.

Oligarchs were especially concerned about the Native community's ability to vote for representatives in the coup state. In its final form, articles that designated the requirements for electing a representative stipulated that the prospective voter must be a male citizen of the republic or, if naturalized prior to January 17, 1893, be of a country that had treaty relations with the monarchy; speak, read, or write either English or Hawaiian; be over twenty years of age; and take an oath of allegiance not to aid in restoring the Hawaiian monarchy. Added to these requirements for the right to vote for senators was a stiff real property requirement of either three thousand dollars or an annual income of six hundred dollars.[58]

Kānaka Maoli quickly understood that the property requirements would disenfranchise a majority of the Indigenous population and that, as William Russ, Jr. argues, this "constitutional system was . . . devoted to the purpose of keeping the [white] American minority in control of the Republic."⁵⁹ Poʻe aloha ʻāina accordingly continued their protests during the convention proceedings. The women of Hui Aloha ʻĀina once again deployed the rhetoric of civil rights and liberty familiar to those in the United States, claiming that the constitution was despotic because it was designed to keep as many Kānaka Maoli from voting as possible, to prevent Asians from voting, and to restrict the rights to freedom of speech and of the press.⁶⁰

WOMEN'S SUFFRAGE IN HAWAIʻI

During the convention, members of the coup government had to grapple with one of the most politically divisive issues of the day: a woman's right to vote. In Hawaiian society, women are seen as "powerful autonomous beings" and during the late nineteenth century, they held significantly more social and political power than their Euro-American counterparts.⁶¹ Indeed, the actions and leadership of Kanaka Maoli women demonstrate that in many ways, Hawaiian society is egalitarian rather than patriarchal.

While the oligarchy could not limit Hawaiian membership in their nation, during the convention, white racial anxiety over the Indigenous population intersected with the structures of patriarchy to withhold the right to vote from all women. The debate over women's voting rights in the islands articulated the complex relationships among gender, indigeneity, and imperialism, as white settler anxieties about Kanaka Maoli potential access to the ballot influenced the outcome of the voting campaign. Convention delegates worried that acquiescence to the women's suffrage movement would open up a "dangerous way to invite a larger group of Native Hawaiians into the political arena."⁶² In other words, Kanaka Maoli women's autonomy posed a threat not just to patriarchal power, but also to the white supremacist state.⁶³

Kēhaulani Kauanui argues that gender oppression was a primary mode of imperialism throughout the history of Hawai'i.[64] Kanaka Maoli women lost political power and voting rights during the first decades of the nineteenth century, when settler colonial agendas began to reshape the archipelago's political landscape. Beginning in the 1820s, Anglo-American Calvinists introduced Western ideas into Hawaiian society, like the law of coverture, that dictated the domestic subjugation of women in social, political, and economic realms.[65] By the mid-nineteenth century, writes Kauanui, "male prominence had manifested itself in the Western political structure of the kingdom" and women lost access to the ballot box.[66] The 1852 constitution, for example, limited the right of franchise to "male subjects over twenty years of age, whether native or naturalized, and every male denizen of the kingdom who paid their taxes."[67]

Although women in Hawai'i no longer held the right to vote in 1893, their counterparts in the United States had been agitating for voting rights for over forty years and progress was being made. In 1890, two major suffrage associations—the American Woman Suffrage Association and the National Woman Suffrage Association—consolidated to create the National American Woman Suffrage Association, and women won the right to vote in Wyoming. From this point forward, supporters of the suffrage movement lobbied state-by-state in order to win voting rights. As the "western frontier" was gradually settled and incorporated into the United States, the new territories proved especially receptive to women's suffrage. Western boosters often supported the suffrage movement in their attempt to lure greater numbers of white settler families. White women's votes were also viewed as a way to negate the political influence of men from Southern and Eastern Europe, and some suffragists turned to racism and bigotry to make their case for enfranchisement.

Following the failed attempt at US annexation of Hawai'i, white American suffragists realized that as part of establishing the legal basis of their newly proclaimed republic, the men who instigated the coup would have to rewrite the electoral entitlements. Although it was not a part of the United States, the creation and negotiation of the Republic of Hawai'i's constitution presented itself as an opportunity for women to (re)gain the right to vote in the islands. Yet as in much of the United States, the suffragists' campaign for gender equality worked to reinforce, and even strengthen, the existing racial hierarchy.

During the first half of 1894, the Hawai'i-based Woman's Christian Temperance Union (WCTU), whose members were either descendants of or married to descendants of the first ABCFM missionaries, held a series of well-attended meetings to gather support for the women's vote. They formed a committee to meet with convention delegates and on June 12, 1894, delivered a petition for suffrage that was signed by one hundred and seventy-three white American women and eighty-three men.[68] Upon receiving the petition, convention delegates questioned whether it would "complicate our suffrage question . . . between the Chinese and the Japanese and the Portuguese . . . we are pretty well in a pili kia [conundrum] in that respect."[69] Delegates also acknowledged the autonomy and power of Native women—albeit dismissively—when they contended that "one great difficulty of the Hawaiian people is that they do not appreciate the privileges or the value of the franchise . . . to go on and add as many more in the shape of Hawaiian women would go to make a great deal more trouble."[70] Convention delegates understood that granting women's suffrage would mean enfranchising Kanaka Maoli women, and as a result, haole elites would be even more outnumbered.

A week later a delegation of the WCTU attended the public hearings of the convention in order to draw support for women's right to vote. In her speech, Mrs. Whitney, one of the suffragists in attendance, called attention to women's voting rights in Wyoming and Colorado as an example of the "civilizing effect" that the "fairer sex could have on the frontier."[71] Although convention delegates continued outwardly to express their support for claims of equality, their fear of Indigenous political power trumped all, and they continued to vote down women's suffrage.

In an attempt to reach a compromise, the suffrage committee proposed an education and property requirement designed to restrict Native women's access to the ballot box. Convention members, however, were well aware that unlike their white American counterparts in the United States, a large number of Kanaka Maoli women owned property and would meet any and all education requirements. They explained that "if all the women who asked for the franchise were of the same class as the committee, there would be no trouble," but as there were "about seven Hawaiian women to one white woman here . . . this would give a big majority of undesirable votes."[72] Some delegates questioned whether the issue of women's suffrage should even be considered, as they favored ignoring the entire matter. Others joked that a greater percentage of married men had signed on to the petition because they are "afraid of having their hair pulled out when they get home."[73]

Ultimately, women did not regain the right to vote under the republic, a right that they once held under the monarchy, because, as Patricia Grimshaw argues, "elite white men feared that doubling the Hawaiian vote would have negative implications on their hope for a prosperous, American, business-oriented future." Instead, the constitution included a vague provision for the matter to be considered at some other time by the legislature. As white women lamented the republic's denial of suffrage to themselves they "appeared oblivious to the irony entailed in their applause for the republic that removed a queen and other highborn Hawaiian women from positions of authority."[74]

CONCLUSION: THE CONVENTION AS REACTIVE ANXIETY

While the haole-led oligarchy debated the sociopolitical boundaries of the nation-state during convention proceedings, Liliʻuokalani and members of the Hawaiian Patriotic Leagues continued their protest through the production, publication, and dissemination of texts that positioned the constitutional monarchy as the rightful government of choice for the majority of Kānaka Maoli and Hawaiian nationals.[75] Throughout the 1890s, images rooted in views of US Reconstruction, slavery, and European imperialism reflected deep-seated biases toward Indigenous populations and people of color.[76] The blackening of Liliʻuokalani painted the queen and her government as incapable of rule while simultaneously legitimizing haole oligarchs as more capable statesmen. The writings that the queen and her fellow royalists circulated challenged these dominant racist depictions and correlated ideas of Kanaka Maoli depravity. They also emphasized that the convention was in no way creating a truly democratic form of government.[77]

As soon as the coup occurred, the queen and poʻe aloha ʻāina began using their extensive knowledge of politics and principles of democratic government to make the case for Hawaiʻi's independence. In March 1893 Liliʻuokalani wrote a piece for the *San Francisco Examiner* titled "A Queen's Appeal." She used this article, Silva writes, to turn the "tables on the oligarchy by deploying the very discourse that they attempted to use against her."[78] The "circumstances of the case do not call for a change of Government. Annexation is repugnant to the feelings of every native Hawaiian," Liliʻuokalani wrote. "Annexation is not necessary for the ends of peace or of civilization, or of commerce, or of security."[79]

These discursive tactics worked to flip the script of countersovereignty, reaffirm the Hawaiian Kingdom's right to political autonomy, and frame haole oligarchs as uncivilized, disruptive, and detrimental aliens. In their 1894 resolution against US annexation, Hui Aloha ʻĀina o Nā Wāhine members strategically echoed the language of white nativists and positioned themselves as "mothers, wives, and sisters. . . . whose country has been seized and whose liberty and rights are being trampled upon by a faction of Aliens." They explained that they wrote to "preserve the National Independence" through "restoration of our beloved Queen Lili'uokalani . . . and the legitimate Hawaiian monarchy."[80] This framing positioned the queen and poʻe aloha ʻāina as moral and just, and emphasized the incongruities between the republic's liberatory rhetoric and its repressive actions. Such language must have struck a nerve around the world and particularly in the United States, which was continuing to pass exclusionary laws to "protect" white Americans from "dangerous" foreign others.

In June 1894, the queen sent official letters of protest to US Minister Willis, as well as to other foreign consuls, that underlined her position as the people's choice through her use of modern ideas of democratic government. She opened each of her letters with the reminder that she would still be the reigning constitutional monarch if not for the illegal actions of the US Armed Forces, and went on to stress her knowledge of free government, highlighting the oligarchy's failure to secure such a platform in the Hawaiian archipelago.[81] The provisional government's actions, Liliʻuokalani noted, were "subversive of the first principles of free government and utterly at variance with the traditions, history, habits and wishes of the Hawaiian people . . . . [They have] set up without the assent of the people [and] . . . ha[ve] not sought to find a permanent basis of popular support." Of the proposed constitution, she stated that it does not "provide for or contemplate a free, popular or republican form of government . . . but does contemplate and provide for a form of government . . . irresponsible to the people, or to the representatives of the people, and which is opposed to all modern ideas of free government."[82] Despite her protests and the president's public condemnation of the overthrow, Cleveland responded to Liliʻuokalani's appeal by noting that since Congress had unanimously passed a resolution against restoration of the monarchy, he could do nothing to help her cause. He had in essence, washed his hands of the matter. For the time being, Hawaiʻi would remain in the interstice between kingdom and colony.

As the coup government's constitutional convention wound down, delegates decided not to ratify the vote. Fearing mass protests, they instead announced the birth of the "Republic of Hawai'i" to a small crowd at a public meeting. In order to accentuate their continued desire for US annexation, they chose as their celebratory date July 4, 1894. While the pro-annexationist *PCA* wrote up the event as a large success and triumph for democracy, the royalist *Holomua* described the crowd and attending delegates as visibly nervous. Opening prayers were passed over in order to hasten the ceremony along, and it was reported that the basement of 'Iolani Palace was filled with armed forces. Although Cleveland had initially declared the provisional government illegal, US Minister Willis immediately recognized the Republic of Hawai'i as the de facto government of the islands.

Though the haole-led oligarchy declared both their convention and the new republic a success, their reactive anxiety was clear. Threatened by movements for women's suffrage, Asian voting, and Indigenous political representation, settlers tried to advance what was revealed to be an incomplete colonial project. Their fears about losing the power they had shored up both before and after the coup led them to restrict voting rights through whatever tools they had at hand, including both US laws and those of the Hawaiian Kingdom. In the meantime, the continued call from po'e aloha 'āina for the return of their nation revealed the limits of countersovereignty as a political mode of authority and fortified the kingdom's right to political independence. These challenges reverberated across the Pacific and strengthened the growing concern in the United States over the lack of race-based jurisdiction for an "other" outside the black-white dichotomy. When eliminating a majority of the Asian and Hawaiian ability to access political power in the republic proved not to assuage white racial anxiety, oligarchs next turned their hopes to manipulating the existing island-based demographics to reflect an increase in the white settler population.

3

HOW THE PORTUGUESE BECAME WHITE

The Search for Labor and the Cost of Indemnity

AFTER THE passage of the 1894 Constitution, haole oligarchs could assert, with relative ease, the compatibility of the coup state's political system with that of the United States. But since the attempted annexation in 1893 had been hindered by the islands' demographics, leaders of the newly formed republic also set out to increase Hawaiʻi's white settler society. One tactic, proposed and later carried out by Sanford Dole, entailed recruiting white American "homesteaders" to colonize Hawaiʻi's Government and Crown Lands (see chapter 5). Another suggested strategy called for finding white laborers from Europe willing to live and work in Hawaiʻi. The latter undertaking fell to Lorrin Thurston, who worked on the twin tasks of recruiting European laborers to Hawaiʻi and convincing the US Senate Foreign Relations Committee that the archipelago's existing population was already suitable for inclusion.

Despite Thurston's assertion that Hawaiʻi was a white republic whose future had to be protected, the 1890 census data made clear that the white community—both American and European—constituted a minority of Hawai'i's residents.[1] The majority of the population, at forty thousand strong, were Kānaka Maoli. As the republic's minister to the United States, Thurston circulated his self-authored booklet, *A Hand-Book on the Annexation of Hawai'i*, with the hope of swaying indecisive American policymakers toward annexation. In it he maintained that Kānaka Maoli were "conservative, peaceful, and generous people, supporters of the Republic and of annexation," and most importantly, able to assimilate into the white population. In his attempt to negotiate the position of Kānaka Maoli in the US racial hierarchy of the time, the haole oligarch asserted that they were "not Africans, but Polynesians. They are brown, not black." Thurston closed his argument stating that "the two races," white and Hawaiian, "freely intermarry one with the other, the results being shown in a present population of some 7,000 of mixed blood. They [Kānaka Maoli] are a race which will in the future, as they have in the past, easily and rapidly assimilate with and adopt American ways and methods."[2] If these "mixed blood Natives" could be counted in the same category as white Europeans and Americans, Thurston argued, the white population in Hawai'i would be enlarged.

The white American populace accepted to at least some degree Thurston's argument regarding the Kanaka Maoli ability to assimilate. But the haole-led oligarchy could not escape the somewhat dissonant fact that they had sought to justify their coup by declaring the Native monarchy unfit, uncivilized, and unjust. To pacify the fears of those who objected to annexation based on Hawai'i's racial demographics, Thurston required a population that could boast European roots. For this he turned to the Portuguese.

Far from being seen as unambiguously European and white, Portuguese laborers in Hawai'i occupied a complex racial and national space. By 1893, the Portuguese comprised the largest group of Europeans in Hawai'i. But because a majority of their population did not come from the European continent and instead hailed from the Azores, Madeira, and Cape Verde islands—Portuguese colonies off the coast of Africa—they were not considered part of Hawai'i's haole ethnic group. Instead, they were often likened to Blacks, with men like South Dakota Senator Richard Pettigrew referring to their community as "the lowest of all the population upon the [Hawaiian] islands except . . . the natives themselves."[3]

Thurston was well aware of this sentiment, which had come up during Congressional debates regarding the "amenability" of Hawai'i's racial demographic to that of the United States. During the proceedings Senator Pettigrew had maintained that "while they speak the language of the Portuguese," the population in Hawai'i were not "Portuguese at all," but were comprised of a "mixture of races—Portuguese and Black and other races of Africa."[4] In truth, Thurston did not have to look as far afield as the Congressional debates to find similar sentiments—Sanford Dole himself wrote to members of US Congress in February 1893 calling for annexation in order to protect the white American population in Hawai'i. According to Dole, among the many dangers that the white American community faced was the islands' fast growing Asian population and the "uncivilized," a category that included the Portuguese.[5]

But by 1894, the oligarchy's perceived needs had changed, and Dole directed Thurston to the Portuguese mainland and colonies, in order to recruit a "European labor source." Four years later, when justifying the annexation of Hawai'i, the 1898 US Senate Committee on Foreign Relations mirrored Dole's change of heart and counted the Portuguese within the 22 percent of the islands' population listed as white. Taking their cue from Dole and Thurston, the committee asserted that in Hawai'i, the Portuguese were "also recognized as white citizens" and called on what they understood to be the population's "Anglo-Saxon qualities" to defend their reasoning. The Portuguese in Hawai'i were, the committee claimed, a "thrifty and law-abiding people" who had "intelligent conceptions of the value of liberty," lived in homes that were "uniformly comfortable and tasteful . . . [and] whose desire to become citizens of the 'Great Republic' [was] very earnest."[6] This was a radical change of heart: the Portuguese, who had not long ago been designated as among the "lowest of all the population," were now described as possessing the "moral" and "aesthetic qualities" of the white race. Their changing racialization served what Dole and Thurston understood to be the needs of the same annexationist cause: white supremacy.

Whiteness, the "white race," and indeed all races are invented categories—constructed for the sake of separating people along lines of presumed phenotypical difference.[7] But race has continued to function as social fact, albeit with different iterations over time and place, and white supremacy has been a constant force in American political culture.[8] In the case of the Portuguese in Hawai'i, articulations of whiteness were manipulated in order to uphold and extend white supremacy throughout occupied territories, and to advance settler colonial possession of the archipelago.[9] Moon-Kie Jung explains that at this time being of "European descent carried the crucial significance of conferring... membership in Hawai'i's political community."[10] For haole oligarchs like Thurston and Dole, the Portuguese embodied the ideal of being "both good laborers and good citizens, a combination devoutly to be desired."[11]

Where scholars of empire have often understood colonial racial formations as "exports" from the metropole, the episodes covered here demonstrate how, to borrow Paul Kramer's phrasing, the "racial remaking of empire and the imperial remaking of race are not separable," and instead exist in a "single, densely interactive field."[12] In Hawai'i, race and empire were mutual formations. The saga surrounding the attempt to recruit Portuguese laborers to Hawai'i reveals that American white supremacy was shaped in part by the interaction between global and local processes of US imperialism in the Pacific, including deliberate reworkings of racial categories and attempts to increase the white labor supply.

Ultimately, the confluence between transpacific imperial formations and local politics of jurisdiction limited the impact of the coup state's efforts to secure labor from Portugal. In January 1895, a counterrevolution intended to restore the Hawaiian Kingdom to political power began against the coup state. In its waning moments, hackdriver Manuel Reis, a Portuguese subject living in Honolulu, was taken into custody for five weeks on suspicion of aiding the counterrevolution. Reis sought redress for his incarceration, and when denied by the coup state he resorted to the same strategy used by Yosaku Imada—he called on his kingdom of birth for legal aid. While the future of one escaped prisoner proved to be of little consequence for the burgeoning Meiji state and its dreams of transpacific empire, for the waning Portuguese monarchy, the fate of this single carriage driver stood for the global contest for power waged between themselves, Great Britain, and the United States—a contest which they were loath to lose. Ultimately, Reis's indemnity case brought Great Britain, the United States, and Portugal into a thirty-year political impasse that greatly affected migration and trade relations around the world.

Because Manuel Reis was incarcerated at this specific place and time—Hawai'i between kingdom and colony—his case came to matter in a particular way. His demand for indemnity pushed forward articulations of state jurisdiction that arose because of the specific geopolitical space that late nineteenth-century Hawai'i occupied. Reis was never compensated for his time served in prison. But by analyzing his case for indemnity alongside that of the attempted recruitment and racialization of Portuguese labor, this chapter broadens the narrative of settler colonialism in Hawai'i to consider the concrete encounters that resulted from the intersecting histories of competing sovereignties, occupation, and resistance.

In March 1896, the Portuguese monarchy halted all emigration to Hawai'i over the question of unresolved reparations for Reis. While this effectively ended the coup government's search for an alternative

European labor source and severely limited its ability to portray itself as a republic aligned with the ideals of American white nationalism, the ban strengthened the local Portuguese community's identity as white Europeans. Faced with an increasing population of Japanese laborers, whom they understood as the cause of their low wages, Hawai'i-based Portuguese emphasized their position as white workingmen through their European heritage. In an ironic twist, Reis's indemnity case led to both the long pause on migration from the Portuguese Empire, as well as the simultaneous push from within the local community to be racialized as white.

The Reis case negotiations and the attempted racialization of Portuguese laborers as white reveal the particular trappings of nation-statehood—white settlement, police force, and international recognition—that haole oligarchs prioritized in order to make the coup state legible to the United States. Bringing together, on the one hand, the oligarchy's attempt to construct a majority-white populace through the racialization and importation of Portuguese labor and, on the other, its simultaneous denial of Portugal's demands for indemnity juxtaposes the coup state's dedication to white supremacy with the disparate power relations between an empire and a fledgling republic. Although both plantation owners and haole oligarchs desperately wanted to secure a new white labor source, the unsuccessful negotiations over the Reis indemnity case speak to the coup state's disavowal of the waning Portuguese Empire and signaled the coming shift to a modern transpacific order.

THE PORTUGUESE IN HAWAI'I

At the time of the overthrow, Portuguese had been residing in Hawai'i for decades.[13] The earliest Portuguese residents were mostly sailors from Madeira, the Azores, and the Cape Verde islands who had who had left whaling ships to settle in the archipelago. Among this community were those known locally as the "Black Portuguese," who were of mixed Portuguese and African descent and hailed from the Cape Verde island of Brava.[14] Approximately four hundred Portuguese people were already living in the kingdom when, in 1878, the first organized shipload of Portuguese contract workers destined for Hawai'i's plantations arrived. By 1896, there had been twenty more such shiploads, bringing approximately 12,780 Portuguese migrants, including women and children, to Hawai'i.[15]

As a population from a European empire, Portuguese migrants were given greater political and social freedoms than Asians within the archipelago. While the Bayonet Constitution of 1887 barred Asians from voting regardless of naturalization status, all nonnatives of European and American ancestry were given the right of franchise, even if they were not subjects of the Hawaiian Kingdom. The only requirement was the ability to read a newspaper in any European language. Jon Van Dyke explains that this carefully "crafted language in the 1887 Bayonet Constitution . . . [was] designed to explicitly allow those of Portuguese ancestry to vote," and helped give the party of haole oligarchs its victory in a critical election held in 1887 against the royalists.[16] On plantations, Portuguese laborers were usually positioned on the upper end of the racial hierarchy. They often served as luna (overseers) to Chinese and Japanese laborers, and were paid more too: in 1886, planters estimated that a Portuguese male laborer cost them roughly forty-five dollars more than a Japanese one.[17] Yet Portuguese laborers had little possibility of advancement—they were stuck in perpetual middle-management. Situated between the haole plantation manager and Asian workforce, luna were expected to maintain the social and racial hierarchy of plantation life.

Although the Portuguese fared relatively better than their Asian counterparts, in 1886, the Portuguese consul general in Hawai'i, Antonio de Souza Canavarro, noted various instances of police abuse directed at the community. In response to his reports, the Portuguese monarchy halted all emigration to Hawai'i beginning in 1888. Despite this act of protest and Portugal's abrogation of all treaties in 1892, on September 15, 1894, Republic of Hawai'i Minister of Foreign Affairs Francis M. Hatch wrote to Thurston and instructed him to travel to Lisbon to negotiate a new immigration treaty.[18] He also directed Thurston to visit the Azores and Madeira to see whether conditions there were favorable for labor recruitment.[19]

At the time of Hatch's initial letters, Thurston was in Washington, DC, promoting the newly formed "Republic of Hawai'i" and defending the coup government against political protest from royalists such as Paul Neumann, who served as Queen Lili'uokalani's private attorney after the overthrow.[20] In one of his many September 1894 communications with Thurston, Foreign Minister Hatch reported that Neumann was in DC, "off on another secret mission to prevent recognition by the European powers."[21] Having just made the official transition from provisional government to a republic in July of that year, the coup state was actively seeking official recognition from various countries and was wary of the continued attempts to reinstate the queen. In addition to official statements of recognition, political treaties served as a way to bolster the international reputation of the questionably formed republic. For the oligarchy an official immigration treaty with Portugal would serve two purposes: it would strengthen the coup state's political footing with recognition from an Old World European empire and solidify a viable source of agricultural labor to counter the ever-increasing Issei population, a group which the haole elite saw as a threat to their control.[22]

SEEKING LABOR ABROAD

To men like Thurston and Hatch, as well as members of the Hawai'i-based Planters' Labor and Supply Company (PL&S), finding any other viable labor source to counter the influx of Japanese was of the utmost importance.²³ Upon stopping in London on his way to Portugal, Thurston was directed by Hatch to "endeavor, unofficially" to ascertain from the British government why Chinese migrants, other than those holding return passports, were prohibited from embarking at Hong Kong for Hawaiʻi. Hatch also requested that Thurston use all his "discretion and charm" to secure the "abrogation of such prohibition."²⁴ As the foreign minister of the republic and an ardent annexationist, Hatch must have known that following the passing of the US Chinese Exclusion Act of 1882, the Hawaiian Kingdom, under pressure from white American business interests and haole plantation owners who had hopes of annexation, had passed its own version of the law in 1886. Beginning in 1888 this Hawaiʻi-based law effectively cut off further importation of Chinese labor to the kingdom and had been carried over to the republic.

The year 1894, however, presented a different political and social climate. Eight years after passing the Chinese Exclusion Act in Hawaiʻi, the perceived need for a cheap, non-Japanese labor source forced the oligarchs in charge to ignore their own legislation. With their plans for incorporation into the United States blocked, republic officials yielded to the plantation owners' demand to withdraw the restrictions on Chinese immigration "to a limited extent," as doing so would "enable [the] planting community to secure the supply of Chinese labor for which it stands so much in need, and would obviate the necessity of adding to [the] Japanese population."²⁵ Haole elite hoped that combined with sources of European labor, the renewed Chinese immigration from Hong Kong would combat the growing "threat" presented by the ever-increasing Japanese presence. They soon found their hopes dashed, however, as Thurston reported that efforts to negotiate with the British had been unsuccessful.²⁶ Thurston set sail for Lisbon with hopes of securing a new immigration treaty and an order for 570 laborers for the PL&S. Fortunately for the haole oligarch, timing, global circumstance, and imperial rivalries were on his side.

Four years before Thurston's arrival in Lisbon, the agricultural and industrial underdevelopment that had plagued Portugal's global economic and political standing had come to a head in a generalized crisis. In 1890 the Portuguese wine industry, which had in large part sustained the national economy, began to experience a massive decline in exports.[27] Without an industry to support its growing population or balance trade with Great Britain, tens of thousands of Portuguese men and women began fleeing to Brazil. The Portuguese monarchy did not attempt to stop the flood of emigration as the remittances the migrants sent home managed to keep the country solvent.

The disaster in the wine industry was magnified by the so-called British Ultimatum of 1890. The two episodes were so far-reaching that together they sounded the death knell to Portugal's status as a global power. During the second half of the nineteenth century, the Portuguese monarchy had focused on laying claim to the land between its two African colonies, Angola and Mozambique, in order to connect them to each other and create a Royal Trans-Africa Railway.[28] In 1890, under pressure from Cecil Rhodes, who founded the British South Africa Company, as well as Church of England and Presbyterian missionaries, British military forces began pushing Portuguese troops out of this area. On January 11, 1890, the British government delivered an ultimatum to the Kingdom of Portugal that demanded the withdrawal of Portuguese troops from Zimbabwe and Malawi—lands where Portuguese and British interests overlapped. Combined with the already waning agricultural and wine industries and the flood of emigration, the acquiescence of King Carlos I to the British fueled growing resentment toward the flailing constitutional monarchy. Two years later, on June 14, 1892, the once-mighty Portuguese Empire declared bankruptcy. By the time Thurston arrived in Lisbon in November 1894, the Portuguese Empire was in the midst of ongoing decline and the representative from Hawai'i found himself poised to take advantage of its fleeing subjects.

When Thurston arrived in Lisbon he immediately secured an audience with the Portuguese minister of foreign affairs. At this meeting, Thurston was informed that because Portugal was a "colonial country" the government was "desirous that their people should go to their various colonies," but they would make no objections if their people wished to emigrate to Hawai'i.[29] Since his officially stated business in Portugal was to negotiate an immigration treaty, Thurston was unable to leave the capital in order to investigate the possibility of recruiting plantation labor from the islands of the Azores and Madeira. He turned to Ernest Hutchinson, who had been sent ahead by the PL&S, to assess the possibilities of importing labor from these Portuguese colonies.

While Thurston waited in Lisbon for an audience with King Carlos I, Hutchinson attempted to recruit plantation labor from the Azores and Madeira. The local governments were ready to cooperate, but as Thurston and Hutchinson soon discovered, the competition with Brazil was formidable. Writing from Madeira, Hutchinson informed PL&S officials that the movement to Brazil "lately resumed is all the rage here again and is the greatest factor against us—the short voyage, identity of language, freedom from contract [underlined] are more than enough to offset the climate—although Brazil is popularly known as the 'Portuguese graveyard.'"[30]

Faced with the possibility of failure, Thurston began to look into other sources of labor recruitment in Portugal. He found one in the northern peninsula city of Porto. Seven to eight hundred men there who had been recruited to work in Portugal's African colonies now found themselves unable to go, because the Portuguese monarchy could no longer afford the amount needed to pay for their shipment. Thurston saw this pool of men, who were already prepared to leave, as a perfect source of labor for the coup state. In his November 14, 1894 communication with Henry F. Glade, the consul general for the republic based in Bremen, Germany, and agent for the Hawaiian Board of Immigration, Thurston lobbied for permission to recruit from the

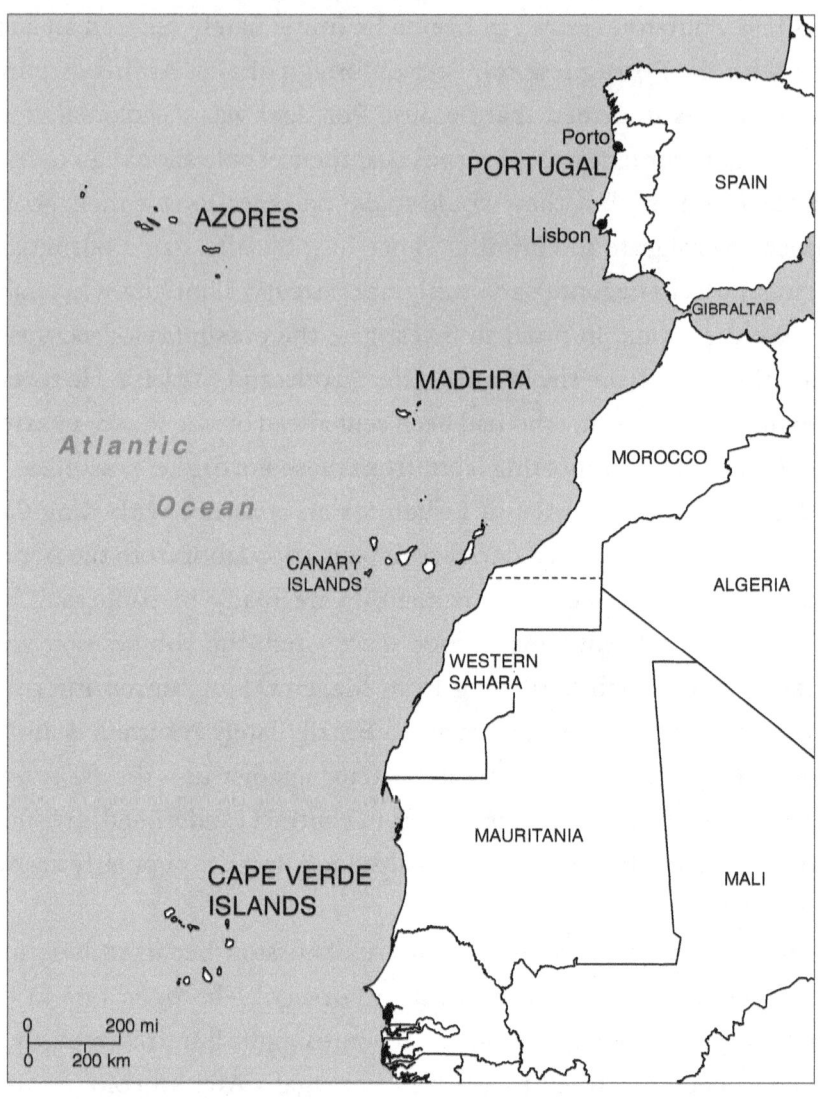

Map 2. Portugal, Madeira, the Azores, and the Cape Verde Islands. Map by Michael Pesses.

Porto-based labor pool, stating that it would "in the strongest way indicate that the government favors emigration to Hawai'i and would strengthen our moral position in the Azores." He also pointed out that as the Portuguese monarchy was "rather in a hole concerning this lot of men," it would most likely "generate a friendly feeling in them if we take them" and perhaps help secure a sorely needed immigration treaty.[31]

To Thurston, it seemed as if he had stumbled upon the perfect solution to his recruiting problems. In Porto he found not only a willing population, but also one that was free of women and children, and would place the republic on good footing with the Portuguese monarchy. Despite the latter's faltering political and economic standing, Thurston understood that labor migration into the republic was greatly needed, and that treaty recognition from an Old World empire could only help the political positioning of the questionably formed coup state.

With a new treaty of immigration between Portugal and the republic drafted in December 1894, Thurston left Lisbon and set sail for Washington, DC, on Christmas Eve. Thinking that he had successfully accomplished his goals of preparing the way for an official immigration treaty and securing a source of reliable, non-Asiatic labor to counter the increasing Japanese population in the islands, Thurston relaxed while at sea. Little did he know that as he was sailing to the United States, war had begun in Hawai'i.

THE COUNTERREVOLUTION AND THE HACK-DRIVER

While Thurston was away in Portugal, those opposed to the republic began to plan the 1895 Kaua Kūloko, or counterrevoultion. In October 1894, they had purchased arms in San Francisco and had secretly shipped them to O'ahu. By December however, the oligarchy had learned of the pending counterrevolution through their paid spies, and had arrested two leaders of Hui Aloha 'Āina, Joseph Nāwahī and John Ailuene Bush.[32] Both Nāwahī and Bush were taken as political prisoners and held without bail for two months between December 1894 and February 1895. During this time, leadership of Hui Aloha 'Āina was held by Robert Kalanihiapo Wilcox and Samuel Nowlein.[33]

Perhaps because they knew that the leaders of the coup state were aware of their plans, Wilcox and Nowlein decided to act quickly. On January 5, 1895, they distributed the purchased arms to those who began to enter Honolulu from outlying districts in anticipation of the counterrevolution. The rest of the munitions were stored at the Lēʻahi-based home of Henry Bertelmann, former major of the Queen's Guards. The counterrevolution was set to occur just after one o'clock a.m. on January 7. But on January 6, republic officials preempted the planned action and sent armed police officers to Bertelmann's home. Counterrevolution forces met the armed officers at Bertelmann's and fighting quickly ensued.

Bertelmann was arrested that day at his residence, but Wilcox and others managed to escape to Lēʻahi. The oligarchy declared martial law on January 7, 1895, and with it, the writ of habeas corpus was suspended. After a week of fighting, Wilcox, Nowlein, and others surrendered in Kalihi Valley on January 14, 1895. In total, roughly four hundred people, most of whom were Hawaiian, were arrested for allegedly supporting the counterrevolution. They were given prison sentences varying from one to thirty-five years and fined anywhere between five thousand and ten thousand dollars.[34] Queen Liliʻuokalani was also taken into custody of the coup state. Among those apprehended for their involvement in the counterrevolution were citizens and subjects of foreign countries including China, Denmark, Macedonia, France, Germany, Great Britain, Japan, and Portugal.[35]

The attorney general for the republic at the time, W. O. Smith, believed that the best strategy following the arrests "was to threaten hanging, frighten as many people as possible, then back off."[36] Accordingly, military tribunals convened by the government sentenced Wilcox and some others to hang, which prompted an outcry from the local and international community.[37] In a letter to President Sanford Dole, Consul General Canavarro situated his plea for leniency for the arrested Portuguese subjects within definitions of "Christian civility," and addressed the president as "the Philosophic Christian who is at the head of the Hawaiian nation."[38] Due to the public outcry and diplomatic pressure for leniency, and perhaps as a gesture of "goodwill" to celebrate the republic's first year of existence, the oligarchy released a few of the prisoners on July 4, 1895. The rest were paroled in January 1896. Many of the European sympathizers who were not citizens of the republic were forcibly deported upon release.

One of the political prisoners who was captured and later released was Portuguese subject and Honolulu resident Manuel Reis. Reis had been born in 1854 in Brava, one of the Cape Verde islands, an archipelago located off the Western Coast of Africa.[39] His father was a port master there. The islands had been colonized by the Portuguese in 1462 and during the next century the population prospered from the transatlantic slave trade. By the time Reis was born, the slave trade was no longer a major economic factor in the islands. Their geographic location along the mid-Atlantic shipping routes however, made the Cape Verde islands an ideal location for resupplying whaling and trading ships. Reis became a crewmember on a whaling vessel, the *Atlantic,* which was whaling off the coast of the Chatham Islands in 1875. It crashed into another vessel, the *Napoleon,* and needed to come to shore for repairs. Although over four thousand miles away, Honolulu proved to be the closest port.[40] The ship sailed for Oʻahu, and Reis arrived in Honolulu on September 12, 1875. While working to discharge the *Atlantic*'s cargo of whale oil in Honolulu, he broke his left arm. He was sent to Queen's Hospital, and while he recovered, the *Atlantic* set sail without him.[41] Although Reis received an honorable discharge from the ship's service, he was unable to sign aboard any other whaling vessel because of permanent weakness in his arm. Stuck in Honolulu at age twenty-five, Reis took on any job that he could and ended up working as coachman and yardman for US Minister General James M. Comly for twenty-five US dollars a month.

In February 1879, Reis became the licensed owner and driver of a carriage for hire in Honolulu. His business soon grew to include three

Figure 8. Manuel and Eugenia Reis at home in Honolulu, 1936. Photo by D. H. Nielen. Courtesy of David Kump and Robert Nielen Ogden.

additional carriages that worked out of a hack-stand known as Honolulu's "290," which was located on the bustling corner of King and Fort Streets. According to Reis, the advent of telephone service in December 1880 served as a boon for business, as it was now possible for customers to call the hack-stand and request a carriage and driver for pickup. At the time of his affidavit in 1895, Reis was averaging "upwards of four thousand (U.S.) dollars a year" and had accumulated property worth an estimated twenty-five thousand dollars.[42] The same year he opened his hack-stand, Reis married Eugenia Keohookalani Pilipo, who came from a prominent Kanaka Maoli family with ties to the monarchy. Due to his wife's connections, Reis's carriages were under royal patronage and his business was often referred to as the "Royalist Hack-Stand."[43] With his prosperous business and his royal ties, Reis was one of the "best known men in Honolulu."[44]

Following the overthrow, Reis's royal patronage soon aroused the suspicions of ruling coup state officials. Beginning in the second half of 1894, his hack-stand was put under secret service surveillance by E. G. Hitchcock, marshal of the provisional government and later of the Republic of Hawai'i. On January 9, 1895, two days after the declaration of martial law and while fighting was still ongoing, Reis was busy transporting patrons around Honolulu. Upon returning to his stables to change horses before the afternoon rush, he was informed that the marshal of the republic had sent for him. Thinking that he was about to receive a business proposition from the republic to supply carriages for their officials, Reis hurried over to the police station. When he gave his name, he was immediately shoved down, searched, and placed in a cell until he was taken to Oahu Prison where he was held with twelve others.[45] While incarcerated, he and those held with him were routinely taunted with death threats by the prison guards.[46] According to statements made by his physicians, Doctors Murray and Brodie, during his time in jail, Reis suffered from delirium brought on by a 105-degree fever. He was moved to the prison hospital and later granted medical leave to recuperate in the more arid climate of Hawai'i Island.[47]

Upon his release, with the aid of former attorney general and prominent royalist Paul Neumann, Manuel Reis made a claim against the coup state and pressed for financial redress. He quickly found out, however, that he was unable to claim indemnity because the oligarchy had passed new laws designed specifically to protect themselves from legal ramifications following the counterrevolution attempt.[48] Left with no other recourse other than diplomatic appeal, Reis, like Yosaku Imada before him, called on his kingdom of birth for protection.

But unlike Imada, Reis was a man with political and economic cachet. He repeatedly drew attention to the fact that he was, "still a subject of the Kingdom of Portugal, never having directly or indirectly forfeited [his] allegiance to or [his] right or protection by said Kingdom."[49] Although Reis noted that he had registered to vote under the Bayonet Constitution of 1887, he, like other residents of Hawai'i at the time, understood that the 1887 document purposefully gave voting rights to residents, as opposed to subjects, of the Hawaiian Kingdom. In other words, the hack-driver benefitted from the political maneuvering that was designed to curtail the powers of the Hawaiian monarchy and bolster the very political leaders who would later imprison him.

With "diplomatic intercession" as the "only avenue of redress left," the Portuguese government initiated a $50,000 indemnity claim against the Republic of Hawai'i on Reis's behalf for damages resulting in disgrace to himself, his family, and his business reputation, as well as permanent injury to his health.[50] In April 1896, fifteen months after Portugal's Consul General Canavarro requested leniency for all detained subjects, during which time he officially discouraged further emigration of Portuguese laborers to Hawai'i, Henry Cooper, minister of foreign affairs for the Republic of Hawai'i, finally detailed the coup state's denial of Reis's indemnity case. Along with his letter to Canavarro, Cooper attached the affidavits of ex-marshal Hitchcock, Johansen, and other detectives who had been charged with the task of monitoring Reis during the months preceding the counterrevolution. According to statements taken from Hitchcock, Manuel Reis was the "continuously trusted hack-driver who took the suspected heads of the conspiracy to their places of secret meeting . . . held at unseemly hours of the night."[51] Reis was also named as a participant at the meetings and held responsible as one of the men who worked to incite people into joining the counterrevolution. C. W. Johansen, a detective hired by Hitchcock, elaborated on the ex-marshal's claim, stating that he had observed Reis at a royalist meeting in September 1894 at which he "spoke very strong against the government and missionaries and wished them all in hell." Johansen also claimed that he heard Reis "telling a kanaka that he was willing to risk everything he had for the royalist cause and to see the provisional government kicked the hell out."[52]

Minister of Foreign Affairs Cooper's superficial reasoning maintained that since Reis had worked with other hack-drivers who had proven their guilt by "choosing" to leave the Republic of Hawai'i when they were given a choice between voluntarily departing and continued imprisonment, he was guilty by association. He asserted that since Reis had allegedly been employed by leaders of the "conspiracy," he had to have knowledge of the event and, "such being the case, it became the duty of Mr. Reis to inform the authorities of what he knew."[53] Cooper also attempted to justify the actions taken by the coup state against Reis by invoking several court decisions following the Morant Bay Rebellion of 1865, which involved the uprising of several hundred Jamaican men and women against their colonial British rulers. According to the minister of foreign affairs, the republic was following international practice and precedent.[54]

Despite Portugal's request, the Republic of Hawai'i refused to grant financial reparations to Reis. In March 1896 the Portuguese monarchy responded by formally halting all emigration from its shores to the Hawaiian archipelago. For the flailing empire, whose subjects were seeking economic opportunity abroad, cutting off a destination for contract labor was not a move to be made lightly. But when put on the diplomatic world stage, the once-mighty Portuguese monarchy did not want to acquiesce to a small, fledgling republic.

THE PORTUGUESE PETITION

The Portuguese monarchy's ban on emigration to Hawai'i led local plantation owners to rely even more heavily on Japanese labor. This ignited both class- and race-based concerns for the Hawai'i-based

Portuguese community. Faced with competition from the increasing numbers of Japanese workers while travel from their home country was barred, members of the Uniao Portugueza, an organization said to represent the Portuguese community throughout the Hawaiian Islands, underlined the similarities between themselves and other European laborers. They stated that it was almost impossible for "European and other workingmen to subsist on the wages offered" now that Asian immigrants had driven pay rates down and singled out the Issei as stealing jobs from other plantation laborers.[55] While Lorrin Thurston worked to convince white Americans that the laboring community from the islands of Madeira, Cape Verde, and the Azores was indeed white and European, the Hawai'i-based Portuguese community was making the same claim.

On Tuesday, March 24, 1896, the *PCA* ran a front-page article covering the recent large gathering of O'ahu's Portuguese community in downtown Honolulu. The meeting's call to halt further Japanese immigration drew interest from both haole laborers and planter elite, as the issue of cheap labor and its impact on wages and overhead costs crossed racial, class, and national boundary lines. In speaking with the press at the gathering, an unnamed Portuguese man described as being "prominent in business circles" voiced his concern about the incoming Japanese migrants as a labor problem. He stated, "For a long time the laboring men have been trying to do something toward stopping the continuous flow of Asiatic laborers . . . the Portuguese . . . are heart and hand with every laboring man barring Asiatics, and we shall continue to be as long as we are on Hawaiian soil."[56] The interviewee then directed further remarks toward the republic's Issei population and cited a scheduled incoming shipment of workers from Japan. To the *PCA* he posed the question, "Does that mean that 1,500 Japanese will step out of the country? . . . Some will come to Honolulu and engage in various occupations . . . . Others will scatter over the islands . . . What are they doing? Taking the bread out of the mouths of the laboring man and his family."[57] Here was the crux of the argument: with cheap Japanese labor flowing into Hawai'i, the Portuguese community argued that their pay was being held down at best, and stolen at worst.

In various public meetings and petitions that circulated over the next several months, leaders of Hawai'i's Portuguese community continued to identify themselves as "workingmen" alongside other European settlers, such as Germans and Norwegians, in opposition to haole elite and Asian labor.[58] In 1896 the Central Committee of the Uniao Portugueza submitted a petition against the further importation of Japanese and Chinese labor to President Sanford Dole and the legislature of the Republic of Hawai'i.[59] This document stated that the over thirteen thousand Portuguese living in Hawai'i defined themselves as both European and settlers, in juxtaposition to the "Asiatics" who were nothing more than a source of cheap, transient labor.[60]

The Portuguese community's opposition to the ban on migration from their home country was focused on planters' policies that used the hiring of Asians to keep wages low for all laborers. But the pro-annexationist press ignored the class-based issue and instead concentrated on racial tensions and differences, championing the Portuguese as white. From March to June 1896, *PCA* editors manipulated the situation to highlight the hostility directed toward Japanese workers by the Portuguese, and to compare the two communities with each other. For example, in a March 31, 1896 article titled "Japan vs. Portugal," the *PCA* stated that "the people here [in Hawai'i] of all nationalities . . . have come to the conclusion that the Hawaiian Islands are too small for the Japanese, and that they should move out . . . for the reason that they are making severe inroads upon the trade of the white storekeepers, and upon the work of mechanics and laborers."[61] While it is possible that the editors of the pro-annexation *PCA* held the interest of the islands' laboring Portuguese population at heart, the series of articles printed over the next few months pointedly promoted both a growing fear of the Japanese population and the hope that the Portuguese community could carry the future of a white republic.

THE INTERNATIONAL EFFECTS OF THE REIS CASE

Undoubtedly the decision by Portugal to halt all emigration to Hawai'i, while Japanese laborers continued to arrive, did not sit well with Lorrin Thurston, members of the Uniao Portugueza, or the laboring island-based Portuguese community. As the first few months of 1896 progressed, tension between the haole-led oligarchy and local Portuguese community continued to escalate, with the latter displaying signs of growing unrest, as merchants and plantation workers alike were reportedly taking part in mass meetings and public rallies.[62] Despite the continued requests for indemnity made by the Portuguese monarchy and escalating pressure from the Hawai'i-based Portuguese population, the haole-led oligarchy held to its decision. In April 1898, while talks of US annexation were in the air, Canavarro sent one last request about the Reis case to the Republic of Hawai'i via Minister Cooper. In his letter, the consul general admonished the minister of foreign affairs for the complete lack of response from the republic and went so far as to accuse the oligarchy of a "veritable violation of the rights of nations." Noting the possibility of annexation to the United States, Canavarro also stated that the indemnity claim would "be maintained whether annexation takes place or not, or whatever the form of government this country may be called to receive."[63]

The Portuguese consul general's letter reveals that his government understood that annexation to the United States carried the possibility of great change. No longer would Portugal be dealing with the fledgling Republic of Hawai'i, but with the United States. On August 4, 1898, with annexation to the United States assured, Cooper finally replied to Canavarro and suggested that if the Republic of Hawai'i had remained an independent country, it would have considered arbitration with the government of Portugal. But given the pending annexation and the imminent transfer of political power, Cooper concluded the republic "no longer [had] the authority to take further steps in the matter."[64] Although Hawai'i would not be formerly annexed until 1900, the republic's political leaders must have thought that, thanks to their strategic stalling, they had successfully passed on the issue of Reis's indemnity.

They were mistaken, however, as the Portuguese monarchy continued to press Reis's claim forward into the international political arena. Following the dismissal from Minister Cooper, Canavarro brought the case to the attention of Viscount de Santo Thryso Carlos Cirilo Machado, the Portuguese minister in Washington, DC, who in turn brought the matter to the attention of John Hay, US Secretary of State. In a November 1898 statement addressed to Hay, Machado pointed out that it was "ridiculous" for Reis to be imprisoned for driving the leaders of the counterrevolution, reminding the secretary that "in general, patrons select the cabmen whom they employ, but cabmen do not select their patrons."[65] Machado also discounted the claims made against Reis by Hitchcock and his detectives by reviewing counter affidavits which described the accusers' poor character. Of C.W. Johansen, Machado claimed that "he never hesitated to catch his man the best way he could, and he always made his money by pleasing his employers . . . . Among his occupations was that of enticing deserters from ships, and hiding them away until the usual reward was offered."[66] With the leading witnesses' character in question, Machado reminded Hay that Reis had never been brought to trial, was not given the opportunity to prove his innocence, and had never been proven guilty. Despite Machado's argument, Secretary Hay was not swayed, and maintained that the United States was not responsible for claims of indemnity against the Republic of Hawai'i. He then referred the matter back to the original source of contention.

Reis was just one among many who called for indemnity. Many of the others who brought cases against the republic were subjects of

Great Britain and France. Following the US annexation of the Hawaiian Islands, Britain applied political pressure to Washington, DC, in order to settle the claims it had pending against the republic as a result of the 1895 counterrevolution.[67] But because Britain had refused to arbitrate the claims of American citizens deported from South Africa during the Boer War, the United States now refused to mediate on behalf of the British citizens.[68] Beginning in 1901, Britain took steps to alleviate the political stalemate between itself and the United States, setting up a commission to address the American claims in South Africa.[69] The US government noted Britain's favorable political response, and by the end of the same year, Secretary of State Hay told Sanford Dole, now territorial governor of Hawai'i, that he would be "pleased" if a similar course could be reached.[70] In 1903, roughly a year after Hay made his request to Dole, the governor sought permission from the territorial legislature to set up a three-man commission to settle all claims stemming from the 1895 counterrevolution. The bill granting the commission passed the through the territorial Senate, but was tabled in the House of Representatives. By this time, the aging Dole had stepped down as governor and could only promise the US State Department that he would encourage the incoming governor, George R. Carter, to follow through on the matter.

Carter, however, refused to provide for a commission and cited the current economic woes of the territory as the reason for his refusal. Britain had been keeping a close eye on the situation, and upon learning of Carter's stance, insisted that when the United States had annexed the islands, it also assumed all legal obligations. In 1911 Britain and the United States agreed upon a schedule of claims for consideration. However, with the onset of World War I, the matter was put on the back burner until 1925, when a three-man arbitration panel was created in Washington, DC.

It had been thirty years since the initial filing of claims and the tribunal wished to expedite the process. Wray Jose explains that in order to do so they "avoided the issue of the propriety of the arrests, and concentrated instead on the question of whether or not one country, in annexing another, [was] liable for the latter's prior obligations."[71] As was expected, Britain argued that it was, while the United States claimed otherwise. On November 10, 1925, after just three days of deliberation, the tribunal came down on the side of the United States and declared that all claims of indemnity were to be rejected. But by avoiding the propriety of the arrests, the tribunal left open the possibility that the Republic of Hawai'i could still be responsible for the indemnity claims. No further claims were pressed however, and after thirty years Manuel Reis saw his case close.

In the three decades that had passed since Reis had first pressed his case, the Old World empires had fallen and been replaced with new nation-states. Portugal, Britain, and the United States had fought together as allies in the Great War. In this new geopolitical configuration, the indemnity claims of a carriage driver from an empire that no longer existed, and provoked questions of jurisdiction between current national allies, became irrelevant. The historical moment of confluence and contingency in which Manuel Reis's claim mattered had passed, and so he lost the backing of his country of origin and along with it, any chance for redress.

CONCLUSION: THE CELEBRATION OF MANUEL REIS

Ironically, during the same decade that Reis lost his case for indemnity, he was also celebrated in prominent local haole-owned newspapers. On December 3, 1929, the *Honolulu Advertiser* ran an article titled "Mr. and Mrs. Manuel Reis to Celebrate Fiftieth Anniversary of Their Wedding Tomorrow."[72] The one-page article recapped Manuel Reis's life history and only briefly mentioned his connection to the 1895 Kaua Kūloko by reducing his jailtime to "a few days in the government prison."[73] Several years later in 1935, the *Honolulu Star-Bulletin* ran a full-page spread on Reis titled, "Whaler, Hack Driver, Citizen: An Old Kamaaina's Romance."[74] While the article covered Reis's experience as a prisoner of the republic, its focus was on his financial success, the scale of his taxi service, and his prominence in Hawaiian society.

After his imprisonment, Reis continued to be a well-respected businessman and notable local figure in Hawai'i. He was the first cab driver to use an automobile, and as in the days of the "Royal Hack-stand," he drove royalty around Honolulu, including several princes of Japan and China, the prince of Wales, and the crown prince and princess of Sweden. He was also entrusted with driving US government officials, such as future president William Howard Taft and Senator Warren G. Harding. Reis's business success was complimented by his social standing and since he was married to Eugenia, he often found himself entertaining both Hawaiian royalty and foreign dignitaries. Of their home, the *Advertiser* wrote in 1935 that upon entering, "you are transported back years to the times of monarchical splendor. For here stand gorgeous kahilis, a score of them, their feathers gently waving in the breeze from Punchbowl."[75] These wistful descriptions by publications like the *Honolulu Advertiser*, a newspaper that had once rallied against those who supported the counterrevolution, speak to the confidence that haole elites had in their relationship with the United States: in the post-WWI geo-political order, both Reis and the Hawaiian Kingdom itself were looked upon as objects of unthreatening nostalgia, held up and glorified as remnants of a past long gone.

Juxtaposing the interpolating power of the emerging US empire to racialize Portuguese laborers as white with the waning Portuguese Empire's lack of ability to maintain the rights of its diasporic subjects reinforces the relevance of Hawai'i's interimperial condition to race-based nationalism. The case of the Portuguese in Hawai'i demonstrates that what being white meant and who could be white was heavily impacted by intersectional geopolitical factors. Weaving together Thurston's quest for a racially malleable labor source with the history of the 1895 counterrevolution and the resultant indemnity case of Manuel Reis, raises the question of how the intersections between transpacific imperial formations and local politics of jurisdiction shaped American white supremacy.

Reis's imprisonment and call for indemnity happened in the liminal space of Hawai'i between kingdom and colony, and his case pushed forward articulations of state jurisdiction that became entangled with processes of racialization. He and the thousands of other Portuguese laborers who crossed oceans and empires to get to Hawai'i found themselves within a hotbed of international conflict that encompassed struggles such as the 1893 overthrow, the counterrevolution of 1895, and multiple immigration bans. Haole oligarchs who were desperate to maintain a white supremacy aligned with race-based nationalism in the United States turned to this local Portuguese population to sustain their illusion of an island-based white majority. At the same time, the 1896 ban on emigration to Hawai'i by the Portuguese Empire, coupled with the rise in Japanese migration, ultimately pressed Hawai'i's Portuguese community to emphasize their status as white workingmen alongside other European migrants. Although they were never considered equals, the local Portuguese community's articulation of whiteness helped to promote the facade of a thriving white settler colony in Hawai'i.

4

THE SHINSHU MARU AFFAIR

Barred Landings and Immigration Detention

ON FEBRUARY 27, 1897, amid heightened awareness and concern over the growing Japanese presence in Hawaiʻi, and just five days before the inauguration ceremony for Republican President William McKinley, the *Shinshu Maru* docked in Honolulu. In accordance with the coup state's health regulations, all people on board were promptly placed in detention on Kamokuʻākulikuli, the same locale where Yosaku Imada had made his attempted escape just three years prior. Of the 670 Japanese passengers on board the Meiji ship, roughly 463, or more than two-thirds, were sent back to Japan after a lengthy detention period. Port authority records reveal that the group was forcibly detained and ultimately turned away not for public health reasons, but because they failed to legitimately possess either preapproved contracts from the republic's Board of Immigration or the equivalent of fifty American dollars. Many of the passengers on board the *Sakura Maru*, which arrived on March 19, 1897, and the *Kinai Maru*, which docked on April 9, met the same fate as their *Shinshu Maru* counterparts. In total, 1,175 migrants were rejected and sent back to Japan.[1]

The Spring 1897 barred landing and detention of Japanese migrants from the *Shinshu Maru*, *Kinai Maru*, and *Sakura Maru*, referred to as the "Shinshu Maru Affair" in news stories of the day, elicited a groundswell of concern from would-be Japanese immigrants, the laboring and merchant Issei in Hawai'i, and Meiji officials. The difference in their objections, however, points to disparities over what each group felt was at stake. To those traveling to the Hawaiian archipelago in search of plantation jobs and other forms of labor, equal treatment, including the basic opportunity to disembark, was essential to their economic subsistence and livelihood. For Issei already living and working in Hawai'i, the prolonged imprisonment of those on board the ships without access to legal counsel emphasized their community's general lack of protection. Denied the ability to naturalize under the coup state, Issei laborers and merchants existed on the boundaries of the body politic and were not afforded legal protections from the republic. Caught in the interstice of empires, these various Issei communities looked to Japan for advocacy and protection. Their agitation was met by Meiji oligarchs who were seemingly more concerned with issues of global positioning than their emigrants' immediate welfare.

In the four years since the diplomatic negotiation with the coup state over Issei franchise rights and the return of Yosaku Imada in 1893, Japan had emerged as a power to be reckoned with. Although the Meiji state had begun its imperial formation in the 1860s with the colonization of Hokkaido (1869) and the Ryukyu Islands (1871), in 1895 Japan shocked the world with a military victory over China. Signed in April of that year, the Treaty of Shimonoseki ended the First Sino-Japanese War (1894–95) and dictated that China would pay an indemnity as well as cede control of Taiwan and the Liaodong Peninsula to Japan.

But even after a victory of this magnitude, for Japan the path to becoming a global power remained uncertain. When the terms of the treaty became public, Russia, France, and Germany immediately intervened in order to stop the spread of "Yellow Peril."[2] Claiming that the Meiji takeover of Liaodong would threaten the Qing government and the independence of Korea, the "Triple Intervention" applied diplomatic pressure on Japan to return the peninsula to China. Despite the Meiji government's attempts to have the United States and Britain intercede on its behalf, barely one month after the signing of the Treaty of Shimonoseki, Prime Minister Hirobumi Itō announced the withdrawal of Meiji troops from Liaodong Peninsula.

Japan had grudgingly acquiesced to the demands of France, Germany, and Russia. But having just over one thousand emigrants barred from entry because they were deemed unfit by the fledgling Republic of Hawai'i was another matter. The action served as a major affront to the emerging empire, especially in light of the fact that just before the coup, Queen Lili'uokalani had ordered an end to unequal treaty rights and relinquished extraterritoriality in Japan.[3] Meiji oligarchs questioned how their government would stand on equal footing with Western powers if their emigrants were rebuffed by the young coup government of Hawai'i. Anxious over the turn against Chinese migrants, they also feared that the Shinshu Maru Affair would lead to a greater global resolve against Japanese settlers, and ultimately, threaten the Meiji state's transpacific imperial ambitions.

Caught in the contingent space shaped by state-based jurisdiction and race-based nationalism, hundreds of Japanese detainees waited out their fate. While they were held at the quarantine station they were allotted only a very small quantity of daily food, subjected to long interrogations, and were reportedly exhausted and unwell. At least one woman was said to have been "driven crazy" by the poor living conditions.[4] While this chapter does not dive into the particular treatment, condition, and lives of the incarcerated migrants, it nonetheless draws attention to the ways that competing forms of

Figure 9. Quarantine station as seen from a ship, ca. 1912. Courtesy of Bishop Museum Archives.

state power reduced the complexities of an individual's and community's existence to a bureaucratic identity in order to be made legible and disciplined.

Republic officials attempted to wield border patrol as a method to maintain white supremacy and state power in Hawai'i on two fronts: limiting the growth of the Japanese population and prolonging the detainment of newly arrived Issei in order to create the impression that they embodied the possibility of a Meiji takeover. One of the unintended consequences of these actions was that they provoked Issei articulations of settler colonialism and bolstered Japan's position on the cusp of transpacific empire. Meiji leaders found themselves pushed to acknowledge the centrality of Hawai'i as a space of direct encounter to their overseas nationalist project. Caught up in the jingoism that surrounded the incident, Hawai'i-based Issei began to articulate their own claim to the archipelago. At a mass community meeting convened in Honolulu in order to discuss the prolonged detainment, for example, an Issei photographer took the stage and claimed that the Issei "made [Hawai'i] what you are and you belong to us.... From what the Japanese have done in this country I am inclined to believe we are entitled to the ownership of it."[5]

The prolonged detention of the Japanese migrants also activated the Meiji government's tactic of relying on international law in order to obtain recognition as a modern and "civilized" global power. At the turn of the twentieth century, the regime of international law embodied the larger method of creating and reinforcing a global order based on the sovereign nation-state. As the young Meiji government stepped out onto the world stage, international law became Japan's new legal discourse of power.[6] Alexis Dudden explains that Meiji officials purposefully engaged Japan in "international terms in hopes of relocating its place in the world and redefining power in Asia."[7] This was a maneuver that the Meiji state had relied on to legitimate violent actions during the First Sino-Japanese War and it once again turned to this tactic in the case of the detained migrants.

From the Meiji oligarchy's viewpoint, Hawai'i provided the perfect place to test a strategy aimed at boosting Japan's global standing through the gradual enhancement of Issei economic and political influence. When this informal approach was inhibited by the legal manipulations of the haole-led oligarchy, Meiji diplomats reacted as they had in the Imada case, and called on the 1871 Treaty of Amity and Commerce with the Hawaiian Kingdom to fortify their argument. One of the consequences of this action was the reinforcement of the Hawaiian Kingdom's state-based sovereignty. Unlike the 1893 negotiations over Yosaku Imada and Issei voting rights, where Japan and the haole-led oligarchy each advocated for their own legal primacy and, in the process, obfuscated the Kanaka Maoli claim to political independence, in this case the Meiji government's repeated reference to the 1871 treaty exposed the coup state's tactics of countersovereignty.

That is, through the "authoritative inviolability" of the regime of international law, which itself is a performative discourse through which sovereign states mutually legitimate each other, the Meiji government exposed the fallacy of the coup state's mode of political authority.[8]

When Japanese Foreign Minister Shigenobu Ōkuma cited the 1871 treaty in order to prove that Japanese were entitled to the same privileges as the citizens or subjects of any other nation, his argument also inherently contended that treaties made and recognized through international diplomacy, like those made between the Meiji emperor and King Kamehameha V, superseded those of the republic. In other words, the Meiji government's response to the barred landing and detention of Japanese emigrants went beyond pronouncing its own civility and legitimacy in the international arena. Invoking the 1871 treaty also reaffirmed the state-based sovereignty of both Japan and the Hawaiian Kingdom, and emphasized the latter's legal primacy over the coup state to the world.

By bringing the practices of border control and racialized state bureaucracy to bear on the incarcerated Japanese migrants, the Shinshu Maru Affair exposed competing visions of a modern transpacific order that were deployed by both white American and Japanese settler colonialisms. At first glance, the imprisonment and forcible return to Japan of one thousand migrants by the Republic of Hawaiʻi may not seem to be of much historical significance. But the treatment of the Japanese migrants was a resolution designed by the coup state to neutralize the problem of those whose presence would otherwise rupture illusions of both capitalism and white supremacy as humanly sustainable.[9] In the face of growing opposition from poʻe aloha ʻāina and others who demanded the restoration of the Hawaiian Kingdom, the coup state used the 1897 barred landings to enforce its terms of white supremacy and signal its compatibility with US race-based nationalism.

JAPANESE CONTRACT AND "FREE LABOR" IN HAWAI'I

By the time the *Shinshu Maru* docked in Honolulu in late February 1897, tensions between the haole-led oligarchy and Meiji government over regulatory mechanisms and the disciplining of foreign (Asian) bodies had been brewing for several years. Between 1885 and 1894, the contract labor system, which was established under the Convention of 1886 between the Hawaiian Kingdom and Japan, balanced the Hawai'i-based plantocracy's need for cheap labor with the Meiji government's desire for economic expansion through emigration.[10] Under this convention, emigration to Hawai'i was to be conducted by contract and occur only between the ports of Yokohama and Honolulu. All emigrants were to receive free steerage on first-class passenger steamers to the Hawaiian Islands. The contracts themselves were to be signed in Japan, and all terms, wages, and types of labor required were to be predetermined in Hawai'i by the planters.[11] A special agent of the Hawaiian Board of Immigration, R. W. Irwin, was to handle the organization of labor shipments. Within this eight-year time span, a total of twenty-six shiploads of contract laborers from Japan arrived on Hawai'i's shores.[12]

When the labor convention was originally executed in March 1886, roughly 150 Issei lived in the Hawaiian archipelago. By 1894, an estimated 28,691 Japanese migrants had come to Hawai'i under the contract system. Because planters often paid laborers with script that could only be used at the plantation store and garnished wages for living items provided, most Issei were unable to afford the return fare back to Japan. As a result of these practices and despite haole and continent-based expressions of white racial anxiety over the growing "Yellow Peril," by 1897 the Asian population in the islands, which comprised both Chinese and Japanese migrants, numbered 45,043 out of an estimated total population of 109,000.

Although the labor convention was heavily revised in 1887, it fell apart after the 1893 overthrow and installation of the coup government.[13]

Oligarchs in charge of the coup state clearly understood that one of the major obstacles to US annexation was white racial anxiety over the islands' Asian- and Native-dominated population. From their seat of power in Honolulu, these men watched as shipload after shipload of migrant Japanese arrived, while across the Pacific, the Meiji state made its mark as an imperial power. At the same time, the McKinley Tariff, which was implemented in the United States in 1890 and imposed a two-cent per pound incentive on all sugar produced domestically, completely erased the advantages that the reciprocity treaty had provided to Hawai'i-based sugar producers. While planters were still reeling from the loss of profits in the US sugar market, Japanese Foreign Minister Munemitsu Mutsu announced that a clause from the contracts that had allowed planters to recuperate $13.17 from each laborer in order to offset their total cost of $53.17 per individual for importation, would soon be eliminated.[14]

Faced with the increasing cost of Japanese workers, Hawai'i-based planters attempted to find an alternative labor source. They first considered Chinese laborers, whose migration had been curtailed but had never ceased entirely.[15] Rebuilding the pipeline to Chinese labor would provide a temporary solution to the shortage in the islands, but leaders of the republic feared the long-term ramification would be another failed attempt at US annexation. Opponents pointed out that importing Chinese labor did nothing to stem the "Asiatic flood" which the United States had just recommitted to excluding through an extension of its Chinese Exclusion Act in 1892.

A second solution focused on enticing white settlers from the North American continent and Europe, but this attempt also proved unsuccessful. Ironically, the effort to bring in white American family farmers to the islands resulted in the creation of the industrial pineapple plantation (see chapter 5), which in turn increased the recruitment of Asian labor. Because the alternative solutions to impending labor shortage and increasing costs failed to bring in the necessary mass of laboring bodies needed to keep industrial plantations up and running, planters sought to find a cheaper way to secure Japanese field workers. This ultimately came in the form of private emigration companies.

In the summer of 1894, a combination of global and domestic concerns brought an end to the convention-based contract labor system. The 1886 convention between Japan and the Kingdom of Hawai'i had stipulated that laborers from either country could migrate freely, but only under contract. Act 66, which was passed by leaders of the coup state on March 1, 1894, changed this requirement by allowing Japanese emigrants to come to Hawai'i if they possessed either a written contract or fifty American dollars upon arrival.[16] The original intent of this law was to limit the number of Issei in Hawai'i, but private emigration companies in Japan and agents in Honolulu saw the "fifty-dollar clause" as the loophole that would enable the flow of migrant "free labor." In light of this change, Japanese emigration not only continued, but underwent large-scale expansion, as the number of private emigration companies mushroomed overnight, competing with each other to give more labor for less money to the ever-eager planters.[17]

In response, coup state officials once again attempted to limit the flow of Issei by passing a February 1895 law, known as Act 17, that required the Honolulu-based Board of Immigration to give its written approval to labor contracts before migrants left Japan. But this stipulation could be applied only to those coming under contract and not to "free laborers."[18] In order to quell the growing apprehension over the constant arrival of Issei while also satisfying their need for a cheap labor source, planters looked to the Portuguese. Their attempt to negotiate around the legal barrier imposed by Act 17 resulted in an agreement to import this "European labor source" at an amount equal to 20 percent of the number of Board of Immigration-approved Japanese contract laborers per shipload.[19] But in spite of the regulatory measures designed to impede Japanese immigration, both contracted and free Issei labor continued to flow into Honolulu. Between 1895 and 1896, just one year after the passing of the fifty-dollar clause, over nine thousand Japanese migrants landed in Hawai'i.[20]

BECOMING "JAPANESE"

Throughout the early months of 1897, government officials from Japan and the Hawai'i-based coup state debated over whether the barred landing and ongoing migrant detention violated international treaty agreements. For the leaders of the republic, it was easier to make and support the argument for blocking the admission of the relatively small number of incoming Japanese who came by contract. Coup state officials claimed that these migrants were attempting to enter the country illegally because their contracts had not been preapproved by their Board of Immigration before traveling to Honolulu, as required by the republic's Act 17.[21]

The real challenge for republic officials however, were the "free Japanese." This group made up the majority of rejected migrants, and the haole-led oligarchy struggled to find a way to "legitimately" bar them from entering the islands. What they finally came up with was a rationale that differentiated between "ownership" and "possession": republic officials claimed that since Japanese emigration companies loaned incoming laborers the money needed in order to land in Honolulu Harbor, the migrants did not actually "possess" the necessary amount and were rightly refused the right to enter the coup state.

Interrogations that ran into the late hours of the night were a routine part of life for the Japanese held at Kamoku'ākulikuli. Republic officials used every excuse they could to enforce their shallow rationale for denying entry while also laying the burden of proof on the incarcerated themselves. They claimed that because the migrants carried the necessary fifty dollars in a pouch separated from the rest of their funds, there was reasonable doubt as to their ownership of the money. Officials also stated that because the separated money was often exactly fifty dollars, or the yen equivalent, this further proved that it did not legitimately belong to the person who held it. Republic Minister of Foreign Affairs Henry Cooper and several other leaders of the oligarchy who conducted detainee interrogations contended that since all the migrants gave the same "parrot-like" answer regarding where they got the money from, namely their mother or father, and what they planned to do with it, that the money must have been loaned to them and the answers pre-rehearsed and untrue.[22] Perhaps the most damning argument out of the numerous examples cited for reasonable doubt, was the fact that many migrants carried with them an agreement by the Kobe immigration company that guaranteed both landing in Honolulu and a job upon arrival for a ten-yen fee. This, coup state officials argued, was proof of the involvement of a third party.

The local Issei community quickly saw through the republic's subjective interrogations and calculated responses. They grew frustrated over the extended detention, poor treatment, and lack of access to legal representation for the Japanese newcomers. Agitation soon led to action, and on March 11, 1897, Honolulu-based Issei held a mass meeting not far from 'Iolani Palace, at the corner of Fort and Queen Streets. At the meeting, members of the Japanese community from various class backgrounds, including merchants, plantation laborers, and religious leaders, voiced their anger over the circumstances of those incarcerated and expressed hope that their detention would soon end. The gathering was surveilled by the coup state and reported on in detail in the local papers, with the *PCA* claiming that "about three hundred Japanese, including one woman, and a number of white people," were present.[23]

On March 16, 1897, with the support of the Issei community, a petition of habeas corpus was filed on behalf of the rejected Japanese by the emigration companies that had brought them over the Pacific. In its attempt to challenge the racial state bureaucracy, the petition claimed that the Japanese migrants were unjustly detained and had been denied the right of legal representation. It also noted that although those held at the quarantine station had asked repeatedly to see an attorney, the oligarchy had refused to comply with this request. The republic's Supreme Court took just one day to review the case and quickly washed its hands of the matter. The court ruled that the Treaty of 1871, which guaranteed Japan "most-favored nation" status as well as the right of Japanese to reside in the islands with "free and easy access to the courts and justice," had not been violated by the imprisonment of those on board the three ships because they were held at the quarantine station and had not technically *landed* in the republic. As a result, the court maintained that the Japanese held at Kamokuʻākulikuli were subject to the port inspector's decision to bar their entry, and that the executive branch could have no say.

The March 17, 1897, Supreme Court statement further infuriated the Hawaiʻi-based Issei. At a mass meeting held in Honolulu later that same day, it was decided that a committee would be formed in order to petition the Meiji government to intervene. Tensions ran high at the gathering as participants voiced their desire to rebel against the republic. To a crowd of several hundred members of the Issei community, one man claimed that he was "perfectly willing to give up my life for those people over in the quarantine station."[24] His statement was reportedly met with thunderous applause.

K. Furuya, a merchant in Honolulu and secretary of the petitioning committee, followed this with a speech that articulated a nationalist project that equated the bodies of Issei laborers with the Meiji nation-state, while also drawing race-based connections between the fate of China's excluded migrants and that of the detained Japanese:

> In Hawaii, Japan is being discriminated against . . . the Government desires to exclude us from the shores of Hawaii. The white races in the world are arrayed against the yellow races. [When] the white races in the world were to be built, China was importuned to send her subjects to California to help out the promoters. But when the interests of the Chinese

conflicted with the whites an exclusion act was passed. When the planters of Hawaii wanted laborers in 1886 the Labor Convention was effectually negotiated, and our people came here. Now our colony has grown and our interests conflict with those of "white residents." This action of the Government is a step toward exclusion.[25]

Both statements made at the gathering reveal the complex ways in which the Issei understood and positioned themselves. On one hand, Japanese settler colonialism worked to create a national identity abroad—here in the interimperial interstice that Issei navigated, nationalism and national identity came to the fore when political protection and advocacy in the international arena were desired. Furuya and others gathered expressed their concerns not as *dekaseginin*, but as citizens of the Japanese nation, or *kokumin*—a category that Jun Uchida explains was not in "full existence at the end of the 1880s."[26]

While it may seem unremarkable now, the ability of an Issei merchant in 1897 Hawaiʻi to speak of a nationalist project that flattened class and regional differences, and conflated the identities of self and nation, is extremely significant. From their position in Honolulu, speaking to an audience of laborers and merchants who hailed from disparate prefectures, villages, and cities in the Japanese archipelago, men such as Furuya not only connected the events in Hawaiʻi to the idea of a Japanese state stretching across the Pacific, but also articulated a unified Issei community's position as state representatives via their shared nationalism.[27] They were in essence, "becoming Japanese" on the Meiji state's periphery.[28]

On the other hand, Furuya's comments simultaneously illuminate the *instability* of national identity and nationalism that persisted despite all efforts by the Meiji state to create a unified "Japan." The merchant's remarks emphasize the relevance of interimperial spaces like Hawaiʻi to our understanding of race-based nationalism and the articulations of the modern nation-state. In particular, Furuya's assertion of the shared predicament faced by the exploited Asian race *vis-à-vis* the white race revealed an understanding of the constructed nature of whiteness that was built on the backs of both Chinese and Japanese laborers. His awareness that Japanese and Chinese migrants shared the burden of Asian racialization in the aftermath of the First Sino-Japanese War, speaks to the complex social relationships that these diasporic communities formed in spite of global contestations and the power of the local racial state bureaucracy.

PROTECT THE "SIMPLE AND IGNORANT" PEOPLE: THE EMIGRANT PROTECTION LAWS

While individuals such as Furuya expressed anger and frustration over their treatment at the hands of the haole-led oligarchy, Meiji officials' concerns reveal the tenuous relationship they held with Japanese emigrants, who were often culled from prefectures and villages far from centers of power. This unease was evident in the letter of protest from Japanese Consul General in Hawai'i Hisashi Shimamura to the republic's attorney general, Henry Cooper. Shimamura wrote, "Does it not seem that a great and an irreparable hardship has been done the simple and ignorant people, in not permitting them to land where they could get employment, and where their services would be beneficial to Hawaii in order that they may repair the loss occasioned by their selling out their effects and breaking up their homes in Japan?"[29] Although Shimamura recognized the harsh conditions that both forced migrants to move away and awaited them in new lands, his patronizing stance underscores the incongruency of his sentiments.

In fact, the discord between the vision of a Japanese empire spreading throughout the Pacific on the backs of educated emigrants and the reality of laborers who were making international headlines in Hawai'i filled Japanese government officials like Shimamura with apprehension.

To the Meiji oligarchy, the living and working conditions of these "simple and ignorant" Issei mattered because of their position as emigrant representatives of the emerging Japanese state. Through their travels, overseas settlers and migrants who would have ordinarily been of little concern to the Meiji government had they stayed home became enmeshed in the ongoing debate over the meaning of Japanese identity and nationhood.

In order to protect its emigrants abroad and gain global recognition as a "civilized" nation-state, the Meiji government turned to the tactic of enforcing strict compliance with international law. In the context of the Shinshu Maru Affair, this maneuver once again brought Japan up against the question of rights for its citizen-subjects caught within spaces of interimperial jurisdiction.[30] In essence, the Meiji state's push for equal standing in the barred landing dispute continued to press the question that began in 1893 over Imada's prison break: How would the individual and nation-state be integrated?

As the Shinshu Maru Affair demonstrates, the concept of rights associated with national membership that gained global currency at the turn of the twentieth century was oftentimes brought to the fore by populations located far from the imperial metropole. Faced with the "dual task of becoming a modern nation-state and empire," citizenship and the rights which this category entailed became relevant in the context of foreign affairs and places for Meiji government leaders and Issei alike.[31] Among the safety measures that the Meiji state instituted in order to protect the Issei community were the emigrant protection laws. Enacted in 1894, these laws required that the emigrant possess a Japanese passport and travel only to countries that had treaty relations with the Meiji state. It also compelled emigrant agents to protect the traveling laborer against financial distress while abroad, as well as fund their trip back to Japan.[32] Consul General Shimamura referenced these laws in his attempt to clarify the misconception that Japanese had entered Hawaiʻi under illegal agreements made with the Kobe Immigration Company. He explained to coup government officials that this law has been enacted in order to shield emigrants against serious suffering in foreign countries. Shimamura also noted that emigration companies were required to use their influence to get employment for those they brought over and, should that fail, to provide free transportation back to Japan.

Although the emigrant protection laws were in theory created to protect Issei, they were also part of the Meiji state's larger strategy of relying on international law to obtain global status and power. In the specific case of Issei in Hawaiʻi, Meiji officials were more anxious than ever that their emigrants should not fall into destitution and thus disgrace Japan.[33] Well aware of what was at stake with the case of Japanese detention, Francis Hatch, minister of foreign affairs for the republic, kept an eye on public opinion in Japan and had newspaper clippings sent to him weekly from Tokyo and Yokohama. In one such article, published on April 8, 1897, a Japan-based journalist stated what Hatch, Meiji officials, leaders of Hawaiʻi's Issei community, and haole oligarchs already knew—that the Shinshu Maru Affair would reverberate across the Pacific and affect Japan's relationship with the United States. The writer claimed that "Japan must . . . insist on the right of landing the Japanese subjects . . . . it appears . . . that with the growth of Japanese influence in the island her [Republic of Hawaiʻi's] desire to rely on the United States has heightened . . . . this question will prove of far more grave and important a nature . . . because it has a great bearing on the rights and interests of tens of thousands of Japanese subjects at present residing in the islands."[34] By recognizing that any political negotiation between the republic and the Meiji government would also be of interest to the United States, the author clearly articulated the precarious condition that the Japanese in Hawaiʻi were caught within and rallied the Meiji government to intercede.

When calling for action on the part of those who were detained and sent back, the same Japan-based journalist invoked the discourse of nation-based rights, asking, "How may our Government recover our national rights? . . . the Japanese-Hawaiian treaty which guarantees the rights of Japanese subjects on the islands has been trampled underfoot . . . the steps that should be taken by the Government are plain enough. As soon as the *Shinshiu* [sic] *Maru* reaches these shores again she had better be sent back to Hawaii with men of war who will repeat the demand for permission to land the emigrants."[35] While the writer's call for physical aggression on the part of Issei is significant, what is more relevant to this analysis is the extension of national rights to those in Hawaiʻi. From their position in Japan, the journalist connected the Hawaiʻi-based incident to the idea of a transpacific Meiji state and called for the protection of emigrant members of the "Japanese nation."

An April 12, 1897, letter sent from Stuart Eldridge, who served as consul for the Republic of Hawaiʻi in Japan, to Attorney General Cooper confirmed this growing nationalist sentiment. Eldridge cautioned leaders of the coup state against the intense negative reaction in Japan and explained that "the exclusion of the emigrants per *Sakura* and *Shinsiu* [sic] *Maru* and their enforced return to Japan has created intense excitement in this country. The temper of the people, as indicated by their newspapers, is most belligerent, and strong pressure is being exercised upon the government in favor of stringent measures."[36] Eldridge went on to warn Cooper of the rumor of warships being deployed to Hawaiʻi. While he claimed that this was in all probability just hearsay, he also noted that Meiji officials had "conceived the idea that the refusal of admission to the emigrants in question was dictated by deliberate intention to stir up trouble with Japan, in the hope that this would facilitate annexation to the United States."[37] Meiji officials had correctly assessed the intentions behind the barred landings, but Eldridge wrote that he tried to convince them otherwise, claiming that the republic was just following the laws regarding "emigration in general."[38]

THE RETURN OF THE *NANIWA*

Understanding the motivation behind the republic's actions, however, did not make maneuvering the political waters surrounding the *Shinshu Maru, Kina Maru,* and *Sakura Maru* barred landings any less complicated for Meiji oligarchs. In fact, their response to the situation worked to expose the competing forms of statecraft at play and underscore how the regulation of state borders via the disciplining of foreign (Asian) bodies was understood as a defining characteristic of Western modernity. On April 19, 1897, Japanese Foreign Minister Shigenobu Ōkuma wrote to Honolulu-based Consul General Shimamura and explained that the "proper regulation of immigration, is a legitimate exercise of the police power of a State . . . reasonably administered by Hawaii will provoke no remonstrance from Japan." He noted, however, that this had not taken place and, to add insult to injury, the right to legal representation had been denied to those detained. Ōkuma also reminded the consul general that under the Treaty of Amity and Commerce of 1871, created and agreed to by the imperial government of Japan and the Hawaiian Kingdom, Japanese subjects were "absolutely and equally" on par with Hawaiian nationals regarding questions of their "right to travel, trade, reside, and exercise every profession or industry in all parts of Hawaii, and complete protection from the Hawaiian government for their persons and property, as well as in regard to civil rights."[39] According to Ōkuma, the Republic of Hawai'i had violated the police power of the state as well as international law, and therefore forfeited its right to political legitimacy within the forming transpacific order.

In response to the coup state's claims that the arriving migrants had violated Acts 66 and 17, which when interpreted together required that all immigrants possess either a written contract preapproved by the republic's Board of Immigration or the equivalent of fifty US dollars, Foreign Minister Ōkuma once again turned to the regime of international law. He maintained that "while such laws might, under certain circumstances, in a national sense be binding upon the authorities of a State, they can never be advanced internationally speaking, as a sufficient answer for the violation of an international compact, and the international question is the only one which concerns the imperial government."[40] Ōkuma's argument reinforced the idea that since the 1871 treaty had been made at the larger level of international diplomacy with the Hawaiian Kingdom, it therefore superseded domestic Acts 66 and 17.[41] According to the Japanese foreign minister, both the rejected migrants and Japan itself were owed an indemnity as a way to make amends for damage inflicted on a personal and national scale.

While an aggressive battle with republic forces was not anticipated nor wanted, both Shimamura and Ōkuma requested that the Meiji government send at least one warship to the Hawaiian archipelago in order to, "exhibit our power and protect 26,000 Japanese, almost one-fourth the total population of Hawaii."[42] This request aligned with Japan's policy of informal colonization: the warship was to protect what was represented by the overseas Japanese, namely the Meiji attainment of equality among nation-states via its political and economic interests in Hawai'i. On May 5, just one week prior to coup state officials receiving Ōkuma's letter of protest, the *Naniwa*, Japan's most formidable warship, once again docked in Honolulu Harbor. On board was Masanosuke Akiyama, counselor of the Japanese Foreign Office, who came to aid in the negotiations between the Meiji government and the republic.

The arrival of the *Naniwa* was meant to enforce Japan's demand for reparations and bring an end to the discord with the republic. But it also played into the haole-led oligarchy's hands and further opened the doorway to annexation to the United States. In Hawai'i, articles such as the series published in the pro-annexationist *Hawaiian Star*, which claimed that the Japanese intended to swarm and overpower the islands, get the vote, and eventually take over, began to appear daily.[43]

The *Daily Bulletin* followed suit and declared that Hawai'i would become a Japanese colony if the United States did not annex it because the republic was too weak and small to fend off Meiji aggression.[44]

Alarm over the arrival of the *Naniwa* in Honolulu quickly spread to North America. In Washington, DC, members of the Senate Foreign Relations Committee claimed that the case of the rejected Japanese provided the perfect example of what was to come if the United States did not lay claim to Hawai'i. The committee explained that "the present Hawaiian-Japanese controversy is the preliminary skirmish in the great coming struggle between the civilization and the awakening forces of the East and the civilization of the West. The issue is whether, in that inevitable struggle, Asia or America shall have the vantage ground of control of the naval 'Key of the Pacific.'"[45] Annexationists were quick to use the strong stance taken by Japan to "prove" the existence of a "Yellow Peril" that would engulf Hawai'i and endanger US interests in the Pacific and Asia. In San Francisco, both the *Chronicle* and the *Examiner* disseminated articles that reiterated the fear that Japanese contract laborers were really imperial soldiers in disguise. Across the country, Lorrin Thurston gave a timely interview to the Washington, D C, *Evening Star* in which he claimed that "the present extraordinary movement from Japan . . . is part of a systematic plot, with the full approval of the Japanese government, to gain control of the islands." Adding fuel to the fire, the haole oligarch also claimed that if the republic proved unable to stop the "invasion, Anglo-Saxon civilization will very soon be swamped out of the country."[46] The justification of escalating white racial anxiety was seemingly confirmed two months later in an interview given by Consul General Shimamura, in which he hinted at the use of Japanese force and equated reparations with the country's honor, stating that "Japan asks nothing unreasonable; she wants justice and fairness in the matter . . . if she cannot get it—well, I do not know what will follow . . . the honor of Japan is at stake."[47]

In Washington, DC, Republic Minister Hatch lost no time in making use of the arrival of the *Naniwa* to his advantage and sent a letter to US Assistant Secretary of State William R. Day that played on the fear of a Meiji-ruled Hawai'i. Hatch claimed that the "conviction felt in Honolulu is that, failing annexation, it will become absolutely impossible to maintain an independent existence. Yielding to Japan means the complete and final establishment of their power."[48] Perhaps there was little need for Hatch's jingoism, for three weeks earlier, upon hearing about the deployment of the *Naniwa* to Hawai'i, Assistant Secretary of the Navy Theodore Roosevelt wrote a letter to President McKinley informing him of the types of ships the United States had in the Pacific in case a conflict erupted. As has been well documented, Roosevelt also proceeded to submit a "Special Confidential Problem for [the] War College" in which he asked Navy personnel to determine what type of and amount of force would be needed to intervene if Japan took control over Hawai'i. He added that this strategy should "keep in mind possible complications with another power on the Atlantic Coast (Cuba)."[49]

Roosevelt's actions are often analyzed within the framework of a late nineteenth-century American impulse at overseas expansion. But placing them in the context of the *Naniwa*'s arrival in Honolulu underscores the importance of the barred landing and detention debacle. In fact, the negotiations between haole oligarchs and Meiji government officials around the whole Shinshu Maru Affair were carefully watched by global powers of the day. As a result, the question of what was to become of Hawai'i was ushered into the consciousness of a broad international community. The republic's refusal to let Japanese migrants into Honolulu in the spring of 1897 and the diplomatic maneuvers between the coup state and Meiji government that followed emphasized the geopolitical importance of Hawai'i and brought the question of its future alliances and position in the Pacific to center stage.

CONCLUSION: THE LIMITS OF DIPLOMACY

On June 16, 1897, just six weeks after the *Naniwa* docked at Honolulu Harbor, the McKinley administration signed a treaty of annexation with coup state officials Lorrin Thurston, Francis Hatch, and William Kinney. According to both US officials and the republic's haole oligarchs, one of the compelling factors that led to the signing of the treaty was the fear of a potential negative international reaction against annexation that could be sparked by the Meiji protest already in play.[50] At the signing ceremony, US Assistant Secretary Day suggested to Minister Hatch that "he ought to interview Hoshi, Envoy Extraordinary and Minister Plenipotentiary from Japan to the United States, and try to agree upon a settlement of the immigration claims in order to help the treaty along towards ratification," as it was believed that further negative reactions from Meiji officials might stall the ratification process.[51] Whether Hatch agreed with Day or not is unknown, but by this time the former statesman understood that Japan's objections to annexation could also be used to prime white racial anxiety and win the American public's support for ratification of the annexation treaty.

On June 19, just three days after the treaty was signed, Japan announced its official objection to the US annexation of Hawai'i. As part of its protest, the Meiji government once again used the same strategy as it had with its rejected emigrants and turned to the regime of international law. Among the concerns listed by the Meiji officials were the continuance of treaty rights between Japan and the Hawaiian Kingdom, the commercial and industrial rights of Issei in the islands, and, finally, that annexation might lead to the postponement of claims and liabilities "already existing in favor of Japan under treaty stipulations."[52] When these objections seemed ineffectual, Minister Hoshi went so far as to suggest to Count Ōkuma that Japan could occupy the islands "by dispatching without any delay some powerful ships under the name of reprisal."⁵³ Ōkuma's response revealed that what the Meiji government valued most was not the well-being of the Issei, Kānaka Maoli, or the legitimacy of the Hawaiian Kingdom. Instead, Ōkuma explained to Hoshi that "continuation without interruption or disturbance of our intercourse with the United States is of vastly more importance to Japan than interests that will be menaced by annexation. Consequently good policy dictates that our opposition to annexation should be within the limits of diplomacy."⁵⁴

Hawai'i proved to be one of the first instances where the Meiji state's practice of informal colonization officially failed. The fact that this failure was against the United States made it an even harder pill to swallow for the many Japanese involved. Masanosuke Akiyama, the diplomat who had been sent onboard the *Naniwa* to aid in the redress negotiations, was so disgusted by his government's inability to prevent US annexation that he attempted suicide on his return home.⁵⁵ For government officials like Akiyama, who would not invest themselves in the lives of the farming or merchant class at home, the Hawai'i-based Issei proved to be important because they were, in essence, representatives of the Japanese nation-state. As such, how they were treated, and what the Meiji government accepted as fair and equal treatment, not only spoke to the affiliation between state and subject, but also commented on Japan's relationship with the United States and the world.

The 1897 Shinshu Maru Affair pushed at articulations of Western modernity through intersecting "regimes of authenticity" such as policing, detention, and international law, brought together by the practices of border control.⁵⁶ These formulations were exacerbated by competing settler colonialisms, forcing leaders of Japan, the United States, and the Republic of Hawai'i to define the borders of their nation-states within the interimperial space of Hawai'i. While the haole-led coup state used the 1897 barred landing to enforce its terms of white supremacy, it also induced Meiji leaders to acknowledge the centrality of this interimperial space of direct encounter to an overseas nationalist project. Through their protest over a perceived violation of political rights, Issei began to affiliate themselves with a Japanese nation, referring to it as a single entity to which they owed allegiance and from which they expected protection.

In December 1897, Japan withdrew its protest over US annexation, and in return, the coup state accordingly paid seventy-five thousand dollars to the Meiji government, emigration companies, and passengers of the *Shinshu Maru*, *Kinai Maru*, and *Sakura Maru*. In an ironic twist, the US annexation of Hawai'i brought about the largest wave of Japanese migration to the archipelago. With the continent-based Chinese Exclusion Acts enforced in the islands, planters were again forced to look to Japan for a cheap and willing labor supply. These "free laborers" came in such abundance that by 1900 the islands' Japanese population exceeded sixty-one thousand—an increase of over forty thousand from the era of the advertised "Yellow Peril" and "Japanese menace."

One of the unintended consequences of the Meiji state's tactic of deploying international law to settle this dispute with the haole-led oligarchy was the reinforcement of the Hawaiian Kingdom's state-based sovereignty. During the same month that the Meiji government withdrew its objections to US annexation, members of the Hawaiian Patriotic Leagues presented their petition, with over twenty-one thousand signatures from Kānaka Maoli and Hawaiian nationals against annexation, to the US Senate Committee on Foreign Relations.[57] Just two months later, in February 1898, it seemed as if the call for the return of the Hawaiian Kingdom to its people had proved enough to defeat the proposed treaty, which was unable to garner the two-thirds majority vote in Congress necessary for ratification. Instead, riding on the imperialist fervor that followed the Spanish-American War, pro-annexation forces submitted a proposal to annex Hawai'i by joint resolution, which sidestepped the two-thirds vote requirement with a simple majority vote in both houses of Congress. On July 7, 1898, five and a half

Figure 10. People on Kamokuʻākulikuli, or "Quarantine Island," ca. 1895. Photo by J.J. Williams. Courtesy of Hawaiʻi State Archives.

years after the overthrow, the Hawaiian Islands became an official territory of the United States when the "Newlands Resolution" was signed into law by President McKinley.

At the heart of this chapter should be the detained migrants themselves, and their story of interrogation and incarceration. After all, it was their predicament that brought these transpacific empires-in-formation into diplomatic negotiations. But their individual troubles and experiences as they were detained and then ultimately denied entry were of little concern to the coup state, Meiji government, or the United States. Instead, the complexities of each individual's existence were reduced to a state-based bureaucratic identity in order to fit into a negotiation between competing forms of statecraft and build support for nationalist projects. While Hawaiʻi was not returned to its people at this time, the political encounters that occurred in this interimperial space pushed Kānaka Maoli, white American settlers, haole oligarchs, and Japanese citizen-subjects and settlers, whether at "home" or abroad, to envision their place in a Pacific world. As the next and final chapter demonstrates, for haole oligarchs this process entailed the re-creation of a particular imaginative geography—that of the empty frontier, primed for white settlement.

5

HISTORICIZING THE HOMESTEAD IN WAHIAWA COLONY

From "American Family Farm" to Industrial Plantation Economy

IN FEBRUARY 1893, a journalist with the *New York Herald* asked, "How can the United States admit the 20,000 Chinese residents of Hawaii to citizenship? How can we extend the invitation to these people to come into our fold while our present laws remain on the statute books?"[1] The journalist's query pointed to a fundamental question regarding articulations of race, citizenship, and the US nation-state at the time: How could the United States ban Asian naturalization, as stated in the 1790 Naturalization Act and upheld again in the 14th Amendment, and still consider allowing more than thirty thousand Chinese and Japanese people into the country?[2] What legal status would these people possess? And what of Kānaka Maoli who were subjects of the Hawaiian monarchy? What would their status be? Writing on this topic the *New York Herald* journalist commented, "it would be a curious thing indeed . . . to some day have a close election for President of the United States settled by the votes of semi-barbaric Sandwich Islanders, whose grandfathers were cannibals, aided by Chinese and Japanese and Papuan laborers."[3]

For the haole-led oligarchy who pushed for annexation to the United States, expressions of white racial anxiety over Hawai'i's population were nothing new.[4] Anti-Asian and anti-Black racisms were one of the primary processes of colonialism that shaped the boundaries of the coup state. Congressional debates over whether the United States should develop close ties to the Hawaiian Kingdom had been occurring ever since the 1850s, when the monarchy agitated for a reciprocity treaty.[5] In many American politicians' minds the issue of reciprocity was linked to annexation, which in turn was inextricably tied to the question of Hawai'i's racial makeup and fear of the injection of "coolies" into the US populace.[6] When the 1893 annexation attempt failed, Honolulu-based oligarchs responded by creating a republic designed to control both Kānaka Maoli and Asians—populations that simultaneously were deemed outside of the national body and yet ruled by the state. While this may have eased some of the fears of white Americans on the continent, it did not address the racial demographic, or more specifically, the lack of white workingmen and farmers, in the islands themselves.[7] To remedy this "problem," haole oligarchs looked to change the face of Hawai'i's population. While Lorrin Thurston attempted to racialize Portuguese migrants as white, Sanford Dole deployed a "homesteading" settler program that he assumed would entice the "Euro-American family farmer" to Hawai'i.

Dole believed that the most effective way to counteract the "dangerous" Asian element was the "development of a hardy, intelligent, peaceful agricultural population" and he challenged the oligarchy to propose a better way to do this than through the "opening up of public lands to settlers whose limited means would be offset by their intelligence, diligence, and determination to achieve their goals."[8] His effort to make Hawai'i more demographically "palatable" to the United States resulted in the creation of a white settler colony in the district of

Wahiawā, O'ahu.[9] Because all of the original thirteen white American families who settled in "Wahiawa Colony" hailed from Southern California, they were often referred to locally as the "California Colony."[10]

The myth of the open and empty frontier played an integral role in the narration of the colony's origins and obfuscated the centrality of Wahiawā within Kanaka Maoli culture and history. Located in central O'ahu, in the ahupua'a (wedge-shaped land section) that stretches between the Wai'anae and Ko'olau mountain ranges, Wahiawā is home to one of the most sacred sites for Kānaka Maoli, the Kūkaniloko birthstones and heiau. Since time immemorial they have served as the cultural center, or piko, of O'ahu.[11] In years past, when the wooded land was free from the din of military vehicles and cars rushing by, it was said that on the plains of Wahiawā, or the "place of noise," you could hear the roar of the ocean coming from the North Shore more than ten miles away.

It was here, in Wahiawā, an area favored by ali'i because of its cool climate, abundance of game, and lush mountainsides, that white American settlers positioned themselves as "pioneers" setting out to tame the wild "frontier." This re-creation of a particular imaginative geography in Wahiawā, that of the empty frontier primed for white settlement, normalized one of the ongoing functions of the US colonial project in the islands: attempting to break the Kanaka Maoli connection to place and consequently, their claims to sovereignty.[12] Manu Karuka explains that the frontier is not "simply a place; like capital, it can be understood as a process and a relationship."[13] Historicizing Wahiawa Colony underscores its impact as a "colonial moment," or a moment that reinforces and normalizes "white domination and accent[s] the reality of the settler colonial process . . . as a system that depends on the continued occupation of stolen lands."[14] In other words, placing the colony within the context of continental dispossession and the oligarchy's sustained effort to possess Hawai'i's Government and Crown Lands exposes the coup state's connections to a larger transpacific project of racialized state violence and the structures of settler colonialism.[15]

Indeed, Sanford Dole's land claim program carried the logic of continental elimination out into the Pacific: it required both the erasure of the Native presence, rationalized through the "racialized concepts of Manifest Destiny and *terra nullius*, which presumed white entitlement to 'empty lands' of the West," and the confiscation of Crown and Government Lands.[16] Writing to the Hawai'i-based commissioner of public lands in 1900 from Usk in Washington State, John B. Renshaw, one of the many people who expressed interest in settling in Hawai'i, articulated this transpacific connection when he referenced the US Homestead Acts, asking whether owning 160 acres of land on the continent would "debar him from acquiring lands" in the recently annexed islands.[17]

This final chapter also takes up questions regarding the cultivation of "American space," and considers how this rhetoric manifested and transformed spatial relations in the islands.[18] Asian American racialization and the mapping of spatial relations in Hawai'i were often co-constitutive. Like its continental namesake, the "California Colony" prohibited Asians from purchasing land; they were instead relegated to small farms on limited leaseholds, positioned as low-wage pineapple plantation and cannery labor, and pushed to live in makeshift labor camps. In addition to enforcing this restrictive land policy, members of the Wahiawa Colony demonstrated their "Americanness" by not just excluding Asians, but also denying their presence: though Japanese plantation labor greatly outnumbered white farmers in the colony, they were legally and culturally erased from the narrative of domesticity, agrarianism, and civility at work in the settlement.

The Wahiawa Colony and Settlement Association experiment proved to be short lived: its demise began in 1939, when a member of the Association brought suit against all the others. By this time, many of the original "California Colonists" had either sold their land or simply defaulted on their payments and returned to the continental United States. Through this process, land that had been designated for colony settlement was turned over to yet another iteration of settler colonialism: the industrial pineapple plantation. During the first half of the twentieth century, as pineapple cultivation merged with the structures of settler colonialism already in play in the colony, Wahiawā grew to become the pineapple production capital of the world.

With a few notable exceptions, most of the "California Colonists" have long been forgotten. But physical manifestations of Wahiawa Colony still mark the landscape: the city's main thoroughfare is named "California Avenue," and streets maintain the names of settlers such as Clark, Dole, and Eames. While it might not be as readily visible today, the discourse created around the colony impacted the future of Hawai'i and the Pacific. Romanticized notions of the "empty western frontier" helped to sell not just Wahiawa Colony but all of Hawai'i to the United States, by connecting geographic articulations of a whiteness that equated an "Americanness" suitable for annexation. At the same time, the cultivation of American spatial organization, cultural imaginaries, and the industrial plantation system in Wahiawā held greater global ramifications: a successful white American settlement in Hawai'i disproved the popular nineteenth-century belief that Anglo-Saxons could not survive in tropical locales while still holding on to their "civilized" ways of life. Ultimately, creating and sustaining a colony in Wahiawā, O'ahu, proved not just the feasibility of white American settlement in Hawai'i, but also hailed the possibility of an "American Pacific."

SANFORD DOLE AND THE "AMERICAN FAMILY FARM"

Throughout his fourteen-year political tenure, spanning from his election to the Hawaiian Legislature in 1884 and culminating with his yearlong presidency of the Republic of Hawai'i, Sanford Dole maintained that the ability to cultivate a "civilized" island-based body politic rested on the recruitment of a "hardy, intelligent, [and] peaceful" white American agricultural population that would work to own the land, instead of planters who brought in great numbers of Chinese and Japanese laborers to farm their large leaseholds.[19] He argued that if given the opportunity to farm and own small parcels of land, white American families would settle in Hawai'i and constitute the "most effective of influences" against Asians and their "infectious habits."[20]

With US annexation as his goal, Dole ignored the Hawaiian Kingdom's cultural and political right over the Crown and Government Lands. These lands, which constituted roughly 1.8 million acres across the Hawaiian archipelago, were created during the Māhele of 1846–48.[21] To Dole, this acreage represented a treasure trove that was mistakenly being leased out to plantation owners, an action that he felt constituted "perhaps the greatest obstacle to a comprehensive homestead system of settlement."[22] Starting in 1872 while still a practicing attorney, he began to rally against laws that gave preference to long-term leasing over the sale of these lands. Emphasizing the close connection between the Crown Land tenure policy and the large influx of Asian labor, Dole contended that the success of commercial sugar production had enabled planters to dictate Hawai'i's immigration policy since the 1860s without regard for the family farmer.[23] Homesteading, and its ability to lure white American families to populate the islands through the promise of land ownership offered, he argued, a solution that would resettle Hawai'i's land in the familiar American pattern of family farming, rather than through the development of industrial plantations worked by "alien" labor.[24]

Twelve years later, as a newly inducted legislator for the Hawaiian Kingdom, Dole introduced the Homestead Act of 1884.[25] Designed to address the "problem" of the large Chinese and Japanese population as voiced in the debates regarding reciprocity, he modeled the Hawaiian Kingdom's Homestead Act after the US law of the same name—in effect carrying out a transpacific project of racialized state violence against Indigenous populations.[26] Under the 1884 Hawai'i law, individuals were allowed to obtain plots of up to twenty acres and were required to live on and build a residence on the site within a period of three years in order to claim ownership.[27] They were also given ten years to pay back the purchase price. To Dole's dismay, the program attracted few settlers and for this he blamed the Hawaiian monarchy, stating that they were "so little in sympathy with the policy that no action was taken under it until 1888," when the administration that had come into power under the Bayonet Constitution of the previous year took "vigorous measures to carry out its provisions."[28] In the end, Dole's protests against long-term leasing of large tracts of land to sugar planters went unheeded, and his 1884 land legislation proved ineffective against the waves of Japanese and Chinese laborers that continued to enter Hawai'i between the 1870s and 1890s.

As the decade that would mark the United States' official entry into overseas colonial expansion opened, both Sanford Dole, by now a leading member of the kingdom's legislature under the haole-led oligarchy, and US Minister to Hawai'i John L. Stevens pinned their hopes of territorial incorporation upon white settlement of the Government and Crown Lands. Like Dole, Stevens shared in the belief that the key to securing Hawai'i as an American territory lay with the white American family farmer. In November 1892, Stevens cabled Secretary of State Foster and informed him of the impending "crisis" that would soon engulf the Hawaiian Kingdom: the islands, he warned, would either be going to Asia or the United States and unless the demographic was addressed promptly, they would become "unfit to be an American Territory or American State under our constitutional system." According to US Minister Stevens, what was needed immediately was a plan to "Americanize the islands" through US "control of the Crown Lands." He suggested that the acreage be disposed "in small lots for . . . [American] settlers and freeholders."[29] This, he claimed, "will make the islands like Southern California . . . bringing everything here into harmony with American life and prosperity."[30]

The overthrow of the monarchy and the implementation of the coup state gave Sanford Dole the opportunity to make major changes to the

Hawaiian land policies he felt were undermining the likelihood of annexation by the United States. On July 26, 1894, several weeks after he was inaugurated as the republic's first president, he wrote to his brother George and revealed that his next goal was to "pass a new land law providing for the management and disposition of Government lands including Crown Lands," and that he "intend[ed] to provide for different methods of furnishing land to settlers, and to make it well-nigh impossible for speculators to get a chance at the public lands."[31] Roughly one year later, Sanford Dole passed the Land Act of 1895.

Through this 1895 law, Dole attempted to increase the immediate number of white American farmers relocating to Hawai'i and implement measures that would mediate their experience and promote long-term settlement. This would, he hoped, result in a large family-anchored white agrarian community suitable for annexation to the United States. Although the Land Act of 1895 was similar to the 1884 Homestead Act in encouraging white American families to settle and farm in Hawai'i, it had two significant differences: the 1895 law targeted the Crown Lands and provided for "settlement associations." In order to create access to the Crown Lands, the 1895 law encouraged Indigenous land dispossession by repealing the 1865 Inalienable Land Statute, a Hawaiian Kingdom law that prohibited the sale of these lands and limited their lease to no more than twenty-one years for general purposes and thirty years for commercial ventures. The 1895 law also combined the Crown and Government Lands into the category of "Public Lands," which were made available to citizens and denizens in parcels of six hundred to one thousand acres through general leases, cash freehold, or right of purchase lease, overseen by three commissioners representing the republic.[32] Lastly, the Land Act positioned the government against the planter class, by promoting the sale and lease of these "Public Lands" to individuals and settler associations rather than speculators, and stipulated that all commercial leases could be cancelled without compensation for the purpose of homesteading.[33] In an effort designed to foster the development of small family farming rather than large industrial plantations, outright sale of land was restricted to parcels of less than one thousand acres.

Perhaps of greatest importance to the development of the Wahiawa Colony was the 1895 Land Act's "settlement association provision," which was one of the first official systematic efforts made by the Republic of Hawai'i to court large numbers of white Americans to farm and settle in the archipelago. Under the provision, groups of six or more who qualified for cash freeholds could apply for "holdings in one block of land," with the number of lots within the block corresponding to the "number of persons forming such association in agricultural or pastoral land or both."[34] Dole explained that through the "association provision" he hoped to attract persons from the continental United States who would not otherwise have ventured to Hawai'i. The value of this system he claimed, could be found "in regard to the settlement of strangers ... from the mainland" as it was "an almost impracticable thing to think of bringing farmers here from the mainland to settle singly in these islands with the idea that they will make a success of it; the loneliness of it ... the different social conditions, would all combine to discourage such a settler with his family ... and to finally cause failure."[35]

During its existence, the Land Act of 1895 distributed more than thirty thousand acres of family farm-size tracts to approximately eight hundred individuals.[36] Although it was never explicitly stated in the law itself, because the 1895 Land Act was open only to citizens and denizens, or those who had access to rights of citizenship in the republic without declaring sole allegiance to it, Asians were effectively barred from taking part in this program.[37] Between 1896 and 1899, those with American citizenship lay claim to 139 holdings, totaling 10,084 acres. This averaged to roughly 72.54 acres per holding and equated to over a third of the total acreage settled in that time period. Kānaka Maoli, who had been systematically dispossessed of their lands since the Māhele, claimed 230 holdings. While the number of plots claimed was greater than those of American citizens, the actual land settled by Kānaka Maoli equated to 6,502 acres, with each plot averaging 28.26 acres.[38] The remaining 13,500 acres were distributed to those with Portuguese, British, Russian, German, Norwegian, French, and Italian citizenship. In effect, through this one law, coup state officials enacted a system to both dispossess Kānaka Maoli of the Government and Crown Lands and put the majority of the acreage in the hands of European and American settlers.

THE "CALIFORNIA COLONY" OF WAHIAWĀ

Fancying himself a "pioneer," in 1897 forty-two-year-old Byron Orlando Clark, an agriculturalist from Southern California and former owner of the forty-acre Altadena Nursery, for which the city is named, traveled to Oʻahu to seek his fortune. He had been born in Hartwick, Iowa, in 1855 and had spent his early career years as an active horticulturalist, landscaping the estates, parks, and streets of Pasadena.[39] After a heavy frost wiped out most of his plant stock, Clark left his business in California for sunnier Hawaiʻi with the intent to purchase enough land to begin commercial farming.[40]

He spent his first year in the islands as the republic's commissioner of agriculture, a position that allowed him to study the lay of the land. During this year, Clark realized that while he did not have the capital needed to buy or lease a suitable amount of land from private individuals for his commercial venture, a 1,350 acre plot of "Public Land" was available for homesteading via the 1895 Land Act's settlement association provision. In January 1898, Clark, along with J. F. Brown, the commissioner of public lands for the Republic of Hawaiʻi, surveyed a parcel of third-class pasture land in Wahiawā, Oʻahu. It had formerly been leased to James Robinson, a businessman who had used it as grazing pasture. But according to the new land laws of the coup state, when leases of government land expired, preference had to be given to individual farmers and settlement associations before the contract would be renewed to the former tenant. It was this preference system that allowed Clark to claim the acreage.

The proposed site of the Wahiawa Colony was located five hours outside of Honolulu and required a ten-mile haul over dirt roads to reach the nearest railroad terminus, at Pearl City. Clark was advised that the land was "sour," ill-suited to farming, and the "whole of Wahiawā would not support a respectable family of pigs" by Kānaka Maoli and others who lived in the area.[41] Despite the multitude of warnings, he told the commissioner not only that he could "subdue the land" and make it produce, but that he "could get others to join [him] in settlement."[42] Clark was quickly assured by the commissioner that the Land Department would lend "any assistance practicable for the colonization of the land," including the building of bridges and paved roads.[43]

Commissioner Brown and President Sanford Dole were especially eager to have the tract occupied by a white American settler association because momentum was once again growing for US annexation of Hawai'i. The sinking of the *Maine* on February 15, 1898, set up a series of events that made annexation of the Hawaiian archipelago seem increasingly likely and with their goal within reach, leaders of the coup state were willing to go to extreme lengths to accommodate potential white American settlers. Although Clark did not have the number of settlers required to be able to lease the entire 1,350-acre tract, he and the others he represented were aware of the coup state's situation. Emboldened by the state of affairs, on June 14, 1898, Clark sent a letter to the republic's Land Commission asking that the tract be set aside for the future purpose of a settlement association which he expected to organize within a year's time.[44] His request was granted three days later, giving those coming from California the security of a contract approved before the annexation to the United States, thus alleviating any possible confusion regarding land rights in the transition period that followed.[45]

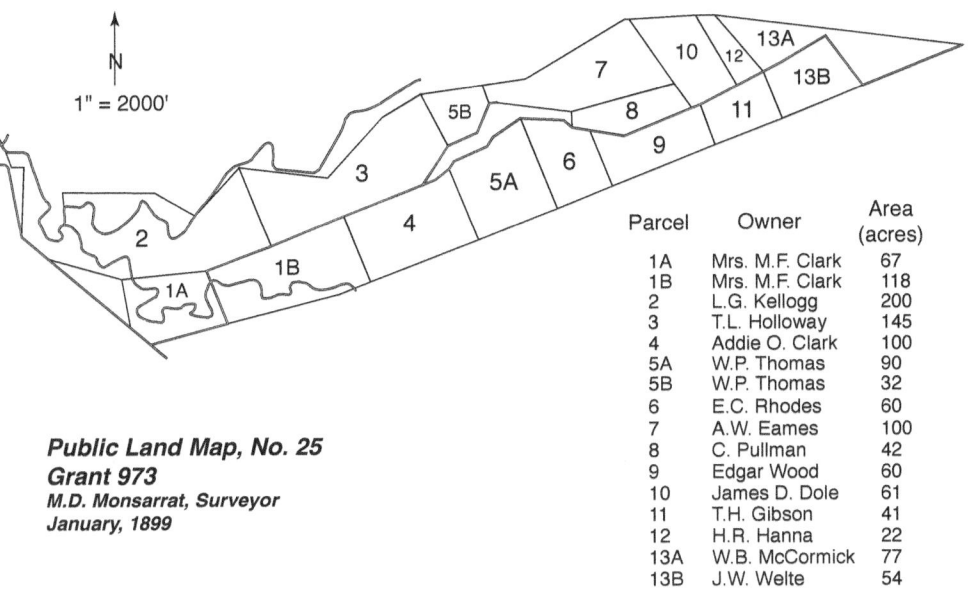

Map 3. Wahiawa Colony, 1899. Map by Michael Pesses.

In August 1898, the first group of thirteen white American settler families left San Francisco for Wahiawā, bringing with them livestock, cuttings from orange and lemon trees, wheel plows, and other farm equipment. By 1900, they reported having plowed over four hundred acres.[46] The original colonists decided on a system that distributed acres of land according to the number of people in a family. Men were to receive the right of purchase to twenty acres, with an additional twenty acres for a wife and for each child. They also intended to have a common central village, with each family living on a town lot of five acres and the rest of their farming land situated away from the community. This experiment in communal living proved short-lived, however, and they soon decided to settle on their own homesteads. Town lots were held in reserve by the Wahiawa Settlement Association, which was to use the land, including sale of the lots, for the "good of the colony."[47]

Contrary to Sanford Dole's vision of the small farmer working the frontier to cultivate "Anglo-Saxon ideas of family life," at this time the majority of white settlers in Hawai'i came to the islands with another American dream: commercial gain. An examination of the numerous inquiries written during the years immediately following the passing of the 1895 Land Act from all areas of the continental United States reveals that interested parties were overwhelmingly concerned with three main issues: the potential for an economically successful coffee plantation, the amount of capital needed to get a plantation off the ground, and whether land settlement laws under the Land Act of 1895 would remain in effect if annexation to the United States were to take place.[48]

The members of the "California Colony" proved no exception to the rule: they constituted the first systematic effort made on O'ahu by a settler association to grow a variety of crops and fruit solely for commercial purposes.[49] Upon arriving in Wahiawā, they soon formed an agricultural cooperative called the Hawaiian Fruit and Plant Company, whose primary purpose was to raise fruits and vegetables for the Honolulu and San Francisco markets.[50] By October 1898, just two months after their arrival, the land was cleared and sown with various citrus plants including oranges, grapefruit, and lime. Grapes, melons, bananas, peaches, figs, pears, avocados, and pineapples were also planted, as were grains, such as wheat, barley, and sorghum for the workhorses. As one writer for the *Honolulu Advertiser* aptly described, in the initial search for a marketable crop, each one of the homesteads became an "experiment station."[51]

After the first growing season, however, colonists had yet to cultivate enough fodder "to feed even a span of horses," and most of the other crops had also failed. Livestock could not fatten on the sparse grass that grew in the red dirt, and insects destroyed what little did grow. The lack of a reliable irrigation system proved to be a serious problem not only for the crops, but also for the colonists' daily life: when it did not rain, water had to be carried up from the two nearby streams to their homes.⁵² As a result of the harsh living conditions, some of the original colonists and investors in the colony decided to cut their losses and sell their plots of land. Others, like Clark and A. W. Eames, focused their energy on cultivating pineapple, the one crop that demonstrated great economic promise.

PINEAPPLE COMES TO WAHIAWĀ

The earliest Western written record of pineapples in Hawai'i is found in Don Francisco de Paula Marin's 1813 journal entry stating, "This day I planted pineapples and an orange tree."⁵³ Nearly thirty years later, Commodore Charles Wilkes, who was traveling as part of the United States Exploring Expedition of 1838–42, reported pineapples being cultivated at Kealakekua Bay on Hawai'i Island in 1840. By the time of the California Gold Rush, pineapples from Hawai'i could be found in small quantities on West Coast market shelves.

For the Hawaiian monarchy, facing mounting pressure from sugar interests, pineapple cultivation and general agricultural diversification offered a way to break the haole-led oligarchy's economic and political hold. As one of their last acts before the coup, both houses of the Kingdom's Legislative Assembly passed a law to "encourage the cultivation, canning, and preserving of pineapples in an attempt to diversify the economy away from sugar."⁵⁴ Despite the monarchy's support, late nineteenth-century technology was not capable of transporting pineapples from Hawai'i to San Francisco, the nearest US port, before they began to spoil.⁵⁵ Having no other options, Hawai'i-based pineapple cultivators turned to canning as a means to get their product to larger global markets.

Before the agricultural development of the US West occurred, a combination of factors, including westward expansion and the California Gold Rush, fueled the growth of the canning industry on the East Coast. By the time pineapple canning began in Hawai'i, Americans on the West Coast were familiar with the consumption of canned fruit. One of the first ventures in Hawai'i-based pineapple canning was started by John Kidwell and John Emmeluth, from England and the United States respectively.[56] In 1892, Kidwell, who had been experimenting with pineapple cultivation in the archipelago for a number of years, and Emmeluth, who began canning the fruit in 1889, partnered to form the Hawaiian Fruit and Packing Company.[57] Despite marketing fourteen thousand cases of pineapple, totaling roughly four hundred thousand fresh fruits, during its six years of existence immense shipping charges and the high US tariff made their venture barely profitable. In 1898 the Hawaiian Fruit and Packing Company succumbed to pressure from sugar planters, sublet their fields to a neighboring sugar plantation, and sold the cannery.

Close examination of the pineapple industry's development in Wahiawa Colony demonstrates that as in the continental United States, "the core institutional forms of plantation, corporation, and frontier post often blended in the same entity."[58] It was not until pineapple came to the "California Colony" and merged with the structures of settler colonialism already in play there that the planting and canning industry grew to a large commercial scale. According to local lore, after John Kidwell leased his plantation to a neighboring sugar company, the new owners ripped out the existing pineapple plants and threw them into a gulch that was adjacent to the main road. On his way back from Honolulu, Byron O. Clark happened upon the discarded plants and brought them to his farm. Because he did not have a large labor force, he replanted the slips in long rows that were spaced seven feet apart as opposed to the recommended method of placing individual plants two feet away from each other in beds of ten to twelve rows in length. Clark's method allowed the small farmer to cultivate pineapples using minimal manpower and horse-drawn equipment and also led to the relatively easy transition to industrial pineapple farming. After some experimentation, Clark found that the Smooth Cayenne variety of pineapples flourished without needing much irrigation. By December 1900, there were reportedly forty thousand pineapples harvested in the colony, their first harvest of such scale.[59]

By July 25, 1902, in a letter to E. S. Boyd, commissioner of public lands, Clark reported that over two hundred thousand pineapples were growing on his homestead and that he hoped to have over half a million planted by the end of that year. He explained that "the growing of pineapples for canning will be the leading industry of the colony" and, in that spirit, the "original small farmer" moved quickly to capitalize on this newly discovered cash crop.[60] Less than two months later, Clark formed a pineapple plantation and cannery, the Tropic Fruit Company. It marketed itself through its unique "high end" canned pineapple—instead of cutting the fruit horizontally, Tropic Fruit cut vertical spears, canned them in their own juices instead of in processed syrup, and sealed everything in specially designed glass jars. While this packaging may have been visually appealing, it was Clark's access to the acreage and other agricultural resources needed for large-scale pineapple cultivation and canning that enabled his company's significant growth.[61] In 1906 Tropic Fruit merged with the Wahiawa Settlement Association's agricultural cooperative, Hawaiian Fruit and Plant Company, to become Consolidated Pineapple Company. Leonard G. Kellogg, another one of the original colonists, and Clark's brother-in-law, served as president.

Nearly a year and half after the first colonists arrived in Wahiawā, James D. Dole, Sanford Dole's second cousin, arrived in Honolulu from Massachusetts. He had with him his life savings of fifteen hundred dollars and all the advantages of belonging to "the mission boys" network.[62] After receiving a tip from Sanford about a sixty-one acre tract of land that had been put up for auction by a disillusioned settler returning to California, James wrote home to his father for a two-thousand-dollar loan. Upon obtaining the funds, he secured the tract for four thousand dollars and incorporated the Hawaiian Pineapple Company (HAPCO) in 1901.[63]

Dole's HAPCO, "capitalized in 1901 with $16,240 was small . . . [but] his timing and connections were impeccable."[64] Indeed, James D. Dole seemed to have both time and power on his side: his cousin Sanford had given him the inside track on the initial settlement acreage; his resulting membership in Wahiawa Colony enabled his purchase of an additional plot from another colonist, upon which his company built its first cannery; and the recent annexation to the United States meant that duties on imported products from Hawai'i were dropped. James also had friends with links to the oligarchy placed in key company positions. Among them was Walter F. Dillingham, heir to the Oahu Railway and Land Company, who served as a director of HAPCO between 1902 and 1904. In 1905 Oahu Railway and Land Company started construction on a branch line that connected Wahiawā to downtown Honolulu, thereby reducing the transit time by two hours and allowing easier access to seasonal labor.[65] These connections met with circumstance and resulted in a tremendous potential for profits. In 1903 HAPCO packed seventy tons, or 1,893 cases of pineapple. In two years this number jumped to 25,022 cases, and by 1908, Dole's cannery packed 225,320 cases annually—more than half of the entire output of Hawai'i's canned production.[66] As demand skyrocketed, production capacity continued to increase, and in 1920, HAPCO packed 1,775,000 cases annually.[67]

Other white settlers of Wahiawa Colony who witnessed HAPCO's exponential growth such as A. W. Eames, an original member of the colony, looked to replicate Dole's economic success.[68] By the first decades of the twentieth century, several industrial plantations and canneries, three of which were founded by members of the Wahiawa Colony, transformed the area into the largest pineapple-producing center in the world.[69] In the midst of this pineapple fever, the *PCA* predicted that Hawai'i would supply half of the US market for canned pineapples by 1906.[70]

WHITE RACIAL LIMITATIONS AND THE FAMILIAR SOUTHERN CALIFORNIA CLIMATE OF HAWAI'I

In 1921 a writer for the *PCA* commented on the growth of the colony, noting that "from a mere homesteaders' settlement it had reached the proportions of suburban city with all the modern convenience of a municipality."[71] In contrast to the developed conditions of 1921, life during the first years of the Wahiawa Colony was extremely difficult. At the time of his initial settlement, James D. Dole despaired over the severe living conditions and noting the poor construction of homes, wrote about watching the corrugated metal roof fly off of a neighboring house during a strong storm. As one reporter commenting on the colonists' lack of initial progress put it, "they were children in the dark—expecting much and all too frequently realizing little."[72]

Despite actual living conditions, Wahiawa Colony was heavily promoted throughout its existence in nationally circulating magazines such as the *Paradise of the Pacific*, as well as the oligarchy's mouthpiece, the *PCA*. Besides offering descriptions of the agricultural bounty culled from the land, these publications erased the Native presence and cultural significance of the area by repeatedly highlighting the success of the Wahiawa "pioneers" and positioning them as the first peoples in the region.[73] For example, a 1903 *PCA* article claimed that while the "pioneers at Wahiawa . . . lived hard lives during the years that they have been engaged in their experiment . . . they have achieved a large measure of success with vigor of mind and body unimpaired."[74] Writing for the *Paradise of the Pacific*, author Henry Brown reinforced this pioneer discourse, noting that before the colony land had "felt the scratching of plows in the hands of California farmers . . . the most disturbing element had been the hoof-beats of scared cattle . . ."[75]

Journalists also cited similarities between Wahiawa Colony and "familiar Southern California," in both climate and topography, as reasons for settlement. In fact, the same 1903 *PCA* article that celebrated the "pioneers" posited that "it is because of [the] trade wind that the colonists find no difficulty in doing all the work on their farms . . . the nights are comparable in a degree to the cool nights of Southern California."[76] Some settlers even took it upon themselves to state publicly that Wahiawa Colony had no equal in terms of climate and natural beauty. In his 1900 article published in *Paradise of the Pacific*, W. B. Thomas, one of the original colonists and a journalist who wrote for California newspapers, claimed that as a place of residence no more "charming spot could be found the world over . . . the climate the year round is simply perfect. Its elevation from eight hundred to twelve hundred feet removes it from the extremes of heat . . . as for scenery, it would be hard to imagine a lovelier vista. In the rivers that border the settlement are numerous fine swimming pools, embowered in ferns and overhanging tropical trees."[77]

Why was so much emphasis placed on the similarity between Wahiawa Colony and Southern California? In his work on race and American empire, Eric T. L. Love explains that any account of the imperial process must "consider the belief in *white racial limitations* that held great sway in the nineteenth century: boundaries dictated by climate that, for anti-imperialists and imperialists alike . . . marked the limits of territorial expansion."[78] The idea that various races each had their own environment in which they would thrive could be traced as far back as the ancient Greeks: both Hippocrates and Aristotle speculated that physical and temperamental differences between groups of people were caused by climate and geography.[79] According to Hippocrates, the "father of medicine," the hot, tropical climates of Asia prevented the development of industry and instead produced laziness among people. In contrast, the ever-changing climate in Europe favored the development of people who were "hard, lean, well-articulated, well-braced," with natures that are "energetic and vigilant."[80] Centuries later this belief continued to shape the limits of Western imperialism and was notably expressed in Alexis de Tocqueville's 1835 description of the United

States and its political institutions when he wrote, "The geographical position of the British race in the New World . . . is peculiarly favorable to its rapid increase," however, it is "well known that, in proportion as Europeans approach the tropics, labor becomes more difficult for them. Many of the Americans even assert that within a certain latitude it is fatal to them."[81]

In 1893, the belief that members of the white race could not settle and transplant their institutions without suffering some moral or physical calamity in tropical locales was expanded on by former US Secretary of the Interior, Carl Schurz, a staunch anti-imperialist and editor for *Harper's New Monthly Magazine*.[82] In his infamous 1893 article entitled "Manifest Destiny," the editor asked, "What kind of people are those we take in as equal members of our national household? . . . Democratic institutions have never on a large scale prospered in tropical latitudes. The so-called republics existing under the tropical sun constantly vibrate between anarchy and despotism."[83] For the German-born Schurz, issues of climate and race were intricately related through systems of value and behavior. Besides pondering why anyone would want to labor in conditions that made any activity so arduous, Schurz contended that Hawai'i's climate aggravated the already unfit nature of the islands' Asian and Native population. He also believed that the warm weather and bounty of the land fostered an idleness that did not correspond with the hard work required to maintain a civilized government and would breed a type of tropical heathenism in white settlers to Hawai'i.

Like many others at the time, Schurz thought that Hawai'i's tropical climate, in addition to "foster[ing] laziness," was not "congenial to men of Germanic blood," and drew a comparative example with the British colonization of India.[84] He argued that there were no more than "one European to thirty five hundred natives" stationed in military garrisons across India, and that the supply of colonists had to be renewed from time to time because the country's climate made it impossible for English children to survive.⁸⁵ The inability to sustain a permanent community there, claimed Schurz, made British colonization impossible, and he foresaw the same predicament befalling the United States' attempt to annex Hawai'i.

To those who would argue against this comparison, the *Harper's* editor warned that even Anglo-Saxons, despite their "proclivity for hard work and democracy," would not be able to withstand the "immorality" of tropical Hawai'i. He explained that while white men might be able to succeed in making a quick fortune in the area and depart without any change in their moral nature, "when they go there to establish permanent homes for themselves and their posterity, the succeeding generations, if not the first settlers, will always prove a deterioration of the race in physical as well as in mental and moral vigor."⁸⁶ Schurz maintained that any long-term land settlement program in Hawai'i would be reduced to "short-lived attempts by speculators to draw American farmers into agricultural settlements" or get-rich-quick schemes.⁸⁷ These speculators would have no real interest in sustaining white American farmers' morale or well-being in the archipelago. He ended by asking the reading audience to consider what the state of this population would be after living in Hawai'i for long periods of time. What would happen to them? And what were the consequences of annexation for those on the American continent? For the *Harper's* editor, annexing the Hawaiian archipelago could only spell disaster— on one hand through incorporation of a people unfit for democracy, including Kānaka Maoli and Asians, and on the other, through the depravity that would result if white Americans were to try and settle the area and "Americanize" the tropics.

Placed in this perspective, the ability of the Wahiawā colonists not just to sustain their "civility" in the tropics, but also to show economic success, proved vital to demonstrating Hawai'i's possible long-term compatibility with the United States—that is, as a white settler state—and also served to further justify the archipelago's colonization through upholding the ideology of Manifest Destiny. Three years after the official annexation of Hawai'i as a US territory, the *PCA* published a multipage article that spoke to the agricultural success of white American men and women at Wahiawa Colony. The author, Sol N. Sheridan, resident of Hawai'i, and later of California's Ventura County, argued against Schurz's editorial, explaining that the members of the Wahiawa Settlement Association and Colony had accomplished as much in three years, in an area that Kānaka Maoli and local residents claimed possessed "sour soil," as the first white Americans to California had in ten. As to the theory that white men could not survive in the open air in the tropics, Sheridan explained that this was "disproved on the colony every day . . . [they] have shown conclusively . . . there is no labor on the land that a white man cannot do."[88]

"ASIATICS" AND "OTHER NUISANCES"

The "California Colony's" success held the potential to demonstrate not just white American dominance of tropical locales, but also prove unnecessary the presence of Asian, and particularly Japanese, "free labor."[89] In the first years of the twentieth century, this resonated with haole oligarchs who were facing the end of the contract labor system. The passing of the Organic Act in 1900, which established Hawai'i as a territory of the United States, made all labor contracts null and void. This freed the large population of Asian contract laborers from plantations and allowed them to enter the larger island society as merchants, business owners, and independent small farmers.

As if to reassure the local haole population and entice white Americans to settle in Wahiawa Colony, in 1903 Byron Clark reminded the public that the "greatest menace to the American tradesman, laborer, or farmer here [Hawai'i] are the Japanese" and that, in order to counter this "menace," all deeds granted by the Wahiawa Settlement Association contained restrictions against selling to "Asiatics" and prohibiting "other nuisances," such as building a saloon.[90] Membership in the Wahiawa Settlement Association was also restricted to adult owners of land who were citizens of the United States or eligible to become citizens.[91] Although at the time, the question of Japanese and Japanese American landownership in Hawai'i did not pose the same problem that it did on the West Coast because of the oligarchy's virtual monopoly of land, haole oligarchs believed that advertising Wahiawa Colony as a "white-only" settlement would persuade increasing numbers of white Americans to cross the Pacific.[92] They accordingly printed their race-based land policy in publications that circulated the North American continent.[93]

Despite the colony's restrictive land policy and his public assertion denying land ownership to Issei, Clark still found it necessary to refute rumors that colonists were leasing all of their land to the Japanese, and to defend those members who had. For example, in his 1902 letter to E.S. Boyd, Clark maintained that "to the best of his knowledge," none of the original members of the settlement association had leased their land to Issei. One new party, he claimed, had "acquired an option to purchase a small holding" and had leased it to "a Japanese" to plant pineapples. He also noted that some of the colonists had let Issei farmers use a small tract of land for nine months—from January 1 to September 1—to grow "just one crop of melons" because the Issei had agreed clear the land and "put it under cultivation." Clark defended this action and explained that this was "certainly very desirable" because the colonist was getting the land "put in condition for use without expense to himself and a year or more sooner than he would be able to do otherwise."[94]

Even with all that was invested in constructing a depiction of Wahiawa Colony as white-only, inconsistencies between rhetoric and reality soon led to the demise of the settlement. Instead of small family-owned farms, the land was opened to the commercial venture that would come to define Wahiawā to the United States and the world: the industrial pineapple plantation. In a twist of fate, it was Sanford Dole's second cousin, James D. Dole, who brought an end to the former Dole's agrarian fantasy and revealed industrial capitalism's inherent contradiction—that the need for a pliable workforce and the vision of small, white, farming settlements were incompatible.

After the first commercial-scale pineapple harvest in 1899 and the construction of James D. Dole's HAPCO cannery in 1901, Hawaiʻi's, and specifically, Wahiawā's, pineapple industry experienced a period of explosive growth. By 1915 the pineapple industry was second only to "king sugar" in Hawaiʻi and presented the greatest source of labor competition for the latter. However, considerable variances dictated different labor patterns in the pineapple industry than in the sugar business.[95] Because pineapple is largely a seasonal plant and needs little irrigation, it requires only a fraction of the labor per acre used to farm sugar. Edward Beechert explains that while there was a "heavy demand for labor in both harvesting and canning operations during the peak summer months from June through August," only a relatively "small cadre . . . of approximately one-sixth the peak force" was needed year-round.[96]

Due to the seasonal character of its labor needs and its relatively late development, during the formative years of the pineapple industry, owners and colonists such as Dole and Eames were able to hire from the local labor pool. The recruitment of labor away from sugar plantations was initially a point of contention between the two industries. James D. Dole was known to take advantage of local labor troubles to attract his seasonal work force. In the midst of the 1909 Issei-led sugar strike on Oʻahu for example, where approximately seven thousand Japanese men and women struck for equal pay, Dole placed advertisements offering work in his fields in all of the local Japanese-language newspapers.[97] In order to recruit workers away from sugar plantations and onto their fields and canneries, pineapple industry owners often paid more—in general offering a dollar a day for fieldwork at time when sugar pay was around eighty cents.[98] Pineapple work was also considered less physically taxing by those in the fields—animal-drawn cultivators managed the weeding and because the fruit grew at higher elevations than sugar, workers relished the cooler climate.

Despite Clark's attempts to downplay the Asian presence in Wahiawa Colony, their labor was vital to the pineapple industry. Until 1915 pineapple companies relied heavily on independent suppliers, most of whom were Issei farmers who worked on small plots of leased land.[99] Thereafter, the pineapple industry became increasingly integrated and companies like Dole's HAPCO expanded their plantings and phased out independent planters altogether. But in 1906, the presence of Issei farmers was still a cause of great concern—so much so that it was commented on by the US Department of Labor and Commerce. In their report on labor in Hawai'i for that year, they noted that "as in the case of coffee, the cultivation of pineapples is beginning to fall into the hands of Japanese . . . and one of the larger tracts in the Wahiawa Colony, which has made a specialty of pineapple raising, is now leased to a Japanese planter."[100]

Although the pineapple industry began phasing out contracted farming in 1915, individual Issei like Kumeiji and Kame Iwatani continued to lease land well into the late 1920s in order to grow the crop. Kame Iwatani notes that her family leased ten acres of land from a pineapple company in an area that was quite mountainous.[101] This made it difficult to maneuver their horse-drawn plow and wagon. Nevertheless, the Iwatanis and their four Filipino laborers worked to clear the land of the forest growth and plant pineapples. Kame recalls that in order to help cover costs and make more money, she also prepared meals and did the laundry for their contracted laborers. Like many Issei women who also worked as sugar and pineapple field hands, this meant that her days began at 3:30 a.m. and often ended late at night.

Even after businesses like HAPCO began cultivating their own pineapples, they found that they still had to rely on Japanese, Hawaiian, and other migrant laborers in their fields and canneries. Until the passing of the Immigration Act of 1924, Issei and Nisei (second-generation

Figure 11. Hawaiian Pineapple Company (HAPCO) field laborers. Courtesy of Hawai'i State Archives, gift of R. S. Kuykendall.

Japanese American) men and women comprised the greatest percentage of pineapple labor, making up roughly half of the plantation field workforce and one third of labor in the canneries. Hawaiian, Portuguese, Chinese, Filipino, and Korean laborers were also among the groups that were represented in both field and cannery work to varying degrees. Women of all ethnicities were heavily employed by HAPCO and the entire pineapple industry. In fact, it was one of the largest employers of women in Hawai'i. During the summer months, women often found temporary work in the fields as weeders and cultivators, and in canneries as trimmers and packers.[102]

Despite being painted as "easier" than sugar plantation work, laboring in the pineapple fields was incredibly taxing. Harvesting was an arduous process that until the 1950s was done by hand and laborers were often paid by piece. In spite of the physical nature of the work, field hands had to wear multiple layers of clothing in order to protect themselves from injury. According to Venicia Damasco Guiala, who worked at Dole's Wahiawā plantation as a seasonal worker, her daily uniform included a hat and handkerchiefs to cover her head and face because of "the dust.... You will cough. No good for you, the chemicals they put on the plant."[103] Field hands also donned heavy denim clothing, rubber or leather gloves, goggles, and two layers of pants to protect themselves from the sharp pineapple leaves. While these layers of clothing were necessary to protect laborers from injury, they also compounded the intense summer heat and made it difficult to work in the winter rains.

Yone Taniguchi, who lived at Dole's Kipapa-5 (K-5) Camp and worked in the pineapple fields during the 1930s, shares that laborers were given only one thirty-minute break for lunch.[104] Many times they were too tired to talk to each other as they ate. Other than this short period, field hands had no rest breaks. When someone had to use the restroom, Taniguchi explains that "you couldn't go far . . . we would try to go in the gulches . . . we would keep toilet paper in our bags. Also in the pockets of our jackets. We would also carry knives so we can dig the ground and then cover it up." Women often carried sanitary pads with them as well as paper bags for disposal. Taniguchi adds that women had to "wait until lunch time to change our napkins so we could go far away."[105] This often meant that they used all or most of their lunch break for necessary hygiene practices.

Cannery work was often thought of as being easier than field labor, but it also presented a multitude of challenges. At Eames's Hawaiian Islands Packing Company for example, workers handled the fresh fruit for twelve hours a day, six days a week, trimming off the thick skin, slicing, coring, and cutting the fruit. Cannery workers, who were mostly young Asian and Hawaiian women, often reported skin burns and rashes from the acidic pineapple juice.[106] The strong smell of the pineapple made some people ill, and as Sue Kajioka explains, "even if

Figure 12. Pineapple trimmers. Courtesy of Hawai'i State Archives.

you come home, the smell will never go out. It's a smell right through your body."[107] Trimmers, those who trimmed the skin and eyes off the pineapple in order to get it ready for slicing, also suffered from hand and wrist injuries. Kajioka, who worked in the Dole Cannery as a trimmer, remembers that "cutting the [pineapple] skin is very hard. Because the knife is sharp [and] . . . you couldn't cut it too deep." Even though their hands got tired from constant repetitive motions and balancing the weight of the pineapple, Kajioka states that "you just have to continue doing it, till the rest period or lunch."[108]

Labor camps were set up for cannery and field workers in and around Wahiawā and were often segregated by ethnicity. At one point, HAPCO had fifteen separate camps in the area. Robert Ishikawa, a Nisei who as a young boy grew up in a work camp adjacent to Hawaiian Islands

Packing Company's cannery, comments on the camps' segregated and rudimentary nature, stating that the "Chinese [lived] on one end, Koreans on another, and Japanese in the back. There was a community bathhouse and a three-stall outhouse.... Our stove was a square five-gallon can—we burned wood in that."[109] When Yasuko Domai arrived in Oʻahu from Japan she first lived in Dole's K-5 Camp, one of the more "finished" camps, where "each family had their own house." She remembers that the "kitchen, laundry, toilet, and bath were outside. We shared a community bath. There were Filipinos, no Chinese, and a Korean was the cook. The Japanese and Filipino single men used to go to the Korean man's house to eat ... We cooked outside, then brought it all inside to eat."[110]

Domai later moved to Brodie 4, a remote Dole camp several miles north of the center of town. Of life in this workcamp she says, "I don't know what I thought it would be, but when I saw it, I thought what a pitiful way to live .... If I knew I was going to live in this kind of place I would never have come. Not only the conditions were bad, but the distance ... so isolated, way up in the hills and mountains."[111] Field hands like Domai often had to live in crude remote camps that were close to the pineapple fields. These camps were clustered in gulches and along streams, reachable only by poorly maintained dirt roads, far beyond the boundaries of Wahiawā town. Liiko Nouchi recalls how difficult living at Dole's K-5 Camp was because the stores and doctors were so far away. When it rained, "the roads are so muddy and so slippery. Cannot get out from there."[112] Another field hand, Josephine Montalbo, commented on life in the camps saying, "look where I am living, so isolated, nobody knows about us."[113]

CONCLUSION: VEXED PRESENCE

Montalbo's comment speaks to the vexed presence that Asians have historically occupied within the US settler colonial space—in this case, as plantation and cannery workers who were legally and culturally erased from the colonial vision of white domesticity, while simultaneously being part of and supporting the structures of settler colonialism. Gary Okihiro explains that as participants in the plantations, a system that was "essentially anti-Asian . . . because it was designed to control and exploit the[ir] productive labor . . . and then to expel them when their utility had ended," Asian laborers were forced to work under conditions that were understood as intolerable for white settlers.[114] The situation in Wahiawā proved to be no different. While the white American settlers of Wahiawa Colony were credited as "pioneers" who "tamed" the "wild and empty frontier," Asian and Kanaka Maoli laborers were the ones planting, picking, and packing the fruit.

By the mid-1920s, the major pineapple industry owners realized that the island-based labor supply did not meet their needs and they began working together with sugar planters to recruit workers from the Philippines. In exchange for a share of the recruitment costs, pineapple industry owners gained access to one third of the labor recruited by the Hawaiian Sugar Planters' Association. This practice led to a shift in the racial composition of the plantation workforce in Hawai'i as Filipino migrants came to make up a majority of the laboring population in both sugar and pineapple industries.

Over the next several decades, as the plantation economy gave way to the postwar military industrial complex and the tourism industry, the discourse of "local" identity took hold among island residents, as they celebrated the multicultural, mixed-race society that originated on the sugar and pineapple fields. As a rhetorical strategy of self-representation, "local" identity served and continues to serve as a "corrective to Hawai'i's colonial 'past,' the 'divisiveness' of Hawaiian nationalism," and the invisibility of Asian labor on plantations and canneries.[115] During the 1970s, this narrative of different ethnic communities coming together with Kānaka Maoli as "locals" on the plantations to strike against haole owners was used by the working class as a "rallying point in their resistance against forces of commercial, suburban, and resort development," and the onslaught of tourists from the American continent and Asia.[116]

In her work on Asian settler colonialism, Candace Fujikane argues that "it is not colonial intent that defines the status of Asians as settlers but rather the historical context of U.S. colonialism of which they unknowingly became a part."[117] Historicizing Wahiawa Colony works not just to reveal its connections to a continent-based settler colonialism, but also to highlight how Asian settler colonialism grew out of this process of erasure and removal. As this final chapter demonstrates, Native dispossession and the recruitment and subsequent erasure of Asian workers were occurring concurrently within this space in order to facilitate the transformation of Wahiawā into the world's industrial pineapple hub.

Although Wahiawa Colony did not live up to Sanford Dole's dream of small family farmers settling the land, it nonetheless served as an articulation of the triumph of whiteness in the tropics. As such, the settlement demonstrated the suitability of Hawai'i as a colony of the United States. As the members of the "California Colony" positioned themselves as "pioneers" taming the inhospitable and empty frontier, they normalized both the removal of the Indigenous presence and the denial of the Asian worker, while simultaneously enforcing a racial hierarchy designed to discipline those whom they recruited as temporary labor. To those who questioned Hawai'i's compatibility with the racial regime of the US nation-state, Wahiawa Colony provided a vision and model of white settlement and supremacy, one that was based on a broader transpacific practice of racialized state violence and genocide, offering the reassurance and familiarity of the already colonized California.

CONCLUSION

ON SEPTEMBER 6, 1897, Hui Aloha ʻĀina members held a mass meeting at Palace Square in Honolulu. James Keauiluna Kaulia, president of the organization, gave a rousing speech to the crowd of thousands of poʻe aloha ʻāina:

> No laila, mai makau, e kupaa ma ke Aloha i ka Aina, a e lokahi ma ka manao, e kue loa aku i ka hoohui ia o Hawaii me Amerika a hiki i ke aloha aina hope loa.
>
> Do not be afraid, be steadfast in aloha for your land and be united in thought. Protest forever the annexation of Hawaiʻi until the very last aloha ʻāina.[1]

A month after this meeting, in response to a planned visit by pro-annexationist US Senator John Tyler Morgan, a group of Kānaka Maoli in Honolulu formed the Komite o ka Lehulehu (Citizens Committee) and created a statement in both ʻōlelo Hawaiʻi and English that contested US annexation.[2] In it, Citizens Committee members claimed that the annexation treaty extinguished "our existence as a Nation" and that the "project of Annexation . . . would be subversive of the personal and political rights . . . of the Hawaiian people and Nation, and would be a negation of the rights and principles proclaimed in the Declaration of American Independence."[3] By once again deploying the rhetoric of state-based jurisdiction and rights, members of the Hawaiian Patriotic Leagues and the Citizens Committee skillfully rallied against US annexation using the language of the nation-state.

Perhaps the strongest example of this rhetorical strategy was made by Queen Liliʻuokalani herself. In her June 17, 1897, letter of protest to President William McKinley, she linked annexation to the violation of the rights to franchise, property, and liberty, and described it as an

> invasion of the rights of the ruling chiefs, in violation of international rights both toward my people and toward friendly nations with whom they have made treaties . . . . Because neither the above-named commission nor the government which sends it has ever received any such authority from the registered voters of Hawaii . . . . Because my people, about forty thousand in number, have in no way been consulted by those, three thousand in number, who claim the rights to destroy the independence of Hawaii . . . . Because said treaty ignores, not only the civic rights of my people, but, further, the hereditary property of their chiefs.[4]

While it might seem that by 1897 Kānaka Maoli, who argued for the sanctity of the nation-state, had accepted a "structure of Western-style government," Noenoe Silva reminds us that they spoke through this structure because it was a form recognized by Western colonizing powers. Using the argument of state-based sovereignty to justify the existence of an independent Hawaiian Kingdom was both a strategy and "necessity of people surviving against the threats of the armed nations of the West."[5]

This book has argued that both Queen Liliʻuokalani and poʻe aloha ʻāina understood that state sovereignty over Hawaiʻi was a legally defined privilege sanctioned through the regime of international law, and strategically used their claim as a tactic of national defense. As a modern transpacific order developed, terms used in the performative discourse of international law "fed on and were fed by theories of the nation-state." Alexis Dudden explains that "although international law presumed to transcend national distinctions with universalist claims, only governments that successfully subscribed to nation-state theories could participate." Within this relationship, representatives of the nation-state "mutually define[d] one another in a politics of display."[6]

How was the modern nation-state, as a form of political organization, understood and refined within the context of the late nineteenth-century Pacific world? One of the main arguments that this book has made is that by examining how poʻe aloha ʻāina, leaders of the coup state, Meiji oligarchs, and Portuguese and Issei settlers not only engaged in, but also contested the spectacle of nation-state making, we can deepen our understanding of the reflexivity of modern nation building. Thinking through the nation-state as a form reveals that the connections among racial capitalism, white supremacy, and settler colonialism that continue to uphold American empire today were both challenged and refined in the interimperial condition of Hawaiʻi.

I began this book a decade ago with the intention of challenging the assumed inevitability underlining the "Hawaiʻi as fiftieth US state" narrative. What I found was that it was precisely in spaces of instability and rupture that concepts such as nation and state were negotiated and refined. Among the many difficulties I encountered in pursuing this project is that writing about the confluence of ideas necessitates engagement with a number of different understandings of terms we take for granted today. As I hope to have demonstrated, ideas such as "nation" and "citizen" meant different things to various communities residing in Hawaiʻi during this time. For Kānaka Maoli, the nation could be understood to reside within the people and the connection to place. For the Issei community in the archipelago, who at home had identified as members of a certain class, village, or profession, membership in the Japanese nation came into relevance when they were threatened from outside sources or when they attempted to acquire civil and political rights abroad.

The push for the Japanese right to vote, for example, one of the narrative threads that runs through this book, produced this type of challenge for Meiji subjects in Hawai'i and the Japanese imperial government at home, as the former looked to the latter for political protection in the islands. Where they had once identified as members of a certain prefecture or village, in the fight for the right to vote and other legal protections under the laws of the coup government, Japanese laborers came to understand themselves as citizen-subjects of the Meiji empire, living in a world of nation-states. Meiji officials, who were caught up in the quest to secure equal treaties abroad, found themselves advocating for the rights of a class of people who would not merit much consideration at home.

This book has also considered how seemingly insignificant local incidents can lead to larger structural changes. The narrative of Manuel Reis, who called on Portugal, his kingdom of birth, to defend him while imprisoned by the coup state on suspicions of supporting the Native monarchy, serves as one of these examples. Reis's story, along with those of others in this book—such as the over one thousand migrants from the *Shinshu Maru, Kinai Maru,* and *Sakura Maru* who were held in prolonged detention—points to the fact that the structural networks created by late nineteenth-century nation- and empire-making resulted in a world where the local was global, and the global, local. It is only through using this framework that Reis's imprisonment for operating a hack-stand that serviced Hawaiian royalty, and the resultant impasse between the Kingdom of Portugal, the Republic of Hawai'i, and the United States, makes sense.

Ultimately, *Pacific Confluence* contributes to conversations about the importance of Hawai'i in the imperial world of the late nineteenth century, not just as a place that is occupied, but as a node for resistance and the exchange of ideas. It has argued for the unexpected centrality of the most physically isolated island chain on the planet to the development of late nineteenth-century understandings of the modern nation-state. And finally, it has considered how these meanings evolved when they came into contact with each other, ultimately traveling beyond the Pacific and affecting articulations of the nation-state around the world.

In her work, Noelani Goodyear-Kaʻōpua calls for deoccupation through setting the conditions of possibility determined by relationship to place.[7] This book posits that considering the nation-state as just one form of historical consciousness and narrative might change our perspective of the past and broaden the possibilities for the future to encompass nonstatist forms of deoccupation. While *Pacific Confluence* is not meant to supplant national historiography, it asks us to consider how this one mode of historical consciousness came to replace others and become hegemonic, thereby rendering less visible other possibilities and futures that are rooted in Indigenous worldviews and alternative relations to people and place. What I hope has become clear is that through revisiting the constructed nature of the nation-state, this book not only highlights its noninevitability, but also emphasizes its invented capacities, steeped in modes of dispossession, violence, and exploitation.

While the violence inherent in nation-state making often made front-page headlines, it also developed incrementally, cloaked in the language of progress and development. Although most of this book centered itself within a brief five-year period at the end of the nineteenth century, the impact of the history shared here is not confined to the past. Intended as a critical endeavor of history, *Pacific Confluence* pushes us to consider how the past informs our present conditions as well as visions for the future. Consider for example, the recent history of Lānaʻi Island, which attests to the continued connections between white supremacy and settler colonialism that were engendered through the processes of US nation-state making.

In June 2012, Larry Ellison, the cofounder and chief executive of Oracle, purchased the Hawaiian island of Lānaʻi for approximately $350 million. Ellison bought the island from David Murdock, who had acquired it in 1986 when he became chief executive officer of Castle and Cooke, one of the "Big Five" sugar factors which also owned Dole Food Company. A year after his purchase, in an interview for the *Wall Street Journal*, Ellison said that it felt "surreal to think that I own this beautiful island. It doesn't feel like anyone can own Lānaʻi. What it feels like to me is this really cool 21st-century engineering project, where I get to work with the people of Lānaʻi to create a prosperous and sustainable Eden in the Pacific."[8] Ellison's comments are laden with an imperialist nostalgia that conceals his complicity with the historical impact of racial capitalism, white supremacy, and settler colonialism on an island community that was self-sustaining before the arrival of settlers and transients.[9] They also raise the question that many people have asked—how does one person come to own an entire island in the Hawaiian archipelago on which resides a sizeable group of Kānaka Maoli with genealogical ties to the land, as well as settlers who have lived there for multiple generations?

Laura E. Lyons explains that for over a century, the "lives and livelihoods of the residents of Lānaʻi have been tied to the destinies of a succession of white landowners with the resources to change not just the economy but also the geographical terrain of the island in the hope of achieving their singular vision of making the island 'profitable.'"[10] A brief examination into the recent history of Lānaʻi reveals that it has been under the control of white settlers since 1863, when Levi Haalelea sold his land in Pālāwai Valley to Walter Murray Gibson, who claimed to represent the Mormon Church.[11] By 1875, against the protests of resident Kānaka Maoli and officials like Paul Nahaolelua, who served as governor of Maui and Lānaʻi, Gibson gained control over a majority of the island either through fee simple title or the long-term lease of government lands.[12] For over two decades, he and his family used the lands for ranching and farming operations.

In 1917, Alexander and Baldwin, another one of the "Big Five" sugar factors, purchased Lānaʻi for roughly six hundred thousand dollars and like Gibson, attempted large-scale ranching. Five years later, in 1922, James D. Dole bought the land from Alexander and Baldwin for $1.1 million in order to grow his pineapple business. He proceeded to clear the land of native growth, divert water to his irrigation systems, and built a plantation "village" for field hands, the majority of whom were migrant Filipinos. In an articulation of his patriarchal settler colonial practices, Dole often referred to Lānaʻi as his "pineapple kingdom."[13] Plantation management regulated almost every aspect of Lānaʻi life, from the 5 a.m. and 8 p.m. sirens that instructed people when to get up and go to bed, to the regulations pertaining to what plants people could grow in their own backyards.[14] Unfortunately for the "pineapple king," transforming Lānaʻi into his fiefdom caused James D. Dole to leverage himself too heavily, and eventually Castle and Cooke took over HAPCO in the 1960s.[15]

While Ellison's plan to turn Lānaʻi into a self-sustaining, eco-friendly, Pacific-based "garden of Eden" might seem disconnected from the history of a Honolulu-based prisoner escaping to a Meiji warship for jurisdictional protection, the decades-long indemnity case of a Portuguese carriage driver, or the theater of the 1894 constitutional convention, the tech entrepreneur's ability to purchase 98 percent of the island reflects the impact of settler colonialism and white supremacy inherent in the modern Pacific world. One might ask Ellison, "Eden for whom?" In fact, Ellison's vision for what Lānaʻi "could be" is connected to the designs that haole oligarchs and settlers like Sanford Dole and Byron Clark held for Wahiawa Colony over a century ago. As men like Clark, Dole, Gibson, Murdock, and Ellison surveyed the "empty" and "wasted" land of Wahiawā and Lānaʻi, they ignored the thousands of years of cultural, social, and political significance that each place holds for Kānaka Maoli in an attempt to fit these locations into a future that they desired.

Like Ellison's "Eden in the Pacific," and Clark's "California Colony," the annexation of Hawai'i as a territory of the United States represented the attainment of a white settler fantasy built on the exploitation of others. But as I have argued throughout this work, given the reality of the multiple vested interests in the archipelago, US annexation was never a forgone conclusion and at times seemed very unlikely. Despite the much publicized "success" of developments like Wahiawa Colony, the coup state was never able to break the Kanaka Maoli connection to place and expansive understandings of ea continue to exceed state-based definitions of sovereignty.

Conducting research on events that occurred in a place and time in which the sociopolitical future was so uncertain prompts the scholar of history to acknowledge not only the different conceptions of political organization that existed, but to imagine, as many must have done, the multitude of possibilities that "could have been" and still exist today. The histories shared here push us to consider how various articulations of the nation were and are being used as oppositional strategies against imperial state encroachments. Noelani Goodyear-Ka'ōpua explains that settler colonial relations might be "transformed by rebuilding, in new ways, the Indigenous structures that have historically sustained our communities," and engages with the possibilities that emerge when diverse settler groups work in place-based affinity with Kānaka Maoli.[16] If nation-states are narrations, then in the place of these "fossilized pretensions to truth grounded in colonial authority," *Pacific Confluence* challenges us to imagine nonstatist forms of deoccupation with a future that resides outside of the constrained logics of US empire.[17] If there were ever a time for change, it is now. It is my hope that by looking back through this history we might be able to see our way out of the settler nation-state we have become and challenge ourselves to envision a futurity beyond a world of borders, barricades, and walls.

Notes

INTRODUCTION

1. Robert William Kalanihiapo Wilcox grew up on Maui and was of royal lineage. In 1881 he was sent by King David Kalākaua to study at a military academy in Turin, Italy. It was assumed that when he returned he would be placed in a prominent government position. However, after the coup, the ruling oligarchs refused to employ him. Wilcox left for San Francisco and returned to Honolulu in 1889 to protest the Bayonet Constitution and see Kalākaua restored to power. He was later elected as the first delegate to the US Congress for the Territory of Hawai'i. For more on Wilcox, see Noenoe K. Silva, *Aloha Betrayed: Native Hawaiian Resistance to American Colonialism* (Durham, NC: Duke University Press, 2004), 127–28.

2. "Loyalists" were subjects of the Hawaiian Kingdom who supported the continued independence of the nation under Hawaiian rule, but not necessarily the monarchy. Robert Wilcox sometimes considered himself a "loyalist" and not a "royalist." See Ronald Williams Jr., "Incarcerating a Nation: The Arrest and Imprisonment of

Political Prisoners by the Republic of Hawai'i, 1895," *The Hawaiian Journal of History* 55, no. 1 (2021): 167–76.

3. Thomas P. Spencer and Puakea Nogelmeier. Ka hoʻokahuli aupuni kaulana o 1893 : kaua kūloko ma Honolulu, Ianuari 7, 1895: ka hoʻāʻo ʻana e hoʻokahuli i ka Repubalika Hawaiʻi, aupuni hou ko Hawaiʻi Pae ʻĀina: hoʻohiwahiwa ʻia me nā kiʻi. The famous overthrow of 1893: Civil war in Honolulu, January 7, 1895: the attempt to overthrow the Hawaiian government: the new government of the Hawaiian Islands: beautifully illustrated with pictures. Honolulu: Bishop Museum Press, 2000. See also Albertine Loomis, *For Whom Are the Stars? Revolution and Counterrevolution in Hawaiʻi, 1893–1895* (Honolulu: University of Hawaiʻi Press, 1977); Silva, *Aloha Betrayed*.

4. This number includes the 123 men taken into custody from the battlefields as well as the three hundred men and women who were arrested later as "political prisoners." For a list of their names, see Williams, "Incarcerating a Nation," 169–74. See also *Pacific Commercial Advertiser*, July 18, 1895; Silva, *Aloha Betrayed*.

5. I use the terms "Kanaka Maoli," "Hawaiian," and "Native Hawaiian" in reference to people of Hawaiian ancestry, regardless of blood quantum classification. I use "Kānaka Maoli" to refer to the plural and collective form of "Kanaka Maoli." When referencing those who have naturalized to or were born as subjects of the Hawaiian Kingdom, I use the terms "Hawaiian nationals" and "Hawaiian citizen-subjects."

6. Affidavit, "In the Matter of the Claim of Manoel Giel Dos Reis against the Hawaiian Government," July 9, 1895, Attorney General File, Series 506, Hawaiʻi State Archives, Honolulu. According to Reis, there were nine British men, two Greek men, and one Danish man held as prisoners with him.

7. Manu Karuka defines countersovereignty as a "position of reaction," since settler sovereignty requires "recognition of Indigenous modes of relationship . . . in order to maintain any semblance of stability or coherence." Manu Karuka, *Empire's Tracks: Indigenous Nations, Chinese Workers, and the Transcontinental Railroad* (Oakland: University of California Press, 2019), 2.

8. Brian Russell Roberts and Michelle Ann Stephens, "Archipelagic American Studies: Decontinentalizing the Study of American Culture," in *Archipelagic American Studies*, edited by Brian Russell Roberts and Michelle Ann Stephens, 1–54 (Durham, NC: Duke University Press, 2017), 13. Augusto Espiritu challenges scholars to reframe the narrative of Asian American history by using the

interimperial perspective, or the "relations of cooperation, competition, and conflict between empires." I use this framework to analyze seemingly local events and situate empire and nation-state within a global-historical frame that works to reveal them as construction and process. For more on the interimperial perspective see Augusto Espiritu, "Inter-imperial Relations, the Pacific, and Asian American History," *Pacific Historical Review* 83, no. 2 (2014): 238–54.

9. See for example Noelani Arista, *The Kingdom and the Republic: Sovereign Hawai'i and the Early United States* (Philadelphia: University of Pennsylvania Press, 2019); Kamanamaikalani Beamer, *No Mākou Ka Mana: Liberating the Nation* (Honolulu: Kamehameha Publishing, 2014); Lorenz Gonschor, *A Power in the World: The Hawaiian Kingdom in Oceania* (Honolulu: University of Hawai'i Press, 2019).

10. For more on Hawaiian articulations of political independence see J. Kēhaulani Kauanui, *Paradoxes of Hawaiian Sovereignty: Land, Sex, and the Colonial Politics of State Nationalism* (Durham, NC: Duke University Press, 2018). For more on the "Pacific world," see David Igler, *The Great Ocean: Pacific Worlds from Captain Cook to the Gold Rush* (New York: Oxford University Press, 2013).

11. Despite being highly contested and difficult to define, this work conceives nation, state, and empire as historical phenomena and artifacts, and as the products of human association. Members of nations define themselves in terms of "ascriptive criteria" that are embedded in the stories they tell to make sense of an idealized collectivity. The "state" refers to the government apparatus that maintains control over a given territory. I adhere to Duara's definition of the nation-state as a "political form with distinct territorial boundaries within which the sovereign state, 'representing' the nation-people, has steadily expanded its role and power." I also emphasize that the question for the state is always "within what boundaries and over which people can it enforce its will?" For more information, see Lauren L. Basson, *White Enough to Be American?: Race Mixing, Indigenous People, and the Boundaries of the State and Nation* (Chapel Hill: University of North Carolina Press, 2008), 12–13; Prasenjit Duara, *Rescuing History from the Nation* (Chicago: University of Chicago Press, 1995), 8–15; Stuart Hall, "The State in Question," in *The Idea of the Modern State*, edited by George McLennan, David Held, and Stuart Hall, 1–28 (Philadelphia: Open University Press, 1984).

12. Candace Fujikane, "Mapping Wonder in the Māui Mo'olelo on the Mo'o'āina: Growing Aloha 'Āina through Indigenous and Settler Affinity Activism," *Marvels and Tales* 30, no. 1 (2016): 45–69.

13. Here Robert Allen Warrior is commenting on Vine Deloria Jr.'s argument in *We Talk, You Listen* (New York: MacMillan, 1970), 124. Robert Allen Warrior, *Tribal Secrets: Recovering American Indian Intellectual Traditions* (Minneapolis: University of Minnesota Press, 1994), 91.

14. See for example, Manu Karuka, *Empire's Tracks* and Dean Itsuji Saranillio, *Unsustainable Empire: Alternative Histories of Hawai'i Statehood* (Durham, NC: Duke University Press, 2019).

15. Roderick Labrador, *Building Filipino Hawai'i* (Chicago: University of Illinois Press, 2015), 135.

16. Jun Uchida, *Brokers of Empire: Japanese Settler Colonialism in Korea, 1876–1945* (Cambridge, MA: Harvard University Asia Center, 2011).

17. Saranillio, *Unsustainable Empire*, 23.

18. Ann Laura Stoler, "Colonial Archives and the Arts of Governance," *Archival Science* 2, no. 1 (2002): 87–109.

19. Epeli Hau'ofa, "Our Sea of Islands," *The Contemporary Pacific* 6, no. 1 (1994): 141–61.

20. For example see Eiichiro Azuma, *In Search of Our Frontier: Japanese American and Settler Colonialism in the Construction of Japan's Borderless Empire* (Oakland: University of California Press, 2019); Setsu Shigematsu and Keith Camacho, eds., *Militarized Currents: Toward a Decolonized Future in Asia and the Pacific* (Minneapolis: University of Minnesota Press, 2010); Lon Kurashige, ed., *Pacific America: Histories of Transoceanic Crossings* (Honolulu: University of Hawai'i Press, 2017).

21. Kamehameha I inaugurated a political relationship with Great Britain in 1794. For more information see Gonschor, *A Power in the World*, 22.

22. Karuka, *Empire's Tracks*, 2.

23. For more on the making of the modern US-led transpacific order, see Alfred Peredo Flores, "'No Walk in the Park': U.S. Empire and the Racialization of Civilian Military Labor in Guam, 1944–1962," *American Quarterly* 67, no. 3 (2015): 813–35; Simeon Man, *Soldiering through Empire: Race and the Making of the Decolonizing Pacific* (Oakland: University of California Press, 2018); Shigematsu and Camacho, *Militarized Currents*.

24. According to Jonathan Kay Kamakawiwo'ole Osorio, Hawaiian identity is a question of ancestry, kinship, and genealogy. See Jonathan Kay Kamakawiwo'ole Osorio, *Dismembering Lāhui: A History of the Hawaiian Nation*

to 1887 (Honolulu: University of Hawai'i Press, 2002). The federal definition of "native Hawaiian" is a descendant, with at least one-half blood quantum, of individuals inhabiting the Hawaiian Islands prior to 1778. This is referred to as the 50 percent blood quantum rule. The State of Hawai'i defines "Native Hawaiian" as anyone who can trace ancestry to the people who occupied the area that now comprises the state before 1778. J. Kēhaulani Kauanui effectively argues that "blood quantum is a manifestation of settler colonialism that works to deracinate . . . and displace indigenous peoples. . . . It is a colonial project in the service of land alienation and dispossession." J. Kēhaulani Kauanui, *Hawaiian Blood: Colonialism and the Politics of Sovereignty and Indigeneity* (Durham, NC: Duke University Press, 2008).

25. See Osorio, *Dismembering Lāhui*; Sally Engle Merry, *Colonizing Hawai'i: The Cultural Power of Law* (Princeton, NJ: Princeton University Press, 2000).

26. For more information on how Western understandings of the nation-state have influenced current decolonization movements, see Joanne Barker, ed., *Sovereignty Matters: Locations of Contestation and Possibility in Indigenous Struggles for Self-Determination* (Lincoln: University of Nebraska Press, 2006).

27. Osorio, *Dismembering Lāhui*. According to Osorio, pono referred to a "state of balance between numerous dualities," especially in relation to a separation between male and female. For maka'āinana the idea of pono linked them in a system of balance and responsibility to ali'i and Akua. See also, Lilikalā Kame'eleihiwa, *Native Land and Foreign Desires: Pahea Lā E Pono Ai?* (Honolulu: Bishop Museum Press, 1992).

28. Osorio, *Dismembering Lāhui*, 40.

29. Osorio, *Dismembering Lāhui*, 147.

30. Mae Ngai, *Impossible Subjects: Illegal Aliens and the Making of Modern America* (Princeton, NJ: Princeton University Press, 2005), 11.

31. Noelani Goodyear-Ka'ōpua, "Introduction," in *A Nation Rising: Hawaiian Movements for Life, Land, and Sovereignty*, edited by Noelani Goodyear-Ka'ōpua, Ikaika Hussey, and Erin Kahunawaika'ala Wright, 1–34 (Durham, NC: Duke University Press, 2014), 4.

32. For a detailed account of the way Kānaka Maoli understood the world from a Hawaiian-centered perspective, see David Chang, *The World and All the Things Upon It: Native Hawaiian Geographies of Exploration* (Minneapolis: University of Minnesota Press, 2016).

33. Through her reading of Hawaiian-language sources, Noelani Arista argues against the dominant missionary-driven narrative of changes to Hawaiian law. While Kamanamaikalani Beamer also argues against a history that centers missionaries and other Euro-American parties as drivers of change, he contends that aliʻi created a hybrid government and used their agency to modify the existing Indigenous structure with select Euro-American tools of governance. See Arista, *The Kingdom and the Republic* and Beamer, *No Mākou Ka Mana*.

34. Between 1836 and 1839, Britain and France acquired special privileges for their subjects through a series of treaties including the right to trial by a jury from the foreign European community. The Kumu Kānāwai, or the 1839 Declaration of Rights, the 1840 Constitution, and the laws of 1841 and 1842 joined Hawaiian systems of governance with hints of Anglo-American influence. Under these documents Kānaka Maoli and Hawaiian nationals were still subject to the rule of the mōʻī and their aliʻi. A House of Representatives, whose members were selected by the people, joined the House of Nobles, or the council of aliʻi appointed by the mōʻī, as a lawmaking body.

35. In 1843 a rogue British naval officer claimed the Hawaiian Islands for Great Britain. Upon restoration of the government to Hawaiʻi by Britain, Kauikeaouli proclaimed "Ua mau ke ea o ka ʻāina i ka pono" or the "ea of our land is perpetuated through justice and proper acts." Hawaiian language and political science scholars Leilani Basham and Noelani Goodyear-Kaʻōpua make the important observation that instead of reaffirming the sovereignty of the government (ke ea o ke aupuni), Kauikeaouli called on the "sovereignty and life of the land itself (ke ea o ka ʻāina)." Following this proclamation, the Hawaiian Kingdom celebrated Lā Hoʻi hoʻi Ea (Sovereignty Restoration Day), a national holiday that began on July 31, 1843. For more information see Noelani Goodyear-Kaʻōpua, "Introduction," in *A Nation Rising;* and Leilani Basham, "Ka Lāhui Hawaiʻi: He Moʻolelo, He ʻāina, He Loina, a He Ea Kākou," *Hūlili: Multidisciplinary Research on Hawaiian Well-Being* 6 (2010): 37–72.

36. Although it claimed the Hawaiian Islands to be with its "sphere of influence," the United States recognized Hawaiʻi's political independence with the Tyler Doctrine of 1842.

37. Gonschor, *A Power in the World*, 27.

38. This document stated "those who were not born in the islands, born to Natives living abroad, or born aboard a ship belonging to the Sandwich

Islands were aliens unless they took the oath of allegiance to the mōʻī, thereby renouncing citizenship in their former country of origin. Osorio, *Dismembering Lāhui*, 57.

39. These were the Constitutions of 1840 and 1852.

40. According to Beamer, private ownership of land did exist before the Māhele, but this was restricted to a "few select cases where an individual had acquired title through deed, oral or written, granted by either the mōʻī or kuhina nui." For more information see Beamer, *No Mākou Ka Mana*, 142 and Kameʻeleihiwa, *Native Land and Foreign Desires*.

41. Due to the economic restrictions faced by Asians, their land ownership was negligible.

42. Ty Tengan and Mark ʻUmi Perkins cite Lilikalā Kameʻeleihiwa and Jocelyn Linnekin as scholars who support the former view, and Kamanamaikalani Beamer, David Keanu Sai, and Robert H. Stauffer as supporting the latter. See Ty P. Kāwika Tengan, *Native Men Remade: Gender and Nation in Contemporary Hawaiʻi* (Durham, NC: Duke University Press, 2008); Mark ʻUmi Perkins, "Kuleana: A Genealogy of Native Tenant Rights," PhD diss., University of Hawaiʻi, 2013, 43-8.

43. Article 62 of the Constitution required that voters own property of at least $150, or a leasehold with rent of at least $25 per year, or have an annual income of $75 per year. It also required that voters take a literacy test in either Hawaiian or English.

44. At this time, Chinese settlers were the only sizeable Asian population in Hawaiʻi. A majority of them began coming to the islands in 1852 as contract laborers.

45. Tiffany Lani Ing, *Reclaiming Kalākaua: Nineteenth-Century Perspectives on a Hawaiian Sovereign* (Honolulu: University of Hawaiʻi Press, 2019), 100–1.

46. Gonschor, *A Power in the World*, 37.

47. For more information on the pan-Oceanian polity see Gonschor, *A Power in the World*.

48. The Hawaiian League was a secret organization composed of white Euro-American men. The League's executive committee had thirteen members and was known as the "Committee of Thirteen." US Minister to Hawaiʻi Stevens renamed this group the "Committee of Safety" following the overthrow. Insiders referred to this group as the "Annexation Club." For more

information see Ralph S. Kuykendall, *The Hawaiian Kingdom*, Vol. 3, *1874–1893: The Kalākaua Dynasty* (Honolulu: University of Hawaiʻi Press, 1967) and Osorio, *Dismembering Lāhui*.

49. Since the first Constitution of 1840, the king had appointed and dismissed cabinet members, whose job it was to head government departments. However, after the passing of the Bayonet Constitution, the cabinet could be removed only upon a vote of want of confidence by the legislature, a group whose membership was dominated by white American planters.

50. Kauanui, *Hawaiian Blood*, 27 and Donald Rowland, "Orientals and the Suffrage in Hawaiʻi," *Pacific Historical Review* 12, no. 1 (1943), 13–14.

51. *Ahlo v. Smith,* 8 Hawaiʻi 420, 1892.

52. The Hawaiian Patriotic Leagues continue to work to affirm the continuity of Hawaiian independence. Noenoe Silva notes that "aloha ʻāina" means "love of the land," which "differs in connotation and cultural coding from "patriotic." See Silva, *Aloha Betrayed*, 130.

53. The "Committee of Thirteen" is thought to have included the following men: Joseph B. Atherton, John H. Paty, William R. Castle, Peter C. Jones, Charles J. Austin, Benjamin F. Dillingham, Sanford B. Dole, Lorrin A. Thurston, William W. Hall, Henry F. Glade, Thomas May, William H. Bailey, and George N. Wilcox. See Kuykendall, *The Hawaiian Kingdom: 1974–1893* and Osorio, *Dismembering Lāhui*.

54. The McKinley Tariff took effect on April 1, 1891. It removed the tariff on all sugar entering the United States and granted a two-cent subsidy per pound to US growers, thus nullifying the advantage that the 1875 Reciprocity Treaty had given Hawaiʻi-based sugar growers and limiting the amount of sugar exported from the kingdom. For more information on the overthrow, see Tom Coffman, *Nation Within: The History of the American Occupation of Hawaiʻi* (Kihei: Koa Books, 2009); Liliʻuokalani, *Hawaiʻi's Story by Hawaiʻi's Queen* (Honolulu: Mutual Publishing, 1991); Neil Thomas Proto, *The Rights of My People: Liliʻuokalani's Enduring Battle with the United States, 1893–1917* (New York: Algora Publishing, 2009); Silva, *Aloha Betrayed*.

55. Stevens was known for his hostility toward the Hawaiian monarchy and his zealous support of annexation. During his four-year tenure in the islands, he repeatedly demonstrated a willingness to intervene in the Hawaiian Kingdom's activities through the use of the US military. In 1891, after the death

of Kalākaua, Stevens requested a permanently stationed warship in Honolulu to protect American interests. Washington responded and sent the USS *San Francisco*. It was replaced on August 24, 1892, by the USS *Boston*, which was one of the most formidable cruisers of the Navy. The fact that in January 1893 the United States had its newest and most technologically advanced warship docked in Honolulu was not lost on the queen.

56. It would take another five years before the US Congress passed a joint resolution to annex the Hawaiian Islands.

57. The Hawaiian Kingdom was familiar with foreign takeover attempts. Between 1815 and 1817, Russian physician George Anton Shaffer built military structures on Oʻahu and Kauaʻi. Together with Kaumualiʻi, the chief of Kauaʻi, he planned an armed takeover of the Hawaiian Islands for Russia. After meeting heavy resistance Shaffer gave up and left. In 1843 the Hawaiian Kingdom first ceded and then restored its sovereignty. Brandy Nālani McDougall, "We Are Not American: Competing Rhetorical Archipelagoes in Hawaiʻi," in *Archipelagic American Studies*, edited by Brian Roberts Russell and Michelle Ann Stephens, 259–80 (Durham, NC: Duke University Press, 2017).

58. For some, like South Dakota Republican Senator Richard Pettigrew, Portuguese from the islands of Madeira and the Azores were not considered white and belonged in the same racial category as the Irish and Eastern Europeans. Richard Franklin Pettigrew, *The Course of Empire: An Official Record* (New York: Boni and Liveright, 1920).

59. Prasenjit Duara, "The Regime of Authenticity: Timelessness, Gender, and National History in Modern China," *History and Theory: Studies in the Philosophy of History* 37, no. 3 (1998) 287–308. See also Alexis Dudden, *Japan's Colonization of Korea: Discourse and Power* (Honolulu: University of Hawaiʻi Press,) 2005.

60. The Crown Lands consist of nearly one million acres that were put in trust under the Hawaiian monarchy. During the 1848 Māhele, the kingdom transferred roughly 1.5 million acres to itself. This constituted the Government Lands, which were to be used for various public purposes. Substantial amounts were sold during the kingdom period, and about eight hundred thousand acres remained at the time of the overthrow. The Government and Crown Lands were claimed by the Republic of Hawaiʻi and then illegally "ceded" to the United States following annexation. Jon M. Van Dyke, *Who*

Owns the Crown Lands of Hawaiʻi? (Honolulu: University of Hawaiʻi Press, 2008); Kameʻeleihiwa, *Native Land and Foreign Desires.*

61. Gonschor, *A Power in the World*, 7.

62. Lisa Kahaleole Hall, "Navigating Our Own 'Sea of Islands:'" Remapping a Theoretical Space for Hawaiian Women and Indigenous Feminism," *Wicazo Sa Review* 24, no. 2 (2009): 15–38.

CHAPTER 1. EMERGING NATIONS, EMERGING EMPIRES

1. Kamokuʻākulikuli is a small island on the South Shore of Oʻahu. The Hawaiian Kingdom officially designated Kamokuʻākulikuli as a quarantine station in early 1869. It was used as a place where incoming ships could be detained until it was determined that their crew was free of infectious disease. By 1888 it was known as "Quarantine Island." Today it is often referred to as "Sand Island."

2. The *Naniwa* was commanded by Heihachirō Tōgō, who in two years would become renowned for his defeat of the Russian fleet at Tsushima Island. The British-built *Naniwa* was the first protected cruiser acquired by the Imperial Japanese Navy. For more information on the *Naniwa*, see "Recaptured: Expulsion of the Japanese Murderer from Refuge on the Naniwa," *The Daily Bulletin*, March 17, 1893; Kathrin Milanovich, "Naniwa and Takachiho: Elswick-Built Protected Cruisers of the Imperial Japanese Navy," in *Warship 2004*, edited by Antony Preston (London: Conway Maritime Press, 2004), 29–56.

3. Court records give no further information about the victim other than to refer to them as a worker named "Kanazawa, a Jap." *Queen v. Yosaku*, 2nd Cir. 1892.

4. Sanford Dole was born to Protestant missionaries in Oʻahu in 1844. He left the island to attend college and in 1868 was admitted to practice law in Massachusetts. He returned to Oʻahu in 1869. He was elected to the Hawaiian legislature in 1884 and again in 1886 as a representative of the Reform Party. In 1886 he was appointed as associate justice of the Hawaiʻi Supreme Court. Dole later became a leading member of the Hawaiian League. He served as the first and only president of the Republic of Hawaiʻi (1894–1898) and the first governor of the Territory of Hawaiʻi. For more information on Sanford Dole, see Helena G. Allen, *Sanford Ballard Dole: Hawaii's Only President, 1844–1926* (Glendale, CA: A. H. Clark Co., 1988).

5. Saburo Fujii to Sanford Dole, March 16, 1893, Records of the Foreign Office and Executive, Foreign Officials in Hawai'i, Series 403, Hawai'i State Archives, Honolulu.

6. According to the Meiji Constitution, members of the House of Representatives were elected by direct male suffrage with qualifications based on taxes. In general, voting was a right limited to the upper class. Universal adult male suffrage was introduced in 1925.

7. Japan colonized Hokkaido in 1869. In 1879 it enforced claims on the Ryukyu Islands, annexing them as Okinawa Prefecture. For more information on the Hawai'i-based anti-Japanese sentiment, refer to Hilary Conroy, *The Japanese Frontier in Hawai'i* (Berkeley: University of California Press, 1953); Moon-Kie Jung, *Reworking Race: The Making of Hawai'i's Interracial Labor Movement* (New York: Columbia University Press, 2006); Gary Y. Okihiro, *Cane Fires: The Anti-Japanese Movement in Hawai'i, 1865–1945* (Philadelphia: Temple University Press, 1991); William Adam Russ, Jr., *The Hawaiian Revolution 1893–94* (Selinsgrove: Susquehanna University Press, 1959); and Donald Rowland, "Orientals and the Suffrage in Hawaii," *Pacific Historical Review* 12, no. 1 (1943): 11–21.

8. See chapter 3 for information on the 1895 counterrevolution. In order to ground the analysis in Hawai'i, I center the work of Kanaka Maoli scholars and practitioners who have documented this history of resistance, including Lili'uokalani, *Hawai'i's Story by Hawai'i's Queen* (Honolulu: Mutual Publishing, 1991) and Noenoe K. Silva, *Aloha Betrayed: Native Hawaiian Resistance to American Colonialism* (Durham, NC: Duke University Press, 2004).

9. Together these two groups had more than seventeen thousand members. Joseph Nāwahī was born in Puna, Hawai'i Island in 1842. He was a teacher, newspaper editor, artist, lawyer, orator, and legislator. He was known for defending the Hawaiian people against US encroachment and was one of the leaders in the struggle against US colonialism in Hawai'i. Emma Nāwahī was born in Hilo, Hawai'i Island in 1854. Her mother, Kahaoleaua, was the daughter of a Hilo chief and her father, Tong Yee, was from Guangdong, China. Her father adopted the surname A'ii based on the 'ōlelo Hawai'i pronunciation of his given name. As part of Hui Aloha 'Āina o Nā Wāhine, Emma helped to gather over twenty-one thousand signatures for the 1897 Kū'ē petitions. For more information see Silva, *Aloha Betrayed* and David A. Chang, *The World and*

All the Things upon It: Native Hawaiian Geographies of Exploration (Minneapolis: University of Minnesota Press, 2016).

10. The first patriotic league, Hui Kālai'āina, was formed in 1887 in order to restore the Hawaiian Kingdom's Constitution of 1864.

11. The two events covered in this chapter illuminate the new relationship between global and national space as it formed in Hawai'i. For more information on this relationship see Rebecca E. Karl, *Staging the World: Chinese Nationalism at the Turn of the Twentieth Century* (Durham, NC: Duke University Press, 2002), 24, 54.

12. Members of Seikyōsha (Association of Politics and Education, established in 1888) called on the state to promote mass emigration and also advocated for a proactive imperialist policy. Founded in 1881, the first Liberal Party (Jiyū-tō) was Japan's first major political party under the parliamentary system. Its members, mostly landowning farmers, spearheaded the Freedom and Popular Rights movement for democracy. Although the party disbanded in 1884, their members joined with other Japanese nationalist groups, including Seikyōsha, to agitate for open emigration, national expansion, and imperialism. Members of both groups could also be found in the continental United States. Enseisha was formed by exiled Freedom and Popular Rights' activists who resided in San Francisco. The core of the Japanese Patriotic League included over thirty political activists from the former Liberal Party. For more information see Eiichiro Azuma, *In Search of Our Frontier: Japanese America and Settler Colonialism in the Construction of Japan's Borderless Empire* (Oakland: University of California Press, 2019), 37–40; Sidney Xu Lu, *The Making of Japanese Settler Colonialism: Malthusianism and Trans-Pacific Migration, 1868–1961* (Cambridge: Cambridge University Press, 2019), 73.

13. I refer here to the Naturalization Act of 1790.

14. Lauren L. Basson, "Fit for Annexation but Unfit to Vote? Debating Hawaiian Suffrage Qualifications at the Turn of the Twentieth Century," *Social Science History* 29, no. 4 (2005): 576.

15. The Hawaiian Kingdom began negotiations with the United States regarding reciprocity in 1854 and was granted the trade relationship in 1875. Southern sugar interests were against treaties of reciprocity with Hawai'i because it cut into their profit margins. See chapter 2 for more information on the 1875 Reciprocity Treaty.

16. Matthew Frye Jacobson, *Barbarian Virtues: The United States Encounters Foreign Peoples at Home and Abroad, 1876–1917* (New York: Hill and Wang, 2001).

17. Since their arrival in the continental United States, Asians had been scapegoated for depressed wage levels, racialized as disease carriers, and endured countless acts of racial violence. In 1882, white supremacist agitation against "Orientals" resulted in the passing of the Chinese Exclusion Act. Under pressure from white American business interests, the Hawaiian Kingdom passed its own version of the act in 1886. Beginning in 1888, this Hawai'i-based law effectively cut off further importation of Chinese labor to the islands and was carried over to the republic. Japanese migrants inherited this anti-Asian racism in both Hawai'i and the continental United States when they were brought in to fill the low-wage labor vacuum that followed Chinese exclusion.

18. John L. Stevens to John W. Foster, November 20, 1892, Consular Letters, Records of the Department of State, National Archives, Washington, DC.

19. Lorrin A. Thurston, *Memoirs of the Hawaiian Revolution* (Honolulu: Honolulu Advertiser Publishing, 1936), 20.

20. Besides Thurston, the commission included J. Marsden, a member of the House of Nobles in the Hawaiian legislature, William R. Castle, an attorney, Charles L. Carter, son of a former Hawaiian minister to the United States, and W. C. Wilder, president of the Inter-Island Steamship Company of Hawai'i and owner of the *Claudine*, the vessel which carried the group to San Francisco. Also on board was the queen's letter of protest. Her delegation, however, would have to find other means of transportation, as the provisional government required the queen to secure and fund her own vessel. She did this by mortgaging three of her homes to Bishop Bank for a total of ten thousand dollars. For more on the commission, see Thurston, *Memoirs of the Hawaiian Revolution*. For information on the queen's actions, see Lili'uokalani, *The Diaries of Queen Liliuokalani of Hawaii 1885–1900*, ed. David W. Forbes (Honolulu: Hui Hānai, 2019), 318–19.

21. Proceedings on the Executive and Advisory Councils of the Provisional Government, January 20–21, 1893, Hawai'i State Archives, Honolulu.

22. This was reflected by the renewal of the Chinese Exclusion Act in 1892.

23. US Department of State, Papers Relating to the Foreign Relations of the United States (Washington, DC: US Government Printing Office, 1894), 202–5;

Eric T. L. Love, *Race over Empire: Racism and U.S. Imperialism, 1865–1900* (Chapel Hill: University of North Carolina Press, 2004), 77.

24. Love, *Race over Empire*, 78.

25. Secretary Foster understood that in a recession year Congress would not look favorably on any treaty that required large amounts of funding. He insisted that the treaty exclude the stipulations regarding the oceanic cable, Pearl Harbor improvements, and the sugar bounty. See Love, *Race over Empire*, 78; William Michael Morgan, *Pacific Gibraltar: U.S.-Japanese Rivalry over the Annexation of Hawai'i, 1885–1898* (Annapolis: Naval Institute Press, 2011), 110–11.

26. David La'amea Kahalepouli Kinoiki Kawānanakoa was born in Pauoa Valley, O'ahu. His father was David Kahalepouli Pi'ikoi, his birth mother was Victoria Kūhiō Kinoiki Kekaulike. He was granted the title of prince in 1883 by King Kalākaua and declared the third heir to the throne after Lili'uokalani and Ka'iulani. In 1891 he was appointed as a member of Queen Lili'uokalani's Privy Council and after the overthrow, was a supporter of the 1895 counter-revolution. For more information, see George F. Nellist, ed., *The Story of Hawaii and its Builders with Which Is Incorporated Volume III Men of Hawaii: An Historical of Hawaii with Biographical Sketches of Men of Note and Substantial Achievement, Past and Present, Who Have Contributed to the Progress of the Territory* (Honolulu: Honolulu Star-Bulletin, 1925), 139–41.

27. Neil Thomas Proto, *The Rights of My People: Liliuokalani's Enduring Battle with the United States, 1893–1917* (New York: Algora Publishing, 2009), 28.

28. Lili'uokalani to William Henry Harrison, January 18, 1893, *Papers Relating to the Annexation of the Hawaiian Islands to the United States* (Washington, DC: US Government Printing Office, 1893), 23. See also, Lili'uokalani, *Hawaii's Story*, 388.

29. Cleveland became president on March 4, 1893.

30. Walter Q. Gresham to James H. Blount, March 11, 1893, in James H. Blount, "Affairs in Hawaii: Report of the U.S. Special Commissioner James H. Blount to U.S. Secretary of State Walter Q. Gresham Concerning the Hawaiian Kingdom Investigation," 53 Cong. 3rd sess., Executive Document 1 (Washington, DC: US Government Printing Office, 1895). Hereafter cited as Blount Report.

31. Gresham to Blount, March 11, 1893, Blount Report.

32. John Foster to John L. Stevens, February 11, 1893, Papers Relating to the Annexation of the Hawaiian Islands to the United States (Washington, DC: US Government Printing Office, 1893), 44–45.

33. Liliʻuokalani, *Diaries of Queen Liliuokalani*, 335.

34. Blount Report, 1296.

35. Blount Report, 1297.

36. Pele is the Hawaiian god associated with volcanic activity and land formation. Hiʻiakaikapoliopele, often referred to as Hiʻiaka, is Pele's favored younger sister and a primary hula deity. Over five hundred mele (song/chant) dedicated to these two deities are listed in the Bishop Museum Archives mele index. For more information, see kuʻualoha hoʻomanawanui, *Voices of Fire: Reweaving the Literary Lei of Pele and Hiʻiaka* (Minneapolis: University of Minnesota Press, 2014).

37. The Royal Hawaiian Band was formed in 1836 by Kauikeaouli (King Kamehameha III).

38. David W. Bandy, "Bandmaster Henry Berger and the Royal Hawaiian Band," *Hawaiian Journal of History* 24 (1990): 69–90. See also Liliʻuokalani, *Diaries of Queen Liliuokalani*, 336.

39. Albertine Loomis, *For Whom Are the Stars* (Honolulu: University of Hawaiʻi Press, 1976), 44–48; Silva, *Aloha Betrayed*, 134–35.

40. Blount Report, 476.

41. While President Cleveland eventually announced his opinion that the provisional government had acted illegally, this did not occur until December 1893.

42. John L. Stevens to John Foster, No. 88, March 1, 1893, Despatches from American Ministers in Hawaiʻi to the Secretary of State, National Archives, Washington, DC; Russ, *The Hawaiian Revolution*, 158.

43. Russ, *The Hawaiian Revolution*, 159.

44. John L. Stevens to John Foster, No. 93, March 24, 1893, Despatches from American Ministers in Hawaiʻi to the Secretary of State, National Archives, Washington, DC.

45. *Pacific Commercial Advertiser*, March 17, 1893.

46. *Pacific Commercial Advertiser*, March 17, 1893.

47. *Pacific Commercial Advertiser*, March 20, 1893.

48. *Pacific Commercial Advertiser*, March 21, 1893.

49. Most Issei laborers were coming from rural farming villages and while conscription was enforced in the Meiji era, many of these men had migrated in order to escape military service. Franklin Odo, *Voices from the Canefields:*

Folksongs from Japanese Immigrant Workers in Hawai'i (New York: Oxford University Press, 2013), 3–4.

50. Takashi Fujitani, *Splendid Monarchy: Power and Pageantry in Modern Japan* (Berkeley: University of California Press, 1996), 5.

51. Fujitani, *Splendid Monarchy*, 6.

52. See Michael Auslin, *Negotiating with Imperialism: The Unequal Treaties and the Culture of Japanese Diplomacy* (Cambridge, MA: Harvard University Press, 2004) and Peter Duus, *The Abacus and the Sword: The Japanese Penetration of Korea, 1895–1910* (Berkeley: University of California Press, 1995).

53. Because of its late arrival onto the global imperial scene, from the moment of its "restoration," the Meiji state prioritized establishing the structures and policies that would signal to the West that Japan was a modern nation-state and not a candidate for colonization. This included imperialistic practices. For more information on Japanese settler colonialism in the nineteenth and twentieth centuries, see Azuma, *In Search of Our Frontier*; Lu, *The Making of Japanese Settler Colonialism*; Jun Uchida, *Brokers of Empire: Japanese Settler Colonialism in Korea, 1876–1945* (Cambridge, MA: Harvard University Asia Center, 2011).

54. Douglas R. Howland, *Translating the West: Language and Political Reason in Nineteenth-Century Japan* (Honolulu: University of Hawai'i Press, 2002), 186.

55. Howland, *Translating the West*, 187.

56. Between 1885 and 1894, 26,069 Issei migrated to Hawai'i under direct supervision of the Japanese government. Between 1894 and 1900, when the Meiji government ceded control to private emigration companies, approximately 57,000 migrants arrived in Hawai'i. By 1900 the Issei made up 40 percent of Hawai'i's population. For more information see Jung, *Reworking Race*, 78.

57. Azuma, *In Search of Our Frontier*, 50. See also Hiromi Monobe, "From 'Vanishing Race' to Friendly Ally: Japanese American Perceptions of Native Hawaiians During the Interwar Years," *Japanese Journal of American Studies*, no. 23 (2012): 73–95.

58. Betten Nagasawa, "Yankii-Sho," in *Meiji Shisoka Shu* (Tokyo: Kodansha, 1968), 291, translated in Monobe, "From 'Vanishing Race' to Friendly Ally," 78.

59. Betten Nagasawa, "Yankii" (1893) in *Seikyōsha bungakushū*, edited by Matsumoto Sannosuke (Tokyo: Chikuma Shobō, 1980), 339, quoted in Azuma, *In Search of Our Frontier*, 50.

60. Azuma, *In Search of Our Frontier*, 48.

61. Azuma, *In Search of Our Frontier*, 51.

62. Lucien Young was lieutenant in the US Navy who was onboard the USS *Boston* following the overthrow.

63. Consul General Fujii eventually succeeded in dispersing the group and they returned back to the plantations without incident. For more information, see Lucien Young's testimony in *Compilation of Reports of Committees: 1789–1901*, vol. 6, *Senate Committee on Foreign Relations*, February 26, 1894 (United States: U.S. Government Printing Office, 1901), 702.

64. "The Census of 1890 by Age and Nationality, Showing Number of Registered Voters," in T.G. Thrum, ed., *Hawaiian Almanac and Annual for 1894: A Handbook of Information on Matters Relating to the Hawaiian Islands, Original and Selected, of Value to Merchants, Tourists, and Others* (Honolulu: T.G. Thrum, 1894), 14. The 1890 Census figures are as follows: Japanese 12,360; Portuguese 8,602; Americans 1,928; British 1,344; Germans 1,034; Norwegians 227; French 70.

65. Expansionists in Japan also understood this fact and pressed the Meiji government to agitate for the Issei right to vote in Hawai'i. For more information, see Azuma, *In Search of Our Frontier*.

66. The local Chinese population in Hawai'i also pushed for the right to vote on several occasions. After the forced signing of the Bayonet Constitution of 1887, they formed a "self-defense society" and raised enough money to purchase a two-story building that was to serve as the society's headquarters. They petitioned the government twice that year and once again in 1890. During the Constitutional Convention of 1894, Chinese residents petitioned for the right to vote in the newly formed republic. Despite their repeated attempts, they lacked the backing of the Chinese state and the society disbanded. See Cabinet Council Minutes August 1, 1887, Hawai'i State Archives, Honolulu; *Daily Bulletin*, May 15, 1894; Chung Kun Ai, *My Seventy Nine Years in Hawaii* (Hong Kong: Cosmorama Pictorial Publisher, 1960), 173–74; Rowland, "Orientals and the Suffrage in Hawai'i."

67. It should be noted that Japan and Hawai'i had a number of treaties and conventions, including the Emigration Convention of 1886. This was created just one year before the 1887 Bayonet Constitution and focused on the creation of the contract labor system and conditions of the plantation environment.

The convention called for provision of Japanese physicians, interpreters, and inspectors. It did not however, call for equal treatment and privileges. This had previously been agreed to and covered in the 1871 Treaty. For more information, see Treaty of Amity and Commerce between the Kingdom of Hawaii and the Empire of Japan, August 19, 1871, in *Treaties and Conventions of the Hawaiian Kingdom* (Honolulu: Pae 'Āina Productions, 2005).

68. Saburo Fujii to Sanford Dole, March 23, 1893, Records of the Foreign Office and Executive, Foreign Officials in Hawai'i, Series 403, Hawai'i State Archives, Honolulu.

69. Sanford Dole to Saburo Fujii, April 10, 1893, Records of the Foreign Office and Executive, Foreign Officials in Hawai'i, Series 403, Hawai'i State Archives, Honolulu.

70. Azuma, *In Search of Our Frontier*, 52.

71. *Pacific Commercial Advertiser*, April 6, 1893.

72. *Hawaiian Star*, April 8, 1893.

73. Irwin had been appointed consul general to Japan by King Kalākaua in 1881. He also held the position of commissioner of immigration and special agent of the Hawaiian Kingdom's Board of Immigration. It was in this latter position that Irwin organized and controlled the shipment of Japanese laborers to Hawai'i between 1885 and 1894. See Ralph S. Kuykendall, *The Hawaiian Kingdom*, vol. 3, *1874–1893: The Kalākaua Dynasty* (Honolulu: University of Hawai'i Press, 1967), 155–56; Conroy, *The Japanese Frontier in Hawai'i*.

74. Munemitsu Mutsu was the former Japanese ambassador to Mexico and had also served as minister of agriculture and commerce. Robert Irwin to Sanford Dole, April 27, 1893, Records of the Foreign Office and Executive, Foreign Officials in Hawai'i, Series 403, Hawai'i State Archives, Honolulu.

75. Irwin to Dole, April 27, 1893.

76. Robert Irwin to Sanford Dole, June 26, 1893, Records of the Foreign Office and Executive, Foreign Officials in Hawai'i, Series 403, Hawai'i State Archives, Honolulu.

77. The Liberal Party referenced here was formed in 1890 and became the majority party that year. Hoshi was a close ally of Mutsu and a strong advocate for emigrants who traveled to the United States and Hawai'i. He also served as the mayor of Tokyo.

78. Azuma, *In Search of Our Frontier*, 52.

79. Yukichi Fukuzawa, "Beikoku wa shishi no seisho nari," *Fukuzawa Yukichi zenshū* 9:444, cited in Azuma, *Between Two Empires*, 19. Since the process of molding the general population into imperial subjects had only begun in the early 1870s, many of the Hawai'i-bound population had not yet been inculcated into centralized state apparatuses and a resultant national identity.

80. *Pacific Commercial Advertiser*, March 20, 1893.

81. *Pacific Commercial Advertiser*, April 4, 1893.

82. Akira Iriye, *Pacific Estrangement: Japanese and American Expansion, 1897–1911* (Cambridge, MA: Harvard University Press, 1972), 49.

83. *Hawaiian Star*, April 20, 1893.

84. Rowland, "Orientals and the Suffrage in Hawai'i," 20.

85. Shiri Pasternak, *Grounded Authority: The Algonquins of Barriere Lake against the State* (Minneapolis: University of Minnesota Press, 2017).

CHAPTER 2. AT THE BORDERS OF NATION AND STATE

1. Mark Twain, "Scenes in Honolulu, No. 4," *Sacramento Daily Union*, April 19, 1866.

2. Previous attempts at reciprocity between the Hawaiian Kingdom and the United States were made in 1848, 1852, 1855, and 1867.

3. At the time of the debate surrounding the 1875 Reciprocity Treaty there were three distinct classes of sugar producers within the United States—the cane planters of Louisiana, and the beet factories and refiners of the West and the North. They held diverse and often conflicting interests, as each producer demanded the highest possible protection for its product. As a rule, cane sugar planters placed their products on the market raw and sold it to the refiners, whereas beet sugar producers placed their product already refined. Cane sugar producers of Louisiana desired a high duty on imported raw sugar, the beet sugar producer desired a high duty on refined, and the refiner a large differential between the two rates of duty. Lowering the duty on imported raw cane sugar from Hawai'i was thus seen as a threat to the domestic producers of cane sugar in the American South. For more information, see Frank R. Rutter, "The Sugar Question in the United States," *Quarterly Journal of Economics* 17, no. 1 (1902), 44–81, 45.

4. H.R. 1, 44th Cong., 1st Sess. 1876.

5. H.R. 1, 44th Cong., 1st Sess. 1876.

6. For more on "coolies" in the US South, see Moon-Ho Jung, *Coolies and Cane: Race, Labor and Sugar in the Age of Emancipation* (Baltimore: Johns Hopkins University Press, 2006).

7. H.R. 1, 44th Cong., 1st Sess. 1876.

8. For more on the 1893 failed annexation attempt, see chapter 1.

9. See for example the February 17, 1894 cover of *Judge* magazine. Refer to Noenoe K. Silva, *Aloha Betrayed: Native Hawaiian Resistance to American Colonialism* (Durham, NC: Duke University Press, 2004), 173–80 for a detailed discussion of Liliʻuokalani on the covers of *Judge*.

10. For more see J. Kēhaulani Kauanui, "Native Hawaiian Decolonization and the Politics of Gender," *American Quarterly* 60, no. 2 (2008): 281–87; Lisa Kahaleole Hall, "Strategies of Erasure: U.S. Colonialism and Native Hawaiian Feminism," *American Quarterly* 60 no. 2 (2008), 273–80; and Lilikalā Kameʻeleihiwa, *Nā Wāhine Kapu: Divine Hawaiian Women* (Honolulu: ʻAi Pohaku Press, 1992).

11. Manu Karuka, *Empire's Tracks: Indigenous Nations, Chinese Workers, and the Transcontinental Railroad* (Oakland: University of California Press, 2019), 2.

12. Gresham's then confidential message to Willis instructed him to "take advantage of an early opportunity" to inform the queen of the "President's sincere regret that the reprehensible conduct of the American Minister and the unauthorized presence on land of a military force of the United States obliged her to surrender her sovereignty . . . and rely on the justice of this Government to undo the flagrant wrong." Walter Q. Gresham to Albert Willis, in James H. Blount, "Affairs in Hawaii. Report of the U.S. Special Commissioner James H. Blount to U.S. Secretary of State Walter Q. Gresham Concerning the Hawaiian Kingdom Investigation," House Executive Document No. 47, 53 Congress, 3rd Session (Washington, DC: US Government Printing Office, 1894), 21–22. Hereafter cited as Blount Report.

13. Gresham to Willis, October 18, 1893, Blount Report, 43.

14. Liliʻuokalani, *Hawaiʻi's Story by Hawaiʻi's Queen* (Honolulu: Mutual Publishing, 1991), 246. According to the penal code set under the Bayonet Constitution of 1887, anyone who committed treason was sentenced to death by beheading and all property confiscated.

15. Silva, *Aloha Betrayed*, 173; Neil Thomas Proto, *The Rights of My People: Liliuokalani's Enduring Battle with the United States, 1893–1917* (New York: Algora Publishing, 2009), 81.

16. For a detailed discussion of these images see Silva, *Aloha Betrayed*, 173–80. Joyce Pualani Warren writes that "settler efforts to diminish Native political agency by conflating the monarchy with racial blackness spoke directly and effectively to American politicians furthering a nation built on slavery's denial of Black humanity." Joyce Pualani Warren, "Reading Bodies, Writing Blackness: Anti-/Blackness and Nineteenth-Century Kanaka Maoli Literary Nationalism," *American Indian Culture and Research Journal* 43, no. 2 (2019): 49–72, 59.

17. Silva, *Aloha Betrayed*, 173–80.

18. Stephanie Nohelani Teves, *Defiant Indigeneity: The Politics of Hawaiian Performance* (Chapel Hill: University of North Carolina Press, 2018), 130.

19. Rev. Sereno E. Bishop, "A Royal Palace Democratized," *Independent*, July 6, 1893, quoted in Lydia Kualapai, "The Queen Writes Back: Lili'uokalani's Hawai'i's Story by Hawai'i's Queen," *Studies in American Indian Literatures* 17, no. 2 (2005): 32–62.

20. Rev. Sereno E. Bishop, "Freedom in Hawaii at Bay," *Independent*, January 4, 1894. For more, see Michael Dougherty, *To Steal a Kingdom: Probing Hawaiian History* (Waimanalo: Island Style Press, 1992), 166; Silva, *Aloha Betrayed*, 173; Merze Tate, *The United States and the Hawaiian Kingdom* (New Haven, CT: Yale University Press, 1965), 223.

21. *Hawaiian Star*, November 27, 1893.

22. Minutes of the Executive Council, November 27, 1893. For more on the oligarchy's extended protest, see William Adam Russ, Jr., *The Hawaiian Revolution, 1893–94* (Selinsgrove: Susquehanna University Press, 1959), 241.

23. On December 18, 1893, President Cleveland delivered a message to Congress in which he asserted that Lili'uokalani was justified in her protest and condemned the actions of US Minister to Hawai'i Stevens for his aid in the coup. Cleveland referred to the overthrow as an "act of war, committed with the participation of a diplomatic representative of the United States and without authority of Congress." The president reminded Congress that claims of "revolution" by the Honolulu-based, haole-led oligarchy should be met with skepticism until the State Department determined that the overthrow had truly been intended to meet the will of the people. Haole oligarchs claimed that even if the American forces had not aided in the coup, the "revolution" would still have taken place and succeeded. Grover Cleveland, "Written Address to the United States Senate and House of Representatives," Executive

Mansion, Washington, DC, December 18, 1893, available at https://history.state.gov/historicaldocuments/frus1894app2/ch7subch1.

24. Albert Willis to Walter Q. Gresham, December 23, 1893, printed in H.R. Ex. Doc. 70, 53rd Cong., 2 Sess. 1893.

25. Senator John Tyler Morgan, a Democrat and ardent imperialist from Alabama, chaired the hearings that were held between December 27, 1893, and February 7, 1894.

26. Copy of letter from Grover Cleveland to H. A. Widemann, J. A. Cummins, and Samuel Parker, August 15, 1894, Cleghorn Collection, Hawai'i State Archives, Honolulu.

27. In response to disputes over property claims made by British residents, in 1843 British naval officer George Paulet issued an ultimatum to Kauikeaouli (King Kamehameha III). Backed by his warship, the rogue British commander forced the king to cede sovereignty to Great Britain. Kauikeaouli did so under protest, and five months later, under instruction from Queen Victoria, British Rear Admiral Richard Thomas arrived in the archipelago to remove Paulet and restore the Hawaiian Kingdom. On July 31, 1843, Kauikeaouli established the national holiday Lā ho'iho'i Ea (Sovereignty Restoration Day) in order to celebrate the return of the Hawaiian Kingdom. Later that same year, Hawai'i's independence was recognized through a tripartite treaty with Great Britain and France. For more information, see Brandy Nālani McDougall, "We Are Not American: Competing Rhetorical Archipelagoes in Hawai'i," in *Archipelagic American Studies*, edited by Brian Roberts Russell and Michelle Ann Stephens, 259–78 (Durham, NC: Duke University Press, 2017).

28. Proceedings of the Executive and Advisory Councils of the Provisional Government and of the Republic, February 5, 1894, Hawai'i State Archives, Honolulu.

29. Born on October 16, 1875, during the reign of King Kalākaua, Princess Victoria Kawēkiu Ka'iulani Kalaninuiahilapalapa Cleghorn was named for England's Queen Victoria, a longtime friend to Hawaiian royalty.

30. Mary Hannah Krout, *Hawaii and a Revolution: The Personal Experiences of a Correspondent in the Sandwich Islands during the Crisis of 1893 and Subsequently* (London: John Murray, 1898), 175.

31. Stephanie Nohelani Teves, "Princess Ka'iulani Haunts Empire in Waikīkī," in *Detours: A Decolonial Guide to Hawai'i*, edited by Hōkūlani K.

Aikau and Vernadette Vicuña Gonzalez (Durham, NC: Duke University Press, 2019), 70.

32. Reports of the sum offered to the royal women vary. One estimate is $350,000 to the queen in return for abdication papers and $150,000 to Princess Kaʻiulani. W. O. Smith favored paying the queen an annual sum of $10,000 in return for her publicly renouncing all claims to the throne. Spalding to Dole, February 10, 1894, President's Files, Hawaiʻi State Archives, Honolulu. Liliʻuokalani also writes of her annoyance with the provisional government for offering her a sum in return for her abdication. For more see Liliʻuokalani, *The Diaries of Queen Liliuokalani of Hawaii 1885–1900*, ed. David W. Forbes (Honolulu: Hui Hānai, 2019), 326 and Proto, *The Rights of My People*, 96.

33. Tom Coffman, *Nation Within: The History of the American Occupation of Hawaiʻi* (Kihei: Koa Books, 2009), 149.

34. W. O. Smith to Lorrin Thurston, February 18, 1894, Records of the Foreign Office and Executive, Ministers and Envoys to Washington, Hawaiʻi State Archives, Honolulu.

35. Lorrin Thurston to Sanford Dole, March 19, 1894, Records of the Foreign Office and Executive, Hawaiʻi State Archives, Honolulu.

36. Thurston to Dole, March 19, 1894.

37. Senate Executive Document 85, 53rd Cong., 2nd sess. 1894. See also William Adam Russ, Jr., *The Hawaiian Republic, 1894–98, and Its Struggle to Win Annexation* (Selinsgrove: Susquehanna University Press, 1961), 20.

38. Henriques Manuscript Collection, June 1894, Bishop Museum, Honolulu. For more information on the Kanaka Maoli reaction and protest, see Silva, *Aloha Betrayed*, 136.

39. *Holomua*, April 3, 1894.

40. Russ, *Hawaiian Republic*, 22. According to the *Bulletin*, there were only 185 Native Hawaiians who registered, 101 foreigners born in Hawaiʻi, 390 Americans, 120 Germans, 418 Portuguese, 195 from Great Britain, and 98 others.

41. Russ, *Hawaiian Republic*, 27. The American delegates from the island of Oʻahu were A. G. M. Robertson, L. C. Ables, and C. L. Carter; also voted in were J. M. Vivas, A. Fernandes, and A. K. Kunuiakea. The delegates from Hawaiʻi Island were D. H. Hitchcock, F. S. Lyman, D. H. Kahaulelia, H. L. Holstein, and J. Kauhane. Maui sent J. W. Kalua, H. P. Baldwin, J. K. Josepa, and W. Y. Horner. From the island of Kauaʻi were A. S. Wilcox,

G. N. Wilcox, and W. H. Rice. See Russ, *Hawaiian Republic*, for more detailed information on the delegates.

42. Records of the Constitutional Convention 1894, Hawai'i State Archives, Honolulu. There is a draft of his speech in the Sanford B. Dole Papers in the Hawai'i State Archives.

43. *Hawaiian Star*, May 18, 1894.

44. *Hawaiian Star*, May 18, 1894.

45. Between 1842 and 1892, approximately 731 Chinese and 3 Japanese people became Hawaiian nationals. For more information see Hawaii Revised Statutes, Vol. 1, Organic Act, Section 4: Citizenship, available at https://www.capitol.hawaii.gov/hrscurrent/Vol01_Ch0001-0042F/03-ORG/ORG_0004.htm.

46. Federally backed immigrant exclusion came in the form of the 1875 Page Act and 1882 Chinese Exclusion Act. Perhaps one of the most infamous acts of violence was the 1885 massacre of twenty-eight Chinese miners in Rock Springs, Wyoming. While the brutality against Chinese communities was usually perpetuated by white workers, local authorities often offered their cooperation. For more see Beth Lew-Williams, *The Chinese Must Go: Violence, Exclusion, and the Making of the Alien in America* (Cambridge, MA: Harvard University Press, 2018).

47. King Kalākaua appointed Armstrong as attorney general of the Kingdom of Hawai'i in 1880. In 1881, in his new capacity as royal commissioner of immigration, Armstrong joined the king on his world tour, which was partly designed to promote plantation labor migration to the islands. Armstrong was not an advocate for the monarchy nor a supporter of the king and made multiple attempts to undermine the Hawaiian Kingdom. For more information, see Tiffany Lani Ing, *Reclaiming Kalākaua: Nineteenth-Century Perspectives on a Hawaiian Sovereign* (Honolulu: University of Hawai'i Press, 2019), 40–42.

48. *Pacific Commercial Advertiser*, June 14, 1894.

49. *Pacific Commercial Advertiser*, June 14, 1894.

50. Records of the Constitutional Convention, May 9, 1894, Hawai'i State Archives, Honolulu.

51. Records of the Constitutional Convention, May 9, 1894, Hawai'i State Archives, Honolulu.

52. Records of the Constitutional Convention, June 4, 1894, Hawai'i State Archives, Honolulu.

53. Dole did not mention that the haole-led oligarchy had forced this constitution upon Kalākaua.

54. Records of the Constitutional Convention, June 4, 1894, Hawai'i State Archives, Honolulu.

55. Records of the Constitutional Convention, June 4, 1894, Hawai'i State Archives, Honolulu.

56. Lorrin Thurston to Sanford Dole, March 3, 1894, Records of the Foreign Office and Executive, Hawai'i State Archives, Honolulu.

57. The specific stipulations for naturalization were as follows: residency in the Hawaiian Islands for two years; intention to retain permanent citizenship; ability to read, write, and speak English; ability to explain the Constitution in English; origination from a country that had an express treaty of naturalization with Hawai'i during either the monarchy or provisional government; good moral character and not a refugee from justice; lawful employment; possession of at least two hundred dollars in property; and acceptance of the oath of allegiance to the Republic of Hawai'i. For more information on the requirements, see Russ, *Hawaiian Republic*, 33.

58. In 2022, these amounts would be roughly $103,253 in real property and $20,650 in annual income.

59. Russ, *Hawaiian Republic*, 33.

60. Silva, *Aloha Betrayed*, 137.

61. J. Kēhaulani Kauanui, "Native Hawaiian Decolonization and the Politics of Gender," *American Quarterly* 60, no. 2 (2008): 281–87, 283. Lilikalā Kameʻeleihiwa has demonstrated that Kanaka Maoli cosmological traditions include both male and female gods, and that women chiefs ruled as early as 1375. For more information see Kameʻeleihiwa, *Nā Wāhine Kapu* and Lisa Kahaleole Hall, "Strategies of Erasure," 273–80.

62. Records of the Constitutional Convention, June 12, 1894, Hawai'i State Archives, Honolulu.

63. Patricia Grimshaw, "Settler Anxieties, Indigenous Peoples, and Women's Suffrage in the Colonies of Australia, New Zealand, and Hawai'i, 1888 to 1902," *Pacific Historical Review* 69, no. 4 (2000): 553–72, 556.

64. Kauanui, "Native Hawaiian Decolonization," 283.

65. Kauanui, "Native Hawaiian Decolonization," 283–84.

66. Kauanui, "Native Hawaiian Decolonization," 284.

67. David Keanu Sai argues that while the Constitution of 1852 did give the right to vote to men who were subjects of the kingdom, it also did not deny the right to vote to women subjects. The Constitution of 1887, otherwise referred to as the Bayonet Constitution, placed the first racial restrictions on the right to vote. See David Keanu Sai "Memorandum: Suffrage of Female Subjects," HawaiianKingdom.org, March 12, 1998, https://hawaiiankingdom.org/info-suffrage.shtml.

68. According to Patricia Grimshaw, the women of the Hawai'i-based WCTU, which was founded in 1884, "did not have qualms about the 1893 coup." Instead, they "declared American progress and liberty good for Hawaiians and supported their male counterparts in their assumption of power." Grimshaw, "Settler Anxieties," 556.

69. Records of the Constitutional Convention, June 12, 1894, Hawai'i State Archives, Honolulu.

70. Records of the Constitutional Convention, June 12, 1894, Hawai'i State Archives, Honolulu.

71. *Pacific Commercial Advertiser,* June 21, 1894.

72. Grimshaw, "Settler Anxieties," 571.

73. Grimshaw, "Settler Anxieties," 571.

74. Grimshaw, "Settler Anxieties," 571. While men in Hawai'i gained the right to vote in 1900, women in the islands had to wait until the passing of the Nineteenth Amendment in 1920.

75. This was a practice that extended well beyond the period of the constitutional convention. For more information on the discursive practices of the queen and, in particular, the rhetorical and visual strategies she used in her memoir, see Kualapai, "The Queen Writes Back."

76. Teves, *Defiant Indigeneity,* 130.

77. Silva, *Aloha Betrayed,* 178–79. See also Lauren L. Basson, *White Enough to be American? Race Mixing, Indigenous People, and the Boundaries of State and Nation* (Chapel Hill: University of North Carolina Press, 2007).

78. Silva, *Aloha Betrayed,* 178.

79. Lili'uokalani, "A Queen's Appeal," *San Francisco Examiner,* March 9, 1893.

80. Henriques Manuscript Collection, June 1894, Bishop Museum, Honolulu.

81. Liliʻuokalani to Albert Willis, June 20, 1894, RG 59, General Records of the Department of State, US National Archives, Washington, DC.

82. Liliʻuokalani to J. F. Hackfeld, June 1894, Manuscript Group 29, Bishop Museum, Honolulu.

CHAPTER 3. HOW THE PORTUGUESE BECAME WHITE

1. Charles T. Rodgers, *Report of the General Superintendent of the Census, 1890* (Honolulu, HI: R. Grieve, 1891). The 1890 Census recorded the population as follows: Hawaiian: 40,622; Polynesian: 588; Chinese nationals: 15,301; Japanese nationals: 12,360; Portuguese nationals: 8,602; US nationals: 1,928; British nationals: 1,344; German nationals: 1,034; French nationals: 70. It also recorded the number of foreigners who had naturalized as Hawaiian subjects and those of foreign parentage who had acquired nationality by birth.

2. Lorrin Thurston, *A Hand-Book on the Annexation of Hawaii* (Saint Joseph, MI: A. B. Morse, 1897), 32. Thurston's descriptions of Kānaka Maoli must be placed in the context of the coup that he helped to organize and lead, primarily under claims of the Indigenous threat to white American interests and safety.

3. Richard Franklin Pettigrew, "The Islands and Their People," Speech in the Senate, July 2, 1894, reprinted in Richard Franklin Pettigrew, *The Course of Empire: An Official Record* (New York: Boni and Liveright, 1920).

4. Pettigrew, "The Islands and Their People."

5. Sanford B. Dole Papers, Hawaiʻi State Archives, Honolulu.

6. S. Rep. 11, 55th Cong., 2nd Sess. 1898.

7. See, for example, Mathew Frye Jacobson, *Whiteness of a Different Color: European Immigrants and the Alchemy of Race* (Cambridge, MA: Harvard University Press, 1998).

8. Jacobson, *Whiteness of a Different Color*, 4. For more information on the construction and meaning of whiteness in US society, see Lauren L. Basson, *White Enough to Be American? Race Mixing, Indigenous People, and the Boundaries of State and Nation* (Chapel Hill: University of North Carolina Press, 2007); George Lipsitz, *The Possessive Investment in Whiteness: How White People Profit from Identity Politics* (Philadelphia: Temple University Press, 1998); Matthew Frye Jacobson, *Barbarian Virtues: The United States Encounters Foreign Peoples at*

Home and Abroad, 1876–1917 (New York: Hill and Wang, 2001), David R. Roediger, *The Wages of Whiteness: Race and the Making of the American Working Class* (London: Verso, 1991).

9. As Maile Arvin explains, settler colonialism is "fueled by a logic of possession through whiteness." Maile Arvin, *Possessing Polynesians: The Science of Settler Colonial Whiteness in Hawai'i and Oceania* (Durham, NC: Duke University Press, 2019), 3.

10. Moon-Kie Jung, *Reworking Race: The Making of Hawai'i's Interracial Labor Movement* (New York: Columbia University Press, 2006), 73.

11. "The Last and Future Portuguese Immigration," *Planters Monthly*, no. 28 (December 1909), 492, in Hawaiian Collection, University of Hawai'i, Mānoa. See also Moon-Kie Jung, *Reworking Race*, 73.

12. Paul Kramer, *The Blood of Government: Race, Empire, the United States, and the Philippines* (Chapel Hill: University of North Carolina Press, 2006), 3.

13. The first large-scale migration of Portuguese to the United States occurred in the whaling industry boom of the 1870s, with roughly fourteen thousand Portuguese arriving from the Azores within a decade. They settled in New England and later became integral to the fishing industry. During the 1880s some of these Portuguese migrants traveled to California and Hawai'i onboard whaling ships. By the time republic officials began their search for an alternative to Asian labor, the Portuguese population was viewed with a sense of familiarity. For more, see Naleen Naupaka Andrade and Stephanie T. Nishimura, "The Portuguese," in *People and Cultures of Hawai'i: The Evolution of Culture and Ethnicity*, edited by John F. McDermott and Naleen Naupaka Andrade, 81–106 (Honolulu: University of Hawai'i Press, 2011).

14. Andrade and Nishimura, "The Portuguese," 82.

15. Between November 1878 and December 1909, twenty-four ships entered the port of Honolulu bringing more than sixteen thousand Portuguese from Portugal, Madeira, and the Azores. Between 1889 and 1894 and 1896 and 1906, there were no arrivals. See M. G. Santos, *Almanach Portuguez de Hawaii para 1911: Um livro de referencia e informação geral relativo ao territorio de Hawaii, Portugal, Madeira e Açores* (Honolulu: Companhia Editora do Pacífico, 1911), 48–49, translated in J. B. d'Oliveira, "Destination, Sandwich Islands," *Hawaiian Journal of History* 4 (1970): 3–52, 51–52.

16. Jon M. Van Dyke, *Who Owns the Crown Lands of Hawai'i?* (Honolulu: University of Hawai'i Press, 2007), 148.

17. Moon-Kie Jung points out that Portuguese laborers categorized as "potential and actual citizens" escaped the classification of "cheap labor." For more information on the racialization of Portuguese labor in Hawai'i, which continued into the twentieth century, see Jung, *Reworking Race*.

18. Francis Hatch to Lorrin Thurston, September 15, 1895, Records of the Foreign Office and Executive, Hawai'i State Archives, Honolulu.

19. Hatch to Thurston, September 15, 1895.

20. Neumann was born in Prussia in 1839. Before coming to Hawai'i he served three terms as state senator of California. In Hawai'i, he served as legal counsel for the German American Claus Spreckels, who maintained a monopoly over the refining of sugar from California and Hawai'i. He also served as attorney general for the Hawaiian Kingdom under King Kalākaua and Queen Lili'uokalani. He was appointed to the House of Nobles, and after the overthrow, served as the queen's personal attorney.

21. Francis Hatch to Lorrin Thurston, September 20, 1894, Records of the Foreign Office and Executive, Hawai'i State Archives, Honolulu.

22. By this time, the Meiji government had challenged the legitimacy of the overthrow and subsequent provisional government. While still in Washington, DC, Thurston wrote of the "Japanese threat" to Theo Davies, a London-based investor in Hawaiian sugar who also served as guardian to Princess Ka'iulani. Thurston described the "urgent necessity" from the standpoint of both the government and planters of obtaining, at as early a date as possible, laborers from "some other source than Japan." Lorrin Thurston to Theo Davies, October 9, 1894, Records of the Foreign Office and Executive, Hawai'i State Archives, Honolulu.

23. The Planters' Labor and Supply Company was formed in 1882 by plantation owners in Hawai'i to facilitate the importation of laborers.

24. Francis Hatch to Lorrin Thurston, September 15, 1894, Records of the Foreign Office and Executive, Hawai'i State Archives, Honolulu.

25. Planters' Labor and Supply Company to Francis Hatch, September 6, 1894, Records of the Foreign Office and Executive, Hawai'i State Archives, Honolulu.

26. Lorrin Thurston to Henry F. Glade, October 9, 1894, Records of the Foreign Office and Executive, Hawai'i State Archives, Honolulu.

27. In 1850 a fungus began killing the grape vines in Madeira, nearly destroying the archipelago's wine production. See Naleen Naupaka Andrade and Stephanie T. Nishimura, "The Portuguese."

28. This claim was visible in the so-called "Pink Map" or "Rose-Colored Map" of 1885, which represented Portugal's claims to northern and southern "Rhodesia," then claimed by the British, today Zambia, Zimbabwe, and Malawi. For more, see David Birmingham, "The Bourgeois Monarchy and the Republicans," in *A Concise History of Portugal* (Cambridge: Cambridge University Press, 2018), 131–60.

29. Lorrin Thurston to Henry F. Glade, November 10, 1894, Records of the Foreign Office and Executive, Hawai'i State Archives, Honolulu.

30. Ernest Hutchinson to the Planters' Labor and Supply Company, undated, Records of the Foreign Office and Executive, Hawai'i State Archives, Honolulu.

31. Lorrin Thurston to Henry F. Glade, November 14, 1894, Records of the Foreign Office and Executive, Hawai'i State Archives, Honolulu.

32. Bush had been prominent in Kalākaua's cabinet, served as editor of the 'ōlelo Hawai'i newspaper *Ka Leo o Ka Lahui*, and was president of the political organization Hui Kālai'āina. Joseph Nāwahī also worked at the newspaper with Bush. For more on Nāwahī, see chapter 1.

33. Noenoe K. Silva, *Aloha Betrayed: Native Hawaiian Resistance to American Colonialism* (Durham, NC: Duke University Press, 2004), 139; Samuel Nowlein was the former head of the Royal Guard, which had disbanded following the coup in 1893. For more on Wilcox, see the introduction.

34. Roughly four hundred people were arrested in conjunction with the counterrevolution. For a list of their names see Ronald Williams Jr., "Incarcerating a Nation: The Arrest and Imprisonment of Political Prisoners by the Republic of Hawai'i, 1895," *The Hawaiian Journal of History* 55, no. 1 (2021): 167–76; *Pacific Commercial Advertiser*, July 18, 1895; Silva, *Aloha Betrayed*.

35. On January 16, 1895, the ruling oligarchs arrested Queen Lili'uokalani for "misprision of treason," or knowing about the counterrevolution attempt and doing nothing to stop it. The queen was imprisoned at 'Iolani Palace, forced to abdicate the throne under threat of execution, and tried by a military

tribunal. Although she was tried in English, the queen responded to all questions in 'ōlelo Hawai'i and refused to enter a plea, claiming that the tribunal and republic had no right to hold her in court. Despite her acts of resistance, Lili'uokalani was sentenced to five years of hard labor. This was soon changed to eight months' imprisonment in one room of 'Iolani Palace, five months' house arrest at her home, Washington Place, and eight months' confinement to the island of O'ahu. Upon her release and the return of her civil rights, the queen left Hawai'i and traveled to Washington, DC, where she continued to protest against the overthrow of her government and Hawai'i's annexation to the United States. For more see Silva, *Aloha Betrayed*.

36. Tom Coffman, *Nation Within: The History of the American Occupation of Hawai'i*. Kihei: Koa Books, 2009, 171.

37. Silva, *Aloha Betrayed*, 139.

38. Antonio de Souza Canavarro to Sanford Dole, January 26, 1895, Consul General for Portugal, Hawai'i State Archives, Honolulu; see also Wray Anthony F. Jose, "The Manuel Reis Case," *Hawaiian Journal of History* 16 (January 1982):134–48.

39. Affidavit, "In the Matter of the Claim of Manoel Giel Dos Reis against the Hawaiian Government," July 9, 1895, Attorney General File, Series 506, Hawai'i State Archives, Honolulu. Some historical accounts list his place of birth as Porto, but in his affidavit Reis states he was born in Brava.

40. For more information, see the *Honolulu Advertiser*, December 3, 1929.

41. *Honolulu Advertiser*, December 3, 1929.

42. Affidavit, "In the Matter of the Claim of Manoel Giel Dos Reis." Four thousand dollars in 1895 would be worth approximately $137,670 in 2022 and twenty-five thousand dollars in 1895 would be worth $860,443. Needless to say, Reis was doing extremely well with his hack service.

43. *Honolulu Star Bulletin*, June 30, 1934.

44. *Report of the Governor to the Secretary of State*, November 20, 1900, Territorial Departments-State, Hawai'i State Archives, Honolulu, 60; see also Jose, "The Manuel Reis Case," 136.

45. Affidavit, "In the Matter of the Claim of Manoel Giel Dos Reis." According to Reis, there were nine British men, two Greek men, and one Danish man held as prisoners with him.

46. Affidavit, "In the Matter of the Claim of Manoel Giel Dos Reis."

47. Affidavit, "H. V. Murray," July 5, 1895, Attorney General File, Series 506, Hawai'i State Archives, Honolulu.

48. These laws were the Hawaii Indemnity Acts of 1895.

49. Affidavit, "In the Matter of the Claim of Manoel Giel Dos Reis."

50. Jose, "The Manuel Reis Case," 140. Reis's claim was quite large in comparison to most other indemnity cases. According to Jose, the total claim for the nine British cases at the time was $6,400.

51. Affidavit, "E. G. Hitchcock," April 23, 1896, Attorney General File, Series 506 Hawai'i State Archives, Honolulu.

52. Affidavit, "C. W. Johansen," April 23, 1896, Attorney General File, Series 506, Hawai'i State Archives, Honolulu.

53. Henry Cooper to Antonio de Souza Canavarro, August 24, 1896, Attorney General File, Series 506, Hawai'i State Archives, Honolulu.

54. On October 11, 1865 preacher Paul Bogle led several hundred Jamaican men and women into the courthouse of Morant Bay, Jamaica. They were protesting the poor economic and social conditions of Black Jamaicans in the British-ruled islands and more immediately, the unjust imprisonment of a Black Jamaican man for "trespassing" on a plantation. During the rebellion, government troops were sent out to hunt down Bogle and while doing so, killed Jamaicans indiscriminately, regardless of whether they were involved. The scale of the response was debated in Great Britain. Cooper referred to the decisions made in the wake of the Morant Bay Rebellion in order to justify the Republic of Hawai'i's actions on an international level. He used these court decisions to set the precedent for a government's use of force in suppressing rebellion and detain suspected conspirators without trial or charges.

55. *Pacific Commercial Advertiser*, March 26, 1896.

56. "Portuguese Uniting," *Pacific Commercial Advertiser*, March 24, 1896.

57. "Portuguese Uniting," *Pacific Commercial Advertiser*, March 24, 1896.

58. Both Germans and Norwegians began arriving in 1881.

59. "Petition against Japanese and Chinese Immigration," March 26, 1896, Records of the Foreign Office and Executive, Series 401, Hawai'i State Archives, Honolulu.

60. Asserting the detrimental effects of the presence of Japanese and Chinese laborers, the petitioners reiterated their complaint regarding the resulting lowered wages despite their being within the racial and social class of

"Europeans" stating that "the invasion . . . has been such that the remuneration of labor has been reduced to such a figure that it has become almost impossible for European and other workingmen to subsist on the wages offered." *Pacific Commercial Advertiser*, March 26, 1896.

61. "Japan vs. Portugal," *Pacific Commercial Advertiser*, March 31, 1896.

62. For example, on Sunday, April 5, 1896, tensions came to a head in a scuffle between several Portuguese men and republic patrolmen at the corner of Punchbowl and Emma Streets, near downtown Honolulu. Patrolmen were reportedly pelted with stones and fence pickets while two Portuguese men were clubbed with so much force they had to be admitted to the hospital. The confrontation ended when a lieutenant fired a shot from his revolver into the crowd. See *Pacific Commercial Advertiser*, April 6, 1896.

63. Antonio de Souza Canavarro to Henry Cooper, April 7, 1898, Records of the Foreign Office and Executive, Series 403, Hawai'i State Archives, Honolulu.

64. Henry Cooper to Antonio de Souza Canavarro, August 4, 1898, Foreign Office Letter Book, Doc. 81, Hawai'i State Archives, Honolulu. See also Jose, "The Manuel Reis Case."

65. Carlos Cirilo Machado to John Hay, November 25, 1898, Consul General of Portugal, Hawai'i State Archives, Honolulu.

66. Machado to Hay, November 25, 1898.

67. Julian Pauncefote to John Hay, August 14, 1900, Territorial Departments-State, Hawai'i State Archives, Honolulu. See also Jose, "The Manuel Reis Case," 143.

68. Jose, "The Manuel Reis Case," 143. The Second Anglo-Boer War (1899–1902) was fought between Great Britain and the Boer South African Republic. After the British victory in 1902, this area was renamed the Transvaal Colony and was one of the founding provinces of the Union of South Africa.

69. Jose, "The Manuel Reis Case."

70. John Hay to Sanford Dole, December 23, 1901, Territorial Departments-State, Hawai'i State Archives, Honolulu.

71. Jose, "The Manuel Reis Case," 144.

72. *Honolulu Advertiser*, December 3, 1929.

73. *Honolulu Advertiser*, December 3, 1929.

74. *Honolulu Star-Bulletin*, September 7, 1935.

75. *Honolulu Advertiser*, June 30, 1934.

CHAPTER 4. THE SHINSHU MARU AFFAIR

1. Henry Cooper to Sanford Dole, April 13, 1897, Francis M. Hatch Manuscript Collection, Hawai'i State Archives, Honolulu. Tallies of the number of *Shinshu Maru* migrants sent back to Japan range from 413 to 470. For more regarding the numbers of rejected passengers from each ship see Hilary Conroy, *The Japanese Frontier in Hawai'i, 1868–1898* (Berkeley: University of California Press, 1953), 125; Tom Coffman, *Nation Within: The History of the American Occupation of Hawai'i* (Kihei: Koa Books, 2009), 213; and Akira Iriye, *Pacific Estrangement: Japanese and American Expansion, 1879–1911* (Cambridge, MA: Harvard University Press, 1972), 51.

2. In general, the term "Yellow Peril" refers to the fear that Asians, as the "uncivilized and heathen non-white other," would invade the "civilized" West. The term also has a specific historical connection to global anti-Japanese sentiment: at the end of the First Sino-Japanese War, Kaiser Wilhelm II used the term to justify the Triple Intervention against Japan to stop the geopolitical "dangers" of the "Yellow race." He referenced the allegorical lithograph, *Peoples of Europe, Guard Your Most Sacred Possessions* (1895) by Herman Knackfuss, to promote Yellow Peril ideology and justify European colonialism in Asia. For more, see Erika Lee, *The Making of Asian America: A History* (New York: Simon and Schuster, 2015), 109–36.

3. The Hawaiian Kingdom was the first nation to voluntarily renounce extraterritoriality in Japan. For more information, see Lorenz Gonschor, *A Power in the World: The Hawaiian Kingdom in Oceania* (Honolulu: University of Hawai'i Press, 2019), 5.

4. *Pacific Commercial Advertiser*, April 23, 1897.

5. *Pacific Commercial Advertiser*, March 12, 1897.

6. Alexis Dudden, *Japan's Colonization of Korea: Discourse and Power* (Honolulu: University of Hawai'i Press, 2005), 58. When Japanese officials entered the global scene in the 1860s, they encountered the regime of international law. These men quickly understood that in the realpolitik of the nineteenth century, international law was a tool of legitimization that could be used to replace the "old East Asian world order" with modern sovereign states; Junnan Lai, "Sovereignty and 'Civilization': International Law and East Asia in the Nineteenth Century," *Modern China* 40, no. 3 (2014): 297.

7. Dudden, *Japan's Colonization of Korea*, 28.

8. Prasenjit Duara, "The Regime of Authenticity: Timelessness, Gender, and National History in Modern China," *History and Theory: Studies in the Philosophy of History* 37, no. 3 (1998): 287–308. See also Dudden, *Japan's Colonization of Korea*, 28.

9. Sharon Luk, *The Life of Paper: Letters and a Poetics of Living beyond Captivity* (Oakland: University of California Press, 2018).

10. The system was also applied retroactively to those who came to the archipelago on board the *City of Tokyo* and *Yamashiro Maru* in 1885.

11. Labor contracts were to be approved by the governor of Kanagawa. The Hawaiian Kingdom was required to provide a sufficient number of inspectors, interpreters, and doctors to work with the laborers in Hawaiʻi in order to ensure that their working and living conditions were acceptable. The two sides agreed that the Hawaiian Kingdom would provide sufficient hospitals and burial grounds, and that 30 percent of migrants would be women. The convention also provided for Issei living in Hawaiʻi to be able to naturalize as Hawaiian subjects and earn the right to vote. These provisions, however, were soon nullified by the 1887 Bayonet Constitution. Hilary Conroy, *The Japanese Frontier in Hawaii, 1868–1898* (Berkeley: University of California Press, 1953), 68–69.

12. At the time of the immigration convention with Japan, Robert Walker Irwin was serving as Consul General for Hawaiʻi in Tokyo. An American businessman, he had come to Japan in 1886 in search of financial opportunities. Irwin received appointments as commissioner of immigration and special agent of the Board of Immigration of Hawaiʻi. It was in these positions that Irwin facilitated the emigration of Japanese laborers to Hawaiʻi from 1886 to 1894. For more on Irwin, see Conroy, *The Japanese Frontier in Hawaii*, 62–83.

13. The convention was revised in 1887 to require laborers to shoulder a larger amount of the costs of their transportation and medical treatment through a significant increase in the amount paid to the Hawaiian government.

14. Robert Irwin to Sanford Dole, July 28, 1893, Japan Minister and Consul, Records of the Foreign Office and Executive, Hawaiʻi State Archives, Honolulu.

15. In 1883, migration from China to the kingdom was limited to "six hundred in any three-month period." In 1884 the Hawaiian Kingdom revised this policy and instituted stricter restrictions, which limited the number of migrant laborers onboard any ship arriving in Hawaiʻi to twenty-five, in addition to

those who had passports entitling them to enter the kingdom. Under these regulations, passports could be issued either by the Foreign Office in Honolulu or by the Consul General in Hong Kong to Chinese residents of Hawai'i who wished to return to the islands or to wives, female relatives, and children of those residing in the islands. For more information, see Ralph S. Kuykendall, *The Hawaiian Kingdom*, vol. 3, 1874–1893: *The Kalākaua Dynasty* (Honolulu: University of Hawai'i Press, 1967), 146–50.

16. "Memorandum as to Relations between Hawaii and Japan," April 17, 1897, Francis M. Hatch Manuscript Collection, Hawai'i State Archives, Honolulu. Although Act 66 was created in 1894, it was not put into effect until late 1896 when it was used against the Japanese.

17. Conroy, *Japanese Frontier*, 115.

18. Acts of the Republic of Hawai'i, Hawai'i State Archives, Honolulu.

19. This was one year before the Manuel Reis indemnity case prompted the Portuguese monarchy to halt all emigration to Hawai'i. The agreement was subsequently altered to include Chinese laborers and a 10-percent ratio of Portuguese to Chinese and Japanese laborers. Minutes of the Board of Immigration, August 7, 1895, Board of Immigration Record Book 1895, Hawai'i State Archives, Honolulu.

20. Conroy, *Japanese Frontier*, 118.

21. Act 17 passed in February 1895.

22. Immigration, Series 524, vols. 1 and 2, unprocessed, Hawai'i State Archives, Honolulu.

23. *Pacific Commercial Advertiser*, March 11, 1897.

24. *Pacific Commercial Advertiser*, March 18, 1897.

25. *Pacific Commercial Advertiser*, March 18, 1897.

26. Jun Uchida, *Brokers of Empire: Japanese Settler Colonialism in Korea, 1876–1945* (Cambridge, MA: Harvard University Asia Center, 2011), 36.

27. The terms *minzoku* and *Yamato minzoku* began to be used during the Meiji era to express a collective ethnic nationalism. Fuminori Minamikawa writes that after Japan's victory in the 1905 Russo-Japanese War, "Japanese immigrant leaders usually explained events involving them using the term *minzoku* to refer to the nation of Japan." By the 1920s, *minzoku* was a "popular term that described the national identity of the Japanese, a political slogan of the new Meiji government, and a concept in social sciences."

Fuminori Minamikawa, "Vernacular Representations of Race and the Making of a Japanese Ethnoracial Community in Los Angeles," in *Trans-Pacific Japanese American Studies: Conversations on Race and Racializations*, edited by Yasuko Takezawa and Gary Y. Okihiro, 107–32 (Honolulu: University of Hawai'i Press, 2016), 111–13.

28. Uchida, *Brokers of Empire*.

29. Hisashi Shimamura to Henry Cooper, April 6, 1897, Records of the Foreign Office and Executive, Series 403, Hawai'i State Archives, Honolulu.

30. Douglas Howland, "Japanese Neutrality in the Nineteenth Century: International Law and Transcultural Process," *Transcultural Studies* 1, no. 1 (2010): 14–37.

31. Uchida, *Brokers of Empire*, 30.

32. Japanese emigrants who chose to travel independently were required to provide two guarantors who would serve in the same capacity as the emigration agent.

33. Conroy, *Japanese Frontier*; Lai, "Sovereignty and Civilization."

34. Untitled newspaper, Francis M. Hatch Manuscript Collection, January–April 1897, Hawai'i State Archives, Honolulu.

35. Untitled newspaper, Francis M. Hatch Manuscript Collection, January–April 1897, Hawai'i State Archives, Honolulu.

36. Stuart Eldridge to Henry Cooper, April 12, 1897, Francis M. Hatch Manuscript Collection, January–April 1897, Hawai'i State Archives, Honolulu.

37. Eldridge to Cooper, April 12, 1897.

38. Eldridge to Cooper, April 12, 1897.

39. Shigenobu Ōkuma to Hisashi Shimamura, April 19, 1897, Records of the Foreign Office and Executive, Series 403, Hawai'i State Archives, Honolulu.

40. Ōkuma to Shimamura, April 19, 1897.

41. Ōkuma ordered Honolulu-based Consul General Shimamura to pass on a copy of his letters to Henry Cooper, which he did on May 11. In a nod to the political power of the United States in Hawai'i, Ōkuma also ordered the Japanese minister in Washington, DC, to read US Secretary of State Sherman a telegram that voiced the Meiji's government's displeasure at the violation of the Treaty of 1871 and the poor treatment of the rejected emigrants. Shigenobu Ōkuma to Tōru Hoshi, April 14, 1897, Notes from Japan, General Records of the Department of State, National Archives, Washington, DC.

42. Hisashi Shimamura to Shigenobu Ōkuma, April 12, 1897, Records of the Foreign Office and Executive, Series 263, Hawai'i State Archives, Honolulu.

43. *Hawaiian Star,* July 2 and 8, 1897.

44. *Daily Bulletin,* July 16, 1897.

45. Julius W. Pratt, *Expansionists of 1898: The Acquisition of Hawaii and the Spanish Islands* (Baltimore: Johns Hopkins Press, 1936), 320.

46. *Evening Star,* March 19, 1897.

47. *Pacific Commercial Advertiser,* May 25, 1897.

48. Francis Hatch to William Day, May 22, 1897, Francis M. Hatch Manuscript Collection, Hawai'i State Archives, Honolulu.

49. Theodore Roosevelt to Caspar F. Goodrich, May 26, 1897, TLS, DLC-MSS, PTR, roll 313.

50. Haole oligarchs believed that the sanctity of a signed treaty would thwart any attempt made by Japan to stall annexation to the United States.

51. William Adam Russ, Jr., *The Hawaiian Republic, 1894–1898, and Its Struggle to Win Annexation* (Selinsgrove: Susquehanna University Press, 1961), 146.

52. Tōru Hoshi to John Sherman, June 19, 1897, Notes from Japan, General Records of the Department of State, National Archives, Washington, DC.

53. Tōru Hoshi to Shigenobu Ōkuma June 17, 1897, Nihon gaikō bunsho (Diplomatic papers of Japan), 30:978. As quoted in Akira Iriye, *Pacific Estrangement: Japanese and American Expansion 1897–1911* (Cambridge, MA: Harvard University Press, 1972), 53.

54. Shigenobu Ōkuma to Tōru Hoshi, June 19, 1897, Nihon gaikō bunsho (Diplomatic papers of Japan), 30:985–86. As quoted in Iriye, *Pacific Estrangement,* 53.

55. Iriye, *Pacific Estrangement,* 53.

56. Duara, "The Regime of Authenticity." See also Prasenjit Duara, *Rescuing History from the Nation: Questioning Narratives of Modern China* (Chicago: University of Chicago Press, 1995).

57. In response to the 1897 signing of the annexation treaty, members of Hui Aloha 'Āina and Hui Aloha 'Āina o Nā Wāhine organized a series of petition drives that collected over twenty-one thousand signatures from Kānaka Maoli and Hawaiian nationals against American annexation. These documents, known as the Kū'ē petitions, were presented to and accepted by the US Senate Committee on Foreign Relations on December 8, 1897. See Silva, *Aloha Betrayed,* 145–59.

CHAPTER 5. HISTORICIZING THE HOMESTEAD IN WAHIAWA COLONY

1. *New York Herald*, February 2, 1893.

2. The 1890 census figures from Hawai'i are as follows: Hawaiian: 34,436; Part Hawaiian: 6,186; Foreign-born Chinese: 15,301; Foreign-born Japanese: 12,360; Hawaiian-born, foreign parentage: 7,495; Americans: 1,928; Britons: 1,344; Portuguese: 8,602; German: 1,034; French: 70; Polynesian: 588; other foreigners: 419. Although the Hawaiian Kingdom had enacted a Chinese Exclusion Act in 1886 that severely limited the number of Chinese migrants to the islands, at the start of the 1890s, as these numbers demonstrate, the Asian population was much larger than that of Europeans and Americans in Hawai'i. Thomas G. Thrum, ed., *Hawaiian Almanac and Annual for 1896* (Honolulu: Black and Auld, 1896), 11.

3. "Why Should We Annex Hawai'i?," *New York Herald*, February 23, 1893.

4. Eric T.L. Love, *Race over Empire: Racism and U.S. Imperialism, 1865–1900* (Chapel Hill: University of North Carolina Press, 2004), 106.

5. For more on the Reciprocity Treaty of 1875, see chapter 2.

6. By 1875, agitation against Chinese labor had already erupted on the American West Coast, as there were three workers—two white and one Chinese—for every job in San Francisco. Ronald Takaki, *Strangers from a Different Shore: A History of Asian Americans* (New York: Little, Brown and Company, 1989), 105. For more on "coolies" and anti-Asian sentiment, see chapter 2.

7. Thrum, *Hawaiian Almanac and Annual for 1896*, 11.

8. Sanford B. Dole, "The Political Importance of Small Land Holdings in the Hawaiian Islands," paper presented at the Honolulu Social Science Association, Honolulu, March 23, 1891, and reprinted in the *Pacific Commercial Advertiser*, August 14, 1891. Dole often referred to the Crown and Government Lands as "Public Lands."

9. Wahiawā is an area in central O'ahu that was configured into a district in 1913. It is fifteen miles long and two to five miles wide. It was created by taking the ahupua'a (wedged-shaped land section) of Wahiawā and Wai'anae Uka from Waialua. An 'ili (division of land) of Waikele was added to the district in 1925. In 1932 it was again enlarged by adding lands from 'Ewa, which had been included in the "military reservation" of Schofield Barracks. Lloyd J.

Soehren, "Wahiawa," Hawaiian Place Names, http://ulukau.org/cgi-bin/hpn?e=&a=d&c=mahele&cl=search&d=HASHeabdccaf2222f5cbfbfdc5, accessed May 2022; Jonah Laʻakapu Lenchanko, "Kūkaniloko: A Hālau of Ākeaakamai of Kāne" (PhD diss., University of Hawaiʻi, 2015), 6; Lani Nedbalek, *Wahiawa: From Dream to Community* (Mililani: Wonder View Press, 1984), 2.

10. The colony was the one project deemed a success by those invested in Dole's scheme. "Wahiawa: Birthplace of the Pineapple Industry," *Pacific Commercial Advertiser*, February 9, 1921. I use "Wahiawa" without a kahakō (macron) to refer to the name of the colony and "Wahiawā" when referencing the district.

11. Jo-Lin Lenchanko Kalimapau, in discussion with the author, June 2019. Kūkaniloko is one of two places in the Hawaiian Islands specifically designated for the birth of high-ranking children. The other site is Holoholokū on Kauaʻi. For more information on Kūkaniloko, see Lenchanko, "Kūkaniloko: A Hālau of Ākeaakamai of Kāne."

12. Wahiawa Colony was established in Kūkaniloko, an area located between the Koʻolau and Waiʻanae mountain ranges that spans roughly thirty-six thousand acres.

13. Manu Karuka, *Empire's Tracks: Indigenous Nations, Chinese Workers, and the Transcontinental Railroad* (Oakland: University of California Press, 2019), 168.

14. Anne Bonds and Joshua Inwood, "Beyond White Privilege: Geographies of White Supremacy and Settler Colonialism," *Progress in Human Geography* 40, no. 6 (2015): 725.

15. In his work *California and Hawaiʻi Bound: U.S. Settler Colonialism and the Pacific West, 1848–1959* (Lincoln: University of Nebraska Press, 2021), Henry Knight Lozano refers to this process as "transpacific Americanization."

16. Bonds and Inwood, "Beyond White Privilege," 724.

17. John Renshaw to Commissioner of Public Land, February 18, 1900, Public Land Commission Records, Hawaiʻi State Archives, Honolulu.

18. There was an attempt to bring white American settlers from Modesto, California, to Ewa Plantation in 1898. This experiment proved to be a failure, with most settlers leaving after just nine months. For more information on the "California Farmers' Colony," see Lozano, *California and Hawaiʻi Bound*, 170–71.

19. Robert H. Horwitz, Judith B. Finn, Louis A. Vargha, and James W. Ceaser, *Public Land Policy in Hawaii: A Historical Analysis* (Honolulu: State of

Hawai'i Legislative Reference Bureau, 1969); Sanford B. Dole, "The Problem of Population and Our Land Policy," *Pacific Commercial Advertiser*, October 26, 1872.

20. Dole, "The Problem of Population and Our Land Policy."

21. The Crown Lands consisted of nearly one million acres that were put in trust under the Hawaiian Kingdom. During the Māhele, the kingdom transferred roughly one and a half million acres to itself. They constituted the Government Lands and were to be used for various public purposes. The Government and Crown Lands were claimed by the Republic of Hawai'i and then illegally "ceded" to the United States following annexation.

22. Sanford B. Dole, "The Problem of Population and our Land Policy."

23. Horwitz et. al., *Public Land Policy*, 4.

24. Horwitz et. al., *Public Land Policy*, 3.

25. An Act to Facilitate the Acquisition and Settlement of Homesteads, August 29, 1884, available at https://dlnr.hawaii.gov/mk/files/2017/02/Q-14-Homestead-Act-of-1884.pdf. For more on the 1884 Homestead Act, see Jon M. Van Dyke, *Who Owns the Crown Lands of Hawai'i?* (Honolulu: University of Hawai'i Press, 2007), 113; Ulla Hasager and Marion Kelly, "Public Policy of Land and Homesteading in Hawai'i," *Social Process in Hawai'i* 40 (2001): 190–232.

26. The 1862 Homestead Act provided that any adult citizen, or intended citizen, who had never borne arms against the US government could claim 160 acres of surveyed government land. Claimants were required to "improve" the plot by building a residence and working the land. After five years of living on and working the land, and paying a small registration fee, the original filer was entitled to the property. Title could also be acquired after only a six-month residency and trivial improvements, provided the claimant paid the government $1.25 per acre. For more on the 1862 Homestead Act, see Harold Melvin Hyman, *American Singularity: The 1787 Northwest Ordinance, the 1862 Homestead and Morrill Acts, and the 1944 G.I. Bill* (Athens: University of Georgia Press, 1986).

27. Van Dyke, *Who Owns the Crown Lands*, 113.

28. Sanford B. Dole, "Hawaiian Public Lands," in Government for the Territory of Hawaii, H.R. 305, "House Commission on Territories," 56 Cong. (1899), as cited in Van Dyke, *Who Owns the Crown Lands*, 112; Dole was one of the men who coordinated and led the movement for the Bayonet Constitution, which gave the legislature, of which he was a member, control over the Hawaiian

government. Within the eleven years before the passing of the Land Act of 1895, 530 homesteads were acquired, settling 8,500 acres.

29. Dole, "Hawaiian Public Lands."

30. Dole, "Hawaiian Public Lands."

31. Sanford B. Dole to his brother, July 26, 1894, cited in Van Dyke, *Who Owns the Crown Lands*, 192.

32. Act 26 of the Laws of the Republic of Hawai'i, also known as the "Land Act of 1895," Laws of the Republic of Hawai'i, Legislative Assembly, Special Session, 1895. The Land Act defined the category of "Public Lands" to include "all lands heretofore classed as Government Lands, all lands heretofore classed as Crown Lands, and all lands that may hereafter come into the control of the government."

33. Citizens and denizens of the Republic of Hawai'i were eligible for three different programs: cash freehold, right-of-purchase lease, and a 999-year homestead lease. Under the cash freehold program, lots were put up for public auction. Those who had the capital were required to put down 25 percent of the purchase price as a down payment. After three additional annual payments the lessee could apply for a government land patent. For those, the majority, who did not have the capital required for the cash freehold system, the right-of-purchase lease provided the lessee with a twenty-one year lease. If after three years the lessee could prove that they had cultivated the land and maintained a permanent residence there, they were entitled to receive a government land patent which gave them fee simple ownership. Under the 999-year homestead lease, which provided homestead land at little cost, if a lessee met the same residency and cultivation requirements of the first two programs and was not delinquent in taxes within a six-year period, the applicant would receive the lease and was required to pay only the real property taxes assessed on the land. The land was to be passed on to the next of kin after the lessee's death. For more on the 1895 Land Act, see Van Dyke, *Who Owns the Crown Lands*, 192–94.

34. Land Act of 1895.

35. Letter from Sanford B. Dole to A. Lewis Jr., July 31, 1908, Sanford B. Dole Papers, Hawai'i State Archives, Honolulu.

36. Van Dyke, *Who Owns the Crown Lands*, 193. The Land Act of 1895 made approximately 4 percent of the population eligible for homesteads. See also "Report of the Commissioners of Public Lands for the Period of 1896–97" and

"Report of the Commissioners of Public Lands for the Period of 1898–99," quoted in Horwitz et al., *Public Land Policy*, 9–14.

37. Between 1896 and 1899, there were a total of three holdings distributed to Issei, totaling 185 acres. There were no plots recorded to Chinese settlers, and they were not listed as a population in the "Report of the Commissioners of Public Land for 1896–97" or the "Report of the Commissioners of Public Lands for the Period of 1898–99."; they may have been included in the "Hawaiian Born" category. Denizens in this case refer to Euro-Americans who were granted the rights of citizens, but not forced to give up their allegiance of their place of origin. The 1894 Constitution of the Republic of Hawai'i did provide citizenship for Asians born or naturalized in the Republic of Hawai'i. However, because of the reading requirement of the naturalization clause, Asians were effectively barred from naturalizing and as a result, homesteading eligibility. For more, see "Reports of the Commissioners of Public Lands for 1896–97" and "Reports of the Commissioners of Public Lands for 1898–99," quoted in Horwitz et al., *Public Land Policy*, 9–14.

38. Horwitz et al., *Public Land Policy*, 9–14.

39. Over his lifespan, Clark filed multiple patents, some of which pertained to irrigation systems and cutting and juicing pineapples. See for example, Byron O. Clark, "Apparatus for Treating Fruit Juices and the Like," US Patent 1062888A, filed January 22, 1912, issued May 27, 1913; this and other patents are available at https://patents.google.com/?inventor=Byron+O+Clark.

40. Cecilia Rasmussen, "L.A. Redux: The City Then and Now," *Los Angeles Times*, August 1, 1991.

41. While Clark notes these statements in his personal letters, the discouragement from Kānaka Maoli and local residents can also be read as an attempt to keep him and the other white settlers out of the area. Letter from Byron O. Clark to E. S. Boyd, Esq., July 25, 1902, in Commissioner of Public Lands, *Diversified Industries in the Territory of Hawaii* (Honolulu: Paradise of the Pacific Print, 1903), 10.

42. Clark to Boyd, 10.

43. Clark to Boyd, 10.

44. The US House of Representatives passed the resolution for annexation on June 15, 1898 with the Senate following on July 6. President McKinley signed the joint resolution on July 7, 1898.

45. When Clark later described this transition period, he stated that he and the colonists feared that without this contract "opponents of the land system would get all land sales, made subsequent to the ratification treaty, annulled, for we did not get fully organized until after annexation, but we considered this contract sufficient to bind the successors in interests and that the colony could be carried through along the lines originally planned." Letter from Clark to Boyd, July 25, 1902, in Commissioner of Public Lands, *Diversified Industries in the Territory of Hawaii*, 11.

46. The Wahiawa Colony was originally settled by thirteen members and their families who formed the Settler Association. They were T. L. Holloway, E. C. Rhodes, Carl Pullman, T. H. Gibson, H. R. Hanna, W. B. McCormick, Mary H. Clark (Byron O. Clark's sister), W. B. Thomas, Edgar Wood, A. W. Eames, J. W. Welte, L. G. Kellogg, and Byron O. Clark. James D. Dole, the founder of Hawaii Pineapple Company, later to become Dole Pineapple Company, moved into the Wahiawa Colony in 1900. See W. O. Smith to Henry Davis and J. H. Townsend, July 30, 1908, M-453, Hawaiʻi State Archives, Honolulu.

47. Land Surveys, nos. 4600–4624, Series 526, Hawaiʻi State Archives, Honolulu; collection is still in process. See also Sol N. Sheridan, "Small Farming Succeeds to a Demonstration," *Pacific Commercial Advertiser*, March 2, 1903.

48. Public Land Commission Records, Miscellaneous Numbered and Unnumbered Correspondence, May 1898–1900, Hawaiʻi State Archives, Honolulu.

49. Sol N. Sheridan, "Small Farming Succeeds to a Demonstration," *Pacific Commercial Advertiser*, March 2, 1903. See also W. B. Thomas, "The Wahiawa Colony," *Paradise of the Pacific*, December 1900, 37–38.

50. Initially tobacco was also considered as a potential cash crop. See "Wahiawa: Birthplace of the Pineapple Industry," *Pacific Commercial Advertiser*, February 9, 1921.

51. "Byron O. Clark," *Honolulu Advertiser*, June 27, 1929.

52. Although two streams ran nearby, colonists' water rights limited them to household use. Nedbalek, *Wahiawa*, 23.

53. While it is not clear how pineapples were brought into Hawaiʻi, they are thought to have originated in the general region where present-day Argentina, Brazil, and Paraguay meet. For more on the origins of the pineapple and its history, see Richard A. Hawkins, *A Pacific Industry: The History of Pineapple Canning in Hawaii* (London: I.B. Tauris, 2011), 6; Gary Y. Okihiro, *Pineapple Culture:*

A History of the Tropical and Temperate Zones (Berkeley: University of California Press, 2009), 80–92. For information on Marin's journal entry, see Duane P. Bartholomew, Richard A. Hawkins, and Johnny A. Lopez, "Hawaii Pineapple: The Rise and Fall of An Industry," *HortScience* 47, no. 10 (2012): 1390–98.

54. This law exempted from taxes all "tools, machinery, appliances, buildings, and all other personal property . . . used exclusively in the cultivation, canning, or preserving of pineapples or other fruits." *Laws of Her Majesty Liliuokalani Queen of the Hawaiian Islands: Passed by the Legislative Assembly at Its Session 1892* (Honolulu: Robert Grieve, Steam Book and Job Printer, 1892), 126–27. See also Hawkins, *Pacific Industry*, 11.

55. At the time of the overthrow in 1893, there were reportedly thirteen pineapple growers, a majority of which were based on Oʻahu. These growers had roughly four hundred thousand plants in the ground and most of their fruit went to local sellers. During the late nineteenth century, shipping fresh pineapples from Hawaiʻi proved to be problematic because of the lack of modern refrigerated shipping technology. And unlike bananas, pineapples did not become any sweeter if shipped green. The fruit's high spoilage rate meant that it could only be shipped short distances to market, and the twenty-one hundred miles from Honolulu to the nearest American port at San Francisco proved too great a distance. For more, see Bartholomew, Hawkins, and Lopez, "Hawaii Pineapple," 1390–91.

56. Hawaiʻi's first pineapple canning company, Kona Fruit Preserving Company, was founded on Hawaiʻi Island in 1882 by the American John Douglas Ackerman and the German Waldemar Muller. Despite favorable assessment by local press and the support of George Washington Pilipō, a Hawaiian nationalist and the representative for North Kona in the kingdom's legislature, Kona Fruit Preserving Company failed to find a market in the United States and the venture ultimately collapsed. Bartholomew, Hawkins, and Lopez, "Hawaii Pineapple," 1391.

57. In 1891 Emmeluth shipped 600 cans to Boston, 960 cans to New York, and 3,000 cans to San Francisco. He soon discovered that the US duty on canned fruit made it very difficult to compete in that market. See Bartholomew, Hawkins, and Lopez, "Hawaii Pineapple."

58. Karuka, *Empire's Tracks*, 44.

59. *Paradise of the Pacific,* December 1900, 38.

60. Clark to Boyd, 10–14. See also Sheridan, "Small Farming Succeeds to a Demonstration."

61. Hawkins, *Pacific Industry*, 19. Between 1902 and 1906, Tropic Fruit benefitted from land transfers and sales from family and former members of the Settler Association. As a result, the company's acreage increased from five acres in fee simple and two hundred acres under lease, to two hundred acres in fee simple and 340 acres under lease.

62. Okihiro, *Pineapple Culture*, 129. Like his second cousin Sanford Dole, James D. Dole was descended from a line of Congregational ministers.

63. In the first half of 1932, HAPCO sustained losses of $5.5 million. This provided the opportunity for minority shareholder Castle and Cooke to force a reorganization of the company and depose James Dole. One of the assets Castle and Cooke acquired was the brand name Dole. Today, Dole Food Company Inc. is one of the leading brand names in fresh fruit. Richard A. Hawkins, "James D. Dole and the 1932 Failure of the Hawaiian Pineapple Company," *Hawaiian Journal of History* 41, (2007): 149–70.

64. Okihiro, *Pineapple Culture*, 132.

65. "What Does Hawaii Want of Railroads, Anyway?" *Hawaiian Star*, October 28, 1911. For more information on the Dillingham family and the Oahu Railway and Land Company, see Walter Francis Dillingham Papers and Addenda, Huntington Library, San Marino, California.

66. Jan K. TenBruggencate, *Hawai'i's Pineapple Century: A History of the Crowned Fruit in the Hawaiian Islands* (Honolulu: Mutual Publishing, 2004), 27.

67. *1941 Western Canner and Packer Yearbook*, 132, quoted in Hawkins, "James D. Dole," 151.

68. Eames initially grew pineapples for HAPCO, and in 1906 incorporated his own pineapple-canning corporation, Hawaiian Islands Packing Company. This was later taken over by the California Packing Corporation, known locally as CalPak, and later became Del Monte.

69. "Wahiawa, Birthplace of the Pineapple Industry," *Pacific Commercial Advertiser*, February 9, 1921. See also, Bartholomew, Hawkins, and Lopez, "Hawaii Pineapple," 1391.

70. "Hawaii Will Supply Half of Pineapple Demand in US," *Pacific Commercial Advertiser*, February 9, 1921.

71. "Hawaii Will Supply Half of Pineapple Demand in US," *Pacific Commercial Advertiser*, February 9, 1921.

72. "Wahiawa: Birthplace of the Pineapple Industry," *Pacific Commercial Advertiser*, February 9, 1921.

73. See Thomas, "The Wahiawa Colony"; Sheridan, "Small Farming Succeeds to a Demonstration"; "Wahiawa: Birthplace of the Pineapple Industry," *Pacific Commercial Advertiser*, February 9, 1921; and "Wahiawa: The Gateway to Opportunity," *Honolulu Advertiser*, January 31, 1939.

74. Sheridan, "Small Farming Succeeds to a Demonstration."

75. Henry Champion Brown, "Wahiawa," *Paradise of the Pacific*, December 1909, 52.

76. Brown, "Wahiawa."

77. Thomas, "The Wahiawa Colony," 38. Thomas also opened a pineapple company in Wahiawā.

78. Love, *Race over Empire*, 24.

79. For a detailed account of the development of the discourse surrounding climate, geography, and the creation of races, see Okihiro, *Pineapple Culture*, 6–25.

80. Hippocrates, vol. 1, translate by W. H. S. Jones, Loeb Classical Library (Cambridge, MA: Harvard University Press, 1923), 133–35, 137, quoted in Okihiro, *Pineapple Culture*, 6.

81. Alexis de Tocqueville, *Democracy in America*, translated by Arthur Goldhammer (New York: Library of America, 2004), 359–60, 369.

82. In 1852 Schurz left Prussia, where he had embraced radical politics. Upon arriving in the United States he became involved in the antislavery movement and joined the Republican Party. In 1861 Lincoln appointed Schurz ambassador to Spain, where he convinced the Spanish government not to support the South during the American Civil War. Upon his return to the United States, Schurz was commissioned as a brigadier general and took part in the Second Battle of Bull Run. In 1870 he became a Republican senator for Missouri, and served on the Foreign Relations Committee. He also served as secretary of interior under Republican President Rutherford B. Hayes. Schurz was the editorial writer for *Harper's Weekly* from 1892 to 1898. For more on Schurz, see Peter T. Lubrecht Sr., *Carl Schurz, German-American Statesman: My Country Right or Wrong* (Charleston, SC: Arcadia Publishing, 2019).

83. Carl Schurz, "Manifest Destiny," *Harper's New Monthly Magazine* 87 (1893): 737–46.

84. Schurz, "Manifest Destiny," 742. For a detailed account of the development of this discourse, see Okihiro, *Pineapple Culture*, 5–25.

85. Schurz, "Manifest Destiny," 741.

86. Schurz, "Manifest Destiny," 741.

87. Schurz, "Manifest Destiny," 741.

88. Sheridan, "Small Farming Succeeds to a Demonstration."

89. By the time of Wahiawa Colony's founding, Japanese labor presented the greatest "Asiatic threat" to the haole-led oligarchy.

90. Sheridan, "Small Farming Succeeds to a Demonstration."

91. In 1900 this excluded all Asian immigrants.

92. Gary Y. Okihiro, *Cane Fires: The Anti-Japanese Movement in Hawai'i, 1865–1945* (Philadelphia: Temple University Press, 1991), 86.

93. See for example, *Paradise of the Pacific*, December 1909, 52.

94. Clark to Boyd, published in *Diversified Industries*.

95. Edward D. Beechert, *Working in Hawaii: A Labor History* (Honolulu: University of Hawaii Press, 1985), 181.

96. Beechert, *Working in Hawaii*, 181.

97. Beechert, *Working in Hawaii*, 181.

98. Beechert, *Working in Hawaii*, 182.

99. Beechert, *Working in Hawaii*, 182; Okihiro, *Pineapple Culture*, 137.

100. US Department of Commerce and Labor, *Third Report of the Commissioner of Labor on Hawaii, 1905*, US House, 59th Congress, 1st session, no. 580 (1906).

101. Kame (Sakamoto) Iwatani was born in Yamaguchi-ken, Japan on January 10, 1896. In 1922 she left Japan for Hawai'i as a picture bride. She worked in the pineapple fields of Paumalū and Leilehua. Kame could not remember which pineapple company they leased the land from. Kame Iwatani, interview by Michiko Kodama, March 2, 1979, transcript, Women Workers in Hawai'i's Pineapple Industry, University of Hawai'i at Mānoa Center for Oral History, Honolulu, http://hdl.handle.net/10125/30453.

102. Michiko Kodama-Nishimoto, Warren S. Nishimoto, and Cynthia A. Oshiro, eds., *Talking Hawai'i's Story: Oral Histories of an Island People* (Honolulu: University of Hawai'i Press, 2009), 81.

103. Venicia Damasco Guiala, interview by Warren S. Nishimoto, in *Talking Hawai'i's Story*, 84.

104. Kipapa-5 was located in the foothills of the Ko'olau Range, a few miles south of Wahiawā town.

105. Yone Taniguchi, interview by Warren Nishimoto, March 13, 1979, transcript, Women Workers in Hawai'i's Pineapple Industry, University of Hawai'i at Mānoa Center for Oral History, Honolulu, http://hdl.handle.net/10125/30464. Yone (Tanaka) Taniguchi was born in Pe'ahi, Maui on January 8, 1902. Her parents were from Yamaguchi-ken, Japan. She began working at the Haiku Fruit and Packing Company in 1927 and was transferred to the Hawaiian Pineapple Company's Wahiawā plantation in 1938.

106. Diane Sasaki, in discussion with the author, December 2016.

107. Sue Shizuyo Kajioka, interview by Michiko Kodama, March 14, 1979, transcript, Women Workers in Hawai'i's Pineapple Industry, University of Hawai'i at Mānoa Center for Oral History, Honolulu, http://hdl.handle.net/10125/30454. Sue Shizuyo (Takahashi) Kajioka was born in in Lahaina, Maui in 1905. Her parents were from Miyagi-ken, Japan. She began working as a trimmer for the Hawaiian Pineapple Company in 1937.

108. Sue Shizuyo Kajioka, interview by Michiko Kodama.

109. Robert Ishikawa, interview by Lani Nedbalek, November 16, 1983, in Nedbalek, *Wahiawa: From Dream to Community*, 47.

110. Yasuko Domai, interview by Lani Nedbalek and Robert Ishikawa, January 24, 1984, in Nedbalek, *Wahiawa: From Dream to Community*, 52.

111. Yasuko Domai, interview by Lani Nedbalek and Robert Ishikawa.

112. Liiko (Onuma) Nouchi, interview by Warren Nishimoto, March 22, 1979, transcript, Women Workers in Hawai'i's Pineapple Industry, University of Hawai'i at Mānoa Center for Oral History, Honolulu, http://hdl.handle.net/10125/30460. Nouchi was born in Pā'auhau, Hawai'i on January 15, 1917. She began working in the Dole pineapple fields in 1950.

113. Josephine Montalbo, interview by Lani Nedbalek, in Nedbalek, *Wahiawa: From Dream to Community*, 52.

114. Okihiro, *Cane Fires*, xii.

115. Candace Fujikane, "Introduction," in *Asian Settler Colonialism: From Local Governance to the Habits of Everyday Life in Hawai'i*, edited by Candace

Fujikane and Jonathan Y. Okamura, 1–42 (Honolulu: University of Hawai'i Press, 2008), 26.

116. Fujikane, "Introduction," 26.

117. Fujikane, "Introduction," 20.

CONCLUSION

1. Noenoe K. Silva, "Kanaka Maoli Resistance to Annexation," 'Ōiwi: A Native Hawaiian Journal 1, no. 1 (December 1998): 40–75, 60. See also *Ke Aloha Aina,* September 11, 1897, available at http://www.ulukau.org/elib/collect/oiwi1/index/assoc/Do.dir/doc82.pdf.

2. Noenoe K. Silva, *Aloha Betrayed: Native Hawaiian Resistance to American Colonialism* (Durham, NC: Duke University Press, 2004), 152.

3. Department of State, "Memorial to the President, the Congress, and the People of the United States," October 8, 1897, in Despatches from United States Ministers in Hawaii to the Secretary of State 1842–1900, National Archives, Washington, DC.

4. Lili'uokalani to William McKinley, June 17, 1897, Annexation of Hawai'i: A Collection of Documents, Hawaiian Collection, Hamilton Library, University of Hawai'i at Mānoa, http://libweb.hawaii.edu/digicoll/annexation/protest/lilius.php.

5. Silva, *Aloha Betrayed,* 162.

6. Alexis Dudden, *Japan's Colonization of Korea: Discourse and Power* (Honolulu: University of Hawai'i Press, 2005), 29.

7. Noelani Goodyear-Ka'ōpua, *The Seeds We Planted: Portraits of a Native Hawaiian Charter School* (Minneapolis: University of Minnesota Press, 2013) and Noelani Goodyear-Ka'ōpua, "Introduction," in *A Nation Rising: Hawaiian Movements for Life, Land, and Sovereignty,* edited by Noelani Goodyear-Ka'ōpua, Ikaika Hussey, and Erin Kahunawaika'ala Wright, 1–34 (Durham, NC: Duke University Press, 2014).

8. Julian Guthrie, "Larry Ellison's Fantasy Island," *Wall Street Journal,* June 13, 2013.

9. Renato Rosaldo, "Imperialist Nostalgia," *Representations,* no. 26 (1989): 107–22.

10. Laura E. Lyons, "Fantasy Island: From Pineapple Plantation to Tourist Plantation on Lānaʻi" in *Detours: A Decolonial Guide to Hawaiʻi*, edited by Hōkūlani K. Aikau and Vernadette Vicuña Gonzalez, 86–93 (Durham, NC: Duke University Press, 2019), 87.

11. Levi Haʻalelea was born in Lahaina in 1822 and was the son of Haʻaloʻu, governor of Molokaʻi and Kipa. His maternal half-brother was Timoteo Haʻalilio. Gibson was excommunicated by the Mormon Church in 1864. For more on Levi Haʻalelea, see "Another Chief Dead," *Pacific Commercial Advertiser*, October 8, 1864. For more on Walter Murray Gibson, see Jacob Adler and Robert M. Kamins, *The Fantastic Life of Walter Murray Gibson: Hawaiʻi's Minister of Everything* (Honolulu: University of Hawaiʻi Press, 1986).

12. Adler and Kamins, *The Fantastic Life of Walter Murray Gibson*, 78.

13. Lyons, "Fantasy Island," 86.

14. For more information on plantation life in Lānaʻi, see Consuelo Agarpao Gouveia, "Lānaʻi's Community Wealth: Lānaʻi's Futures," in *The Value of Hawaiʻi 2: Ancestral Roots, Oceanic Visions*, edited by Aiko Yamashiro and Noelani Goodyear Kaʻōpua, 82–87 (Honolulu: University of Hawaiʻi Press, 2014).

15. Lyons, "Fantasy Island," 90. See also Richard A. Hawkins, "James D. Dole and the 1932 Failure of the Hawaiian Pineapple Company," *Hawaiian Journal of History* 41 (2007): 149–70.

16. Goodyear-Kaʻōpua, *The Seeds We Planted*, 127.

17. Manu Karuka, *Empire's Tracks: Indigenous Nations, Chinese Workers, and the Transcontinental Railroad* (Oakland: University of California Press, 2019), 19.

Bibliography

ARCHIVAL SOURCES

Bishop Museum Archives:
    Henriques Manuscript Collection
Hawai'i State Archives:
    Acts of the Republic of Hawai'i
    Attorney General File, Series 506
    Board of Immigration Record Book
    Cleghorn Collection
    Foreign Office Letter Book
    Francis M. Hatch Manuscript Collection
    Japan Minister and Consul
    Proceedings of the Executive and Advisory Councils of the Provisional Government and of the Republic
    Public Land Commission Records
    Records of the Constitutional Convention
    Records of the Foreign Office and Executive
    Sanford B. Dole Papers

The Huntington Library:
   Walter Francis Dillingham Papers
University of Hawaiʻi at Mānoa:
   Center for Oral History
   Hawaiian Collection
US National Archives:
   Despatches from American Ministers in Hawaii to the Secretary of State
   RG 59 General Records of the Department of State

NEWSPAPERS AND PERIODICALS

Daily Bulletin (Honolulu)
Evening Star (Washington, DC)
Harper's New Monthly Magazine
Hawaiian Star
Holomua
Honolulu Advertiser
Honolulu Star-Bulletin
Ke Aloha Aina
Los Angeles Times
New York Herald
Pacific Commercial Advertiser (Honolulu)
Paradise of the Pacific
Sacramento Daily Union
San Francisco Examiner
Wall Street Journal

SECONDARY SOURCES

Adler, Jacob, and Robert M. Kamins. *The Fantastic Life of Walter Murray Gibson: Hawaiʻi's Minister of Everything.* Honolulu: University of Hawaiʻi Press, 1986.

Agarpao Gouveia, Consuelo. "Lānaʻi's Community Wealth." In *The Value of Hawaii 2: Ancestral Roots, Oceanic Visions,* edited by Aiko Yamashiro and Noelani Goodyear-Kaʻōpua, 82–87. Honolulu: University of Hawaiʻi Press, 2017.

Ai, Chung Kun. *My Seventy Nine Years in Hawaii.* Hong Kong: Cosmorama Pictorial Publisher, 1960.

Allen, Helena G. *Sanford Ballard Dole: Hawaii's Only President, 1844–1926.* Glendale, CA: A. H. Clark Co., 1988.

Andrade, Naleen Naupaka, and Stephanie T. Nishimura. "The Portuguese." In *People and Cultures of Hawai'i: The Evolution of Culture and Ethnicity*, eds. John F. McDermott and Naleen Naupaka Andrade, 81–106. Honolulu: University of Hawai'i Press, 2011.

Arista, Noelani. *The Kingdom and the Republic: Sovereign Hawai'i and the Early United States.* Philadelphia: University of Pennsylvania Press, 2019.

Arvin, Maile. *Possessing Polynesians: The Science of Settler Colonial Whiteness in Hawai'i and Oceania.* Durham, NC: Duke University Press, 2019.

Auslin, Michael R. *Negotiating with Imperialism: The Unequal Treaties and the Culture of Japanese Diplomacy.* Cambridge, MA: Harvard University Press, 2004.

Azuma, Eiichiro. *Between Two Empires: Race, History, and Transnationalism in Japanese America.* New York: Oxford University Press, 2005.

———. *In Search of Our Frontier: Japanese America and Settler Colonialism in the Construction of Japan's Borderless Empire.* Oakland: University of California Press, 2019.

Bandy, David W. "Bandmaster Henry Berger and the Royal Hawaiian Band," *Hawaiian Journal of History* 24 (1990): 69–90.

Barker, Joanne, ed. *Sovereignty Matters: Locations of Contestation and Possibility in Indigenous Struggles for Self-Determination.* Lincoln: University of Nebraska Press, 2006.

Bartholomew, Duane P., Richard A. Hawkins, and Johnny A. Lopez. "Hawaii Pineapple: The Rise and Fall of an Industry." *HortScience* 47, no. 10 (2012): 1390–98.

Basham, Leilani. "Ka Lāhui Hawai'i: He Mo'olelo, he 'Āina, he Loina, a he Ea Kākou." *Hūlili: Multidisciplinary Research on Hawaiian Well-Being* 6 (2010): 37–72.

Basson, Lauren L. "Fit for Annexation but Unfit to Vote?" *Social Science History* 29, no. 4 (2005): 575–98.

———. *White Enough to Be American? Race Mixing, Indigenous People, and the Boundaries of State and Nation.* Chapel Hill: University of North Carolina Press, 2007.

Beamer, Kamanamaikalani. *No Mākou Ka Mana: Liberating the Nation*. Honolulu: Kamehameha Publishing, 2014.

Beechert, Edward D. *Working in Hawaii: A Labor* History. Honolulu: University of Hawai'i Press, 1985.

Birmingham, David. *A Concise History of Portugal*. Cambridge: Cambridge University Press, 2018.

Blount, James H. "Affairs in Hawaii. Report of the U.S. Special Commissioner James H. Blount to U.S. Secretary of State Walter Q. Gresham Concerning the Hawaiian Kingdom Investigation." House Executive Document No. 47, 53 Congress, 3rd Session. Washington, DC: US Government Printing Office, 1894.

Bonds, Anne, and Joshua Inwood. "Beyond White Privilege: Geographies of White Supremacy and Settler Colonialism." *Progress in Human Geography* 40, no. 6 (2016): 715–33.

Chang, David A. *The World and All the Things upon It: Native Hawaiian Geographies of Exploration*. Minneapolis: University of Minnesota Press, 2016.

Coffman, Tom. *Nation Within: The History of the American Occupation of Hawai'i*. Kihei: Koa Books, 2009.

Commissioner of Public Lands, *Diversified Industries in the Territory of Hawaii*. Honolulu: Paradise of the Pacific Print, 1903.

Conroy, Hilary. *The Japanese Frontier in Hawai'i, 1868–1898*. Berkeley: University of California Press, 1953.

de Tocqueville, Alexis. *Democracy in America*. Translated by Arthur Goldhammer. New York: Library of America, 2004.

d'Oliveira, J.B. "Destination, Sandwich Islands." *The Hawaiian Journal of History* 4 (1970): 51–52.

Dougherty, Michael. *To Steal a Kingdom*. Waimanalo: Island Press, 1992.

Duara, Prasenjit. "The Regime of Authenticity: Timelessness, Gender, and National History in Modern China." *History and Theory: Studies in the Philosophy of History* 37, no. 3 (1998): 287–308.

———. *Rescuing History from the Nation: Questioning Narratives of Modern China*. Chicago: University of Chicago Press, 1995.

Dudden, Alexis. *Japan's Colonization of Korea: Discourse and Power*. Honolulu: University of Hawai'i Press, 2005.

Duus, Peter. *The Abacus and the Sword: The Japanese Penetration of Korea, 1895–1910*. Berkeley: University of California Press, 1995.

Espiritu, Augusto. "Inter-Imperial Relations, the Pacific, and Asian American History." *Pacific Historical Review* 83, no. 2 (2014): 238–54.

Flores, Alfred Peredo. "'No Walk in the Park': US Empire and the Racialization of Civilian Military Labor in Guam, 1944–1962." *American Quarterly* 67, no. 3 (2015): 813–35.

Fujikane, Candace. "Introduction." In *Asian Settler Colonialism: From Local Governance to the Habits of Everyday Life in Hawaiʻi*, edited by Candace Fujikane and Jonathan Y. Okamura, 1–42. Honolulu: University of Hawaiʻi Press, 2008.

———. "Mapping Wonder in the Māui Moʻolelo on the Moʻoʻāina: Growing Aloha ʻĀina through Indigenous and Settler Affinity Activism." *Marvels and Tales* 30, no. 1 (2016): 45–69.

Fujitani, Takashi. *Splendid Monarchy: Power and Pageantry in Modern Japan*. Berkeley: University of California Press, 1996.

Gonschor, Lorenz. *A Power in the World: The Hawaiian Kingdom in Oceania*. Honolulu: University of Hawaiʻi Press, 2019.

Goodyear-Kaʻōpua, Noelani. "Introduction." In *A Nation Rising: Hawaiian Movements for Life, Land, and Sovereignty*, edited by Noelani Goodyear-Kaʻōpua, Ikaika Hussey, and Erin Kahunawaikaʻala Wright, 1–34. Durham, NC: Duke University Press, 2014.

———. *The Seeds We Planted: Portraits of a Native Hawaiian Charter School*. Minneapolis: University of Minnesota Press, 2013.

Grimshaw, Patricia. "Settler Anxieties, Indigenous Peoples, and Women's Suffrage in the Colonies of Australia, New Zealand, and Hawaiʻi, 1888 to 1902." *Pacific Historical Review* 69, no. 4 (2000): 553–72.

Hall, Lisa Kahaleole. "Navigating Our Own 'Sea of Islands': Remapping a Theoretical Space for Hawaiian Women and Indigenous Feminism." *Wicazo Sa Review* 24, no. 2 (2009): 15–38.

———. "Strategies of Erasure: U.S. Colonialism and Native Hawaiian Feminism." *American Quarterly* 60, no. 2 (2008): 273–80.

Hall, Stuart. "The State in Question." In *The Idea of the Modern State*, edited by George McLennan, David Held, and Stuart Hall, 1–28. Philadelphia: Open University Press, 1984.

Hasager, Ulla, and Marion Kelly. "Public Policy of Land and Homesteading in Hawaiʻi." *Social Process in Hawaiʻi* 40 (2001): 190–232.

Hauʻofa, Epeli. "Our Sea of Islands." *The Contemporary Pacific* 6, no. 1 (1994): 147–61.
Hawkins, Richard A. "James D. Dole and the 1932 Failure of the Hawaiian Pineapple Company." *Hawaiian Journal of History* 41 (2007): 149–70.
———. *A Pacific Industry: The History of Pineapple Canning in Hawaii*. New York: I.B. Taurus, 2011.
hoʻomanawanui, kuʻualoha. *Voices of Fire: Reweaving the Literary Lei of Pele and Hiʻiaka*. Minneapolis: University of Minnesota Press, 2014.
Horwitz, Robert H., Judith B. Finn, Louis A. Vargha, and James W. Ceaser. *Public Land Policy in Hawaii: A Historical Analysis*. Honolulu: State of Hawaiʻi Legislative Reference Bureau, 1969.
Howland, Douglas. "Japanese Neutrality in the Nineteenth Century: International Law and Transcultural Process." *Transcultural Studies* 1, no. 1 (2010): 14–37.
———. *Translating the West: Language and Political Reason in Nineteenth-Century Japan*. Honolulu: University of Hawaiʻi Press, 2002.
Hyman, Harold Melvin. *American Singularity : The 1787 Northwest Ordinance, the 1862 Homestead and Morrill Acts, and the 1944 G.I. Bill*. Athens: University of Georgia Press, 1986.
Igler, David. *The Great Ocean: Pacific Worlds from Captain Cook to the Gold Rush*. New York: Oxford University Press, 2013.
Ing, Tiffany Lani. *Reclaiming Kalākaua: Nineteenth-Century Perspectives on a Hawaiian Sovereign*. Honolulu: University of Hawaiʻi Press, 2019.
Iriye, Akira. *Pacific Estrangement: Japanese and American Expansion, 1879–1911*. Cambridge, MA: Harvard University Press, 1972.
Jacobson, Matthew Frye. *Barbarian Virtues: The United States Encounters Foreign Peoples at Home and Abroad, 1876–1917*. New York: Hill and Wang, 2001.
———. *Whiteness of a Different Color: European Immigrants and the Alchemy of Race*. Cambridge, MA: Harvard University Press, 1998.
Jose, Wray Anthony Francisco. "The Manuel Reis Case." *The Hawaiian Journal of History* 16 (January 1982): 134–48.
Jung, Moon-Ho. *Coolies and Cane: Race, Labor, and Sugar in the Age of Emancipation*. Baltimore: Johns Hopkins University Press, 2006.
Jung, Moon-Kie. *Reworking Race: The Making of Hawaiʻi's Interracial Labor Movement*. New York: Columbia University Press, 2006.
Kameʻeleihiwa, Lilikalā. *Native Land and Foreign Desires: Pahea Lā E Pono Ai?* Honolulu: Bishop Museum Press, 1992.

———. *Nā Wāhine Kapu: Divine Hawaiian Women*. Honolulu: 'Ai Pohaku Press, 1992.

Karl, Rebecca E. *Staging the World: Chinese Nationalism at the Turn of the Twentieth Century*. Durham, NC: Duke University Press, 2002.

Karuka, Manu. *Empire's Tracks: Indigenous Nations, Chinese Workers, and the Transcontinental Railroad*. Oakland: University of California Press, 2019.

Kauanui, J. Kēhaulani. *Hawaiian Blood: Colonialism and the Politics of Sovereignty and Indigeneity*. Durham, NC: Duke University Press, 2008.

———. "Native Hawaiian Decolonization and the Politics of Gender." *American Quarterly* 60, no. 2 (2008): 281–87.

———. *Paradoxes of Hawaiian Sovereignty: Land, Sex, and the Colonial Politics of State Nationalism*. Durham, NC: Duke University Press, 2018.

Knight Lozano, Henry. *California and Hawai'i Bound: U.S. Settler Colonialism and the Pacific West, 1848–1959*. Lincoln: University of Nebraska Press, 2021.

Kodama-Nishimoto, Michiko, Warren S. Nishimoto, and Cynthia A. Oshiro, eds. *Talking Hawai'i's Story: Oral Histories of an Island People*. Honolulu: University of Hawai'i Press, 2009.

Kramer, Paul A. *The Blood of Government: Race, Empire, the United States, and the Philippines*. Chapel Hill: University of North Carolina Press, 2006.

Krout, Mary H. *Hawaii and a Revolution: The Personal Experiences of a Newspaper Correspondent in the Sandwich Islands during the Crisis of 1893 and Subsequently*. London: John Murray, 1898.

Kualapai, Lydia. "The Queen Writes Back: Lili'uokalani's *Hawai'i's Story by Hawai'i's Queen*." *Studies in American Indian Literatures* 17, no. 2 (2005): 32–62.

Kurashige, Lon, ed. *Pacific America: Histories of Transoceanic Crossings*. Honolulu: University of Hawai'i Press, 2017.

Kuykendall, Ralph S. *The Hawaiian Kingdom*. Vol. 3, *1874–1893: The Kalākaua Dynasty*. Honolulu: University of Hawai'i Press, 1967.

Labrador, Roderick N. *Building Filipino Hawai'i*. Urbana: University of Illinois Press, 2015.

Lai, Junnan. "Sovereignty and 'Civilization': International Law and East Asia in the Nineteenth Century." *Modern China* 40, no. 3 (2014): 282–314.

Laws of Her Majesty Liliuokalani, Queen of the Hawaiian Islands, Passed by the Legislative Assembly at Its Session, 1892. Honolulu: R. Grieve, Steam Book and Job Printer, 1892.

Lee, Erika. *The Making of Asian America: A History*. New York: Simon and Schuster, 2015.

Lenchanko, Jonah Laʻakapu. "Kūkaniloko: A Hālau of Ākeaakamai of Kāne." PhD diss., University of Hawaiʻi, 2015.

Lew-Williams, Beth. *The Chinese Must Go: Violence, Exclusion, and the Making of the Alien in America*. Cambridge, MA: Harvard University Press, 2018.

Liliʻuokalani. *The Diaries of Queen Liliuokalani of Hawaii 1885–1900*. Edited and annotated by David W. Forbes. Honolulu: Hui Hānai, 2019.

———. *Hawaiʻi's Story by Hawaiʻi's Queen*. Honolulu: Mutual Publishing, 1991.

Lipsitz, George. *The Possessive Investment in Whiteness: How White People Profit from Identity Politics*. Philadelphia: Temple University Press, 1998.

Loomis, Albertine. *For Whom Are the Stars?* Honolulu: University of Hawaiʻi Press, 1976.

Love, Eric Tyrone Lowery. *Race over Empire: Racism and U.S. Imperialism, 1865–1900*. Chapel Hill: University of North Carolina Press, 2004.

Lu, Sidney Xu. *The Making of Japanese Settler Colonialism: Malthusianism and Trans-Pacific Migration, 1868–1961*. Cambridge: Cambridge University Press, 2019.

Lubrecht, Peter T. *Carl Schurz, German-American Statesman: My Country Right or Wrong*. Charleston, SC: Arcadia Publishing, 2019.

Luk, Sharon. *The Life of Paper: Letters and a Poetics of Living Beyond Captivity*. Oakland: University of California Press, 2017.

Lyons, Laura E. "Fantasy Island: From Pineapple Plantation to Tourist Plantation on Lānaʻi." In *Detours: A Decolonial Guide to Hawaiʻi*, edited by Hōkūlani K. Aikau and Vernadette Vicuña Gonzalez, 86–93. Durham, NC: Duke University Press, 2019.

Man, Simeon. *Soldiering through Empire: Race and the Making of the Decolonizing Pacific*. Oakland: University of California Press, 2018.

McDougall, Brandy Nālani. "We Are Not American: Competing Rhetorical Archipelagoes in Hawaiʻi." In *Archipelagic American Studies*, edited by Brian Russell Roberts and Michelle Ann Stephens, 259–80. Durham, NC: Duke University Press, 2017.

Merry, Sally Engle. *Colonizing Hawaiʻi: The Cultural Power of Law*. Princeton, NJ: Princeton University Press, 2000.

Milanovich, Kathrin. *"Naniwa and Takachiho: Elswick-Built Protected Cruisers of the Imperial Japanese Navy."* In *Warship 2004*, edited by Antony Preston, 29–56. London: Conway Maritime Press, 2004.

Minamikawa, Fuminori. "Vernacular Representations of Race and the Making of a Japanese Ethnoracial Community in Los Angeles." In *Trans-Pacific Japanese American Studies*, edited by Yasuko Takezawa and Gary Y. Okihiro, 107–32. Honolulu: University of Hawai'i Press, 2017.

Monobe, Hiromi. "From 'Vanishing Race' to Friendly Ally: Japanese American Perceptions of Native Hawaiians during the Interwar Years." *Japanese Journal of American Studies*, no. 23 (2012): 73–95.

Morgan, William Michael. *Pacific Gibraltar: U.S.-Japanese Rivalry over the Annexation of Hawai'i, 1885–1898*. Annapolis: Naval Institute Press, 2011.

Nedbalek, Lani. *Wahiawa: From Dream to Community*. Mililani: Wonder View Press, 1984.

Nellist, George F., ed. *The Story of Hawaii and its Builders with Which Is Incorporated Volume III Men of Hawaii: An Historical Outline of Hawaii with Biographical Sketches of Men of Note and Substantial Achievement, Past and Present, Who Have Contributed to the Progress of the Territory*. Honolulu: Honolulu Star-Bulletin, 1925.

Ngai, Mae M. *Impossible Subjects: Illegal Aliens and the Making of Modern America*. Princeton, NJ: Princeton University Press, 2005.

Odo, Franklin. *Voices from the Canefields: Folksongs from Japanese Immigrant Workers in Hawai'i*. New York: Oxford University Press, 2013.

Okihiro, Gary Y. *Cane Fires: The Anti-Japanese Movement in Hawai'i, 1865–1945*. Philadelphia: Temple University Press, 1991.

———. *Pineapple Culture: A History of the Tropical and Temperate Zones*. Berkeley: University of California Press, 2009.

Osorio, Jonathan Kay Kamakawiwo'ole. *Dismembering Lāhui: A History of the Hawaiian Nation to 1887*. Honolulu: University of Hawai'i Press, 2002.

Papers Relating to the Annexation of the Hawaiian Islands. Washington, DC: US Government Printing Office, 1893.

Pasternak, Shiri. *Grounded Authority: The Algonquins of Barriere Lake against the State*. Minneapolis: University of Minnesota Press, 2017.

Perkins, Mark 'Umi. "Kuleana: A Genealogy of Native Tenant Rights." PhD diss., University of Hawai'i, 2013.

Pettigrew, Richard Franklin. *The Course of Empire: An Official Record.* New York: Boni and Liveright, 1920.

Pratt, Julius W. *Expansionists of 1898: The Acquisition of Hawaii and the Spanish Islands.* Baltimore: Johns Hopkins Press, 1936.

Proto, Neil Thomas. *The Rights of My People: Liliuokalani's Enduring Battle with the United States, 1893–1917.* New York: Algora Publishing, 2009.

Roberts, Brian Russell, and Michelle Ann Stephens. "Archipelagic American Studies: Decontinentalizing the Study of American Culture." In *Archipelagic American Studies*, edited by Brian Russell Roberts and Michelle Ann Stephens, 1–54. Durham, NC: Duke University Press, 2017.

Roediger, David R. *The Wages of Whiteness: Race and the Making of the American Working Class.* London: Verso, 1991.

Rosaldo, Renato. "Imperialist Nostalgia." *Representations* no. 26 (1989): 107–22.

Rowland, Donald. "Orientals and the Suffrage in Hawaii." *Pacific Historical Review* 12, no. 1 (1943): 11–21.

Russ, William Adam, Jr. *The Hawaiian Revolution, 1893–94.* Selinsgrove: Susquehanna University Press, 1959.

———. *The Hawaiian Republic, 1894–98, and Its Struggle to Win Annexation.* Selinsgrove: Susquehanna University Press, 1961.

Rutter, Frank R. "The Sugar Question in the United States." *The Quarterly Journal of Economics* 17, no.1 (1903): 44–81.

Saranillio, Dean Itsuji. *Unsustainable Empire: Alternative Histories of Hawai'i Statehood.* Durham, NC: Duke University Press, 2018.

Shigematsu, Setsu, and Keith L. Camacho, eds., *Militarized Currents: Toward a Decolonized Future in Asia and the Pacific.* Minneapolis: University of Minnesota Press, 2010.

Silva, Noenoe K. *Aloha Betrayed: Native Hawaiian Resistance to American Colonialism.* Durham, NC: Duke University Press, 2004.

———. "Kanaka Maoli Resistance to Annexation." *Ōiwi: A Native Hawaiian Journal* 1, no.1 (December 1998): 40–75..

Spencer, Thomas P., and Puakea Nogelmeier. Ka hoʻokahuli aupuni kaulana o 1893 : kaua kūloko ma Honolulu, Ianuari 7, 1895: ka hoʻāʻo ʻana e hoʻokahuli i ka Repubalika Hawaiʻi, aupuni hou ko Hawaiʻi Pae ʻĀina: hoʻohiwahiwa ʻia me nā kiʻi. The famous overthrow of 1893: Civil war in Honolulu, January 7,

1895: the attempt to overthrow the Hawaiian government: the new government of the Hawaiian Islands: beautifully illustrated with pictures. Honolulu: Bishop Museum Press, 2000.

Stoler, Ann Laura. "Colonial Archives and the Arts of Governance." *Archival Science* 2, no. 1 (2002): 87–109.

Takaki, Ronald. *Strangers from a Different Shore: A History of Asian Americans.* New York: Little, Brown and Company, 1989.

Tate, Merze. *The United States and the Hawaiian Kingdom.* New Haven, CT: Yale University Press, 1965.

TenBruggencate, Jan K. *Hawai'i's Pineapple Century: A History of the Crowned Fruit in the Hawaiian Islands.* Honolulu: Mutual Publishing, 2004.

Tengan, Ty P. Kāwika. *Native Men Remade: Gender and Nation in Contemporary Hawai'i.* Durham, NC: Duke University Press, 2008.

Teves, Stephanie Nohelani. *Defiant Indigeneity: The Politics of Hawaiian Performance.* Chapel Hill: University of North Carolina Press, 2018.

———. "Princess Ka'iulani Haunts Empire in Waikīkī." In *Detours: A Decolonial Guide to Hawai'i*, edited by Hōkūlani K. Aikau and Vernadette Vicuña Gonzalez, 67–76. Durham, NC: Duke University Press, 2020.

Thrum, Thomas G., ed. *Hawaiian Almanac and Annual for 1894.* Honolulu: T. G. Thrum, 1894.

———, ed. *Hawaiian Almanac and Annual for 1896.* Honolulu: Black and Auld, 1896.

Thurston, Lorrin A. *A Hand-Book on the Annexation of Hawaii.* Saint Joseph: A. B. Morse, 1897.

———. *Memoirs of the Hawaiian Revolution.* Honolulu: Honolulu Advertiser Publishing, 1936.

Treaties and Conventions of the Hawaiian Kingdom. Honolulu: Pae 'Āina Productions, 2005.

Uchida, Jun. *Brokers of Empire: Japanese Settler Colonialism in Korea, 1876–1945.* Cambridge, MA: Harvard University Asia Center, 2011.

Van Dyke, Jon M. *Who Owns the Crown Lands of Hawai'i?* Honolulu: University of Hawai'i Press, 2007.

Warren, Joyce Pualani. "Reading Bodies, Writing Blackness: Anti-/Blackness and Nineteenth-Century Kanaka Maoli Literary Nationalism." *American Indian Culture and Research Journal* 43, no. 2 (2019): 49–72.

Warrior, Robert Allen. *Tribal Secrets: Recovering American Indian Intellectual Traditions*. Minneapolis: University of Minnesota Press, 1994.

Williams, Ronald, Jr. "Incarcerating a Nation: The Arrest and Imprisonment of Political Prisoners by the Republic of Hawai'i, 1895." *Hawaiian Journal of History* 55, no. 1 (2021): 167–76.

Index

Ackerman, John Douglas, 215n56
Akiyama, Masanosuke, 124, 128
Americanness, 135–36
annexation of Hawai'i, 1–3, 10–11, 19–20, 142; advocacy for, 31–37, 39, 80, 178n55, 183n20; Americanness and, 136; anti-Japanese rhetoric and, 30, 37–38, 124–25; Kānaka Maoli resistance to, 129; land policy and, 22, 179n60; Meiji objection to, 127, 129; Morgan Report and, 60; pineapple industry and, 148; race and, 31–32, 65–66, 79, 113, 132–33; racism and, 53; Reis indemnity case and, 100–101; *Shinshu Maru* affair and, 122; treaty of, 33–34, 127, 129–30, 179n56, 184n25, 208n57, 213n44; Yellow Peril and, 125
Arista, Noelani, 176n33
Armstrong, William N., 67–72, 194n47
Arvin, Maile, 198n9

Asian American studies: anti-imperial perspective of, 172n8
Asians: citizenship of, 16, 213n37; disenfranchisement of, 69–70, 85; enfranchisement of, 66; incorporation of, 31; naturalization of, 66–71, 132; suffrage of, 16
aupuni system, 12, 176n35
Azuma, Eiichiro, 42, 46

Basham, Leilani, 176n35
Bayonet Constitution (1887), 60, 171n1, 187n66–67, 211n26; Asian disenfranchisement, 85; penal code, 190n14; racial difference and, 16–17, 178n49, 196n67; suffrage under, 96, 196n67
Beamer, Kamanamaikalani, 176n33, 177n42
Beechert, Edward, 155
Bertelmann, Henry, 92

235

Bishop, Sereno, 58
blood quantum, 172n5, 175n24
Blount, James, 28–29, 34–37
Blount Report, 58–60
Bogle, Paul, 202n54
Boyd, E. S., 147, 154
Brown, J. F., 141–42
Bush, John Ailuene, 91

Canavarro, Antonio de Souza, 85, 92–93, 96, 100–101
capitalism: occupation of Hawaiʻi and, 4–5; nation-state and, 5–6, 165; racial, 7, 111, 165; worker exploitation under, 4
Carlos I, 88–89
Carter, George R., 102
Castle, William R., 178n53, 183n20
Chinese: citizenship of, 69, 132–33; disenfranchisement of, 64; exclusion, 67, 87, 113, 118, 129, 183n17, 183n22, 194n6, 209n2; under Hawaiian Kingdom, 68; labor, 68, 87, 113, 138, 183n17, 202n60, 206n19, 209n6; migration, 205n15; naturalization of, 66, 69; suffrage of, 68, 74, 187n66; violence against, 194n46
citizenship, 132; of Asians, 16, 213n37; of Chinese, 69, 132–33; Issei, 40; of Japanese, 66, 70; land ownership and, 71–72; and Meiji empire, 40–41, 166; Portuguese, 199n17; race-based, 26, 43; suffrage and, 66–67; Wahiawa Settlement Association and, 154
citizenship, Hawaiian, 172n5, 176n38; denizens, 13, 140, 212n33, 213n37; 1887 Constitution and, 16–17; in Hawaiian Kingdom, 13–14, 16–17; of Kānaka Maoli, 32; language requirement, 70–71, 195n57, 213n37; in Republic of Hawaiʻi, 64, 66–71, 195n57, 212n33; US citizenship, 32
Clark, Byron Orlando, 22, 141–47, 153–54, 169, 213n41, 214n45
Clark, Mary H., 214n46
Cleghorn, Archibald Scott, 61
Cleveland, Grover, 29, 33–36, 185n41; opposition to coup, 34, 55, 57–58, 60, 78, 190n12; support of monarchy, 191n23
colonialism: in Hawaiʻi, 5, 13; Portuguese, 93; racism and, 133; worker exploitation under, 4. *See also* settler colonialism
colonialism, US: Hawaiʻi and, 5, 13; subjugation of Kānaka Maoli and Asians, 7. *See also* settler colonialism
colonization: decolonization, 11; erasure and, 24; of Hokkaido, 40, 181n7; Meiji, 40, 107, 110, 124, 128, 181n7
Committee of Thirteen (Hawaiian League), 16, 17, 177n48, 178n53
confluence, 9, 11, 83, 103, 165
contract labor, 45, 187n67, 205n10–13; Japanese, 112–14, 153; Portuguese, 85; Yellow Peril and, 125. *See also* labor
Cooper, Henry, 119, 122, 202n54, 207n41; Reis indemnity case and, 96–97, 100–101, 116
countersovereignty, 3, 55, 62, 110–11, 172n7; Kānaka Maoli and, 71; limits of, 69, 76, 78

Davies, Theo, 62, 199n22
Day, William R., 126, 127

decolonization: nonstatist approaches to, 11
Deloria, Vine, Jr., 174n13
de Tocqueville, Alexis, 150–51
diaspora, 9
Dillingham, Walter F., 148
disenfranchisement: of Asians, 69–70, 85; of Chinese, 64; of Japanese, 64; of Kānaka Maoli, 71–72
dispossession, 7, 11; of Kānaka Maoli, 140–41
Dole, James D., 147–49, 155, 169, 214n46, 216n63
Dole, Sanford B.: *Ahlo v. Smith* decision, 17; annexation efforts of, 43; biography, 180n4; Blount report, reaction to, 58–60; Committee of Thirteen membership, 178n53; counter-revolution, response to, 92–93; homesteading plan, 22, 79, 133–40, 142, 155, 162; *Naniwa* incident and, 26; participation in coup, 16, 211n28; Portuguese labor recruitment, 81; presidency of, 1–2, 26, 69, 136; Reis indemnity case and, 102; Republic of Hawai'i, founding of, 62–63, 65
Dole Food Company, 216n63
Domai, Yasuko, 160
Duara, Prasenjit, 173n11
Dudden, Alexis, 110, 165

ea, 12–13, 23
Eames, A. W., 136, 145, 148, 155, 215n46; Hawaiian Islands Packing Company, 158, 216n68
Eldridge, Stuart, 122

Ellison, Larry, 168–70
emigration: Meiji empire and, 10
emigration, Japanese: 25, 27*fig.*, 45, 47, 98, 114, 120–22, 207n32; emigrant protection laws, 120–21
emigration, Portuguese, 2–3, 83–86, 88, 96–97, 100, 105, 198n15, 206n19
Emigration Convention of 1886, 4, 187n67
Emmeluth, John, 146, 215n57
empire: nation-state and, 5–6, 8–9; race and, 82; white supremacy and, 21, 84
empire, British, 61
empire, Portuguese, 88, 90, 200n28
empire, US, 8; expansion and, 3–4; Hawaiian coup state and, 3–4; in the Pacific, 18
enfranchisement: of Asians, 66; of women, 66, 72–73. *See also* disenfranchisement
erasure: colonization and, 24; of dissent, 4; of Japanese labor, 135; settler colonialism and, 162
Espiritu, Augusto, 172n8
exclusion: Asian, 31; Chinese, 67, 87, 113, 118, 129, 183n17, 183n22, 194n6, 209n2
Expedition Society (Enseisha), 30, 41, 182n12

Foster, John W., 33–34, 37, 138, 184n25
Freedom and Popular Rights movement, 182n12
Fujii, Saburo, 26, 37, 43, 46, 187n63
Fujikane, Candace, 162
Fujitani, Takashi, 40
Fukuzawa, Yukichi, 45
Furuya, K., 117–19

INDEX 237

gender: in precolonial Hawai'i, 54; women's suffrage and, 72–73
Gibson, Walter Murray, 168–69, 221n11
Glade, Henry F., 89, 178n53
Gonschor, Lorenz, 13
Goodyear-Ka'ōpua, Noelani, 12, 167, 170, 176n35
Government and Crown Lands, 23, 32, 79, 134–35, 137, 179n60, 211n21; as "public lands," 22, 133, 139–40, 209n8, 212n32; white settlement of, 138
Gresham, Walter Quintin, 58, 190n12
Grimshaw, Patricia, 75, 196n68
Guiala, Venicia Damasco, 158

Haalelea, Levi, 168, 221n11
Harrison, Benjamin, 33–34
Hatch, Francis M., 86–87, 121, 127
Hau'ofa, Epeli, 9
Hawai'i: colonialism and, 13; demographics of, 80, 197n1, 133–36, 209n2; empire building in, 5; imperialism and, 4–5; independence of, 5, 10, 171n2; interimperial dynamics in, 4–5, 23, 27, 29, 44, 48, 120, 128–30, 166–67; as Japanese space, 44; land ownership in, 177n41; "local" identity, 161–62; modernity and, 29; nationalism and, 23; occupation of, 4–5; settler colonialism and, 4–5, 19, 23, 26. *See also* annexation of Hawai'i; Hawaiian Kingdom; Republic of Hawai'i
Hawaiian Fruit and Packing Company, 146
Hawaiian Fruit and Plant Company, 144
Hawaiian Islands Packing Company, 158, 216n68

Hawaiian Kingdom, 3; attempted takeovers of, 179n57; Chinese exclusion under, 87, 118, 129, 183n17, 183n22, 209n2; citizenship and naturalization under, 13–14, 16–17; Constitution of 1840, 176n34, 177n39, 178n49; Constitution of 1864, 14, 177n44, 182n10; first constitution, 13; governance of, 13, 176n33–34, 177n39; international relations of, 192n27; international support for, 61; Japan, diplomatic relations with, 108, 124; Japan, treaty rights with, 127–28; overthrow of, 8; political independence of, 15; reciprocity debate, 31, 133; recognition of, 13; renouncing of extraterritoriality in Japan, 108, 204n3; restoration movement, 28, 33, 35, 42–43; state-based sovereignty of, 129; suffrage under, 196n67; US, diplomatic relations with, 51, 133; women's political power, 72–73; women's suffrage in, 72. *See also* Hawai'i
Hawaiian League (Committee of Thirteen), 16, 17, 32, 177n48, 178n53
Hawaiian National Band, 36
Hawaiian Patriotic Leagues, 129, 164, 178n52; constitutional convention protests, 75–76; restoration, calls for, 17, 28–29, 182n10
Hawaiian Pineapple Company (HAPCO), 148, 155–57, 157*fig*., 216n61, 216n68
Hay, John, 101–2
Hitchcock, Ernest G., 89, 95–96, 101
Hokkaido: colonization of, 40, 107, 181n7
Holloway, T. L., 214n46
Holomua, 64, 78

hoʻomanawanui, kuʻualoha, 35
Hoshi, Tōru, 45, 127–28, 188n77
Howland, Douglas, 41
Hui Aloha ʻĀina, 17, 28*fig.*, 35–36, 92, 200n32; annexation opposition, 163–64, 208n57
Hui Aloha ʻĀina o Nā Wāhine, 17, 28, 29*fig.*, 36, 63–64, 181n; annexation opposition, 208n57; constitutional convention protests, 72; independence advocacy of, 76–77
Hui Kālaiʻāina (Hawaiian Political Association), 17, 28, 36, 182n10

Imada, Yosaku, 18–19, 25–26, 36–39, 43, 46–49; escape of, 18–19, 30–31, 34; legal strategy of, 83, 95–96
Imada incident, 18–19, 34–39, 43, 46–49, 60, 107
immigration: Act 17, 114, 115; Japanese, 107; sugar industry and, 137
immigration law, US, 30, 52; Chinese Exclusion Act, 67, 87, 113, 183n17, 194n46; Immigration Act of 1924, 156–57; Page Act, 194n46
imperialism: Hawaiʻi and, 4–5; imperial nostalgia, 168; interimperial dynamics in Hawaiʻi, 4–5, 23, 27, 29, 44, 48, 120, 128–30, 166–67; settler colonialism and, 4; white racial limitations, 150–53
imperialism, Japanese, 29, 181n7, 186n53
imperialism, US, 29; white supremacy and, 11
independence: advocacy for, 63–64, 76–77; of Hawaiʻi, 10, 15, 171n2; of Kānaka Maoli, 5, 12, 23, 110; Tyler Doctrine, 176n36

Irwin, Robert Walker, 45, 112, 188n73, 205n12
Ishikawa, Robert, 159–60
Issei: citizenship and, 40; farmers, 156; in Hawaiʻi, 6; labor, 38–40, 45, 185n49, 188n73; Meiji state and, 27; migration to Hawaiʻi, 27, 186n56; naturalization of, 205n11; response to *Shinshu Maru* affair, 116–19; restoration, advocacy for, 42–43; settler colonial claims of, 109–10; suffrage of, 19, 26, 30, 41–45, 47–48, 187n65
Itō, Hirobumi, 108
Iwatani, Kame, 156, 218n101
Iwatani, Kumeiji, 156

Japanese: citizenship of, 66, 70; contract labor, 112–14, 153; disenfranchisement of, 64; immigration of, 107. *See also* emigration, Japanese; Issei
Japanese Alliance (Nihonjin Dōmei), 44
Japanese Patriotic League (Sōkō Nihonjin Aikoku Dōmei), 30, 42, 44, 182n12
Johansen, C. W., 96–97, 101
Jose, Wray, 102–3
Jung, Moon-Kie, 82, 199n17

Kaʻiulani, 37, 184n26; attempted bribing of, 62, 193n32; opposition to Republic, 63; restoration efforts of, 61–62
Kajioka, Sue Shizuyo, 158–59, 219n107
Kalākaua, David, 15*fig.*, 15–17, 38, 178n55, 184n26, 188n73, 194n47
Kameʻeleihiwa, Lilikalā, 177n42, 195n61
Kamehameha I, 12, 174n21
Kamehameha III (Kauikeaouli), 13, 176n35, 179n60, 185n37, 192n27

Kamehameha V, 22, 111
Kamokuʻākulikuli (Quarantine Island), 25, 106, 109*fig.*, 115, 117, 130*fig.*, 180n1
Kānaka Maoli (Native Hawaiians): annexation, resistance to, 129, 163–64, 208n57; assimilation of, 80; citizenship of, 32; counterrevolution of, 1–2; countersovereignty and, 71; disenfranchisement of, 71–72; dispossession of, 140–41; enfranchisement of, 66; incorporation of, 31; independence claims of, 110; nationhood, concept of, 11–12, 165; political independence of, 5, 12, 23; restoration activism of, 28; sovereignty of, 44; state-based sovereignty claims of, 21–22, 27, 30, 35, 41, 48–50, 111; use of term, 172n5; whiteness and, 80
Karuka, Manu, 54–55, 134, 172n7
Kaua Kūloko, 1, 20–21, 83, 91–97, 102–5, 172n4, 200n35
Kauanui, J. Kēhaulani, 73, 175n24
Kauikeaouli (Kamehameha III), 13, 176n35, 179n60, 185n37, 192n27
Kaulia, James Keauiluna, 163
Kaumualiʻi, 179n57
Kawānanakoa, David, 33, 184n26
Kellogg, Leonard G., 147, 214n46
Kidwell, John, 146
Komite o ka Lehulehu (Citizens Committee), 163–64
Kramer, Paul, 82
Kumu Kānāwai, 176n34

labor: Asian, 33, 53, 153, 156, 198n13; Chinese, 68, 87, 113, 138, 183n17, 202n60, 206n19, 209n6; colonial exploitation of, 4; Filipino, 161; pineapple industry and, 155–61, 169–70; sugar industry and, 155–56, 157. *See also* contract labor
labor, Issei, 38–39, 185n49, 188n73; Emigration Convention, 45
labor, Japanese, 86–87, 97–100, 107, 138, 153, 166, 202n60, 206n19; erasure of, 135
labor, Portuguese, 81–82, 84, 89, 96, 114, 206n19
Lā hoʻihoʻi Ea (Sovereignty Restoration Day), 192n27
lāhui, 12, 36
Lānaʻi Island, 167–70
land: 1848 Māhele, 14, 137, 140, 211n21; sovereignty and, 176n35
Land Act of 1895, 22, 139–40, 144; settlement association provision, 140–41
land ownership, 14; annexation and, 22, 179n60; citizenship and, 71–72; of Government and Crown Lands, 134–35, 137; in Hawaiʻi, 177n41; of Lānaʻi Island, 167–70; suffrage and, 12
land policy: coup and, 137–38; Homestead Act of 1884, 137–39, 211n26; Land Act of 1895, 22, 139–40, 144, 211n28, 212n36; of Sanford Dole, 22; sugar industry and, 137–38
Liberal Party (Jiyū-tō), 30, 45, 182n12, 188n77
Likelike, 61
Liliʻuokalani, 1–2, 56*fig.*, 184n25; arrest of, 92, 200n35; attempted bribing of, 62, 193n32; independence advocacy of, 76–77; opposition to Republic, 63; overthrow of, 17; protest of coup, 44, 75–76, 164, 191n23, 200n35; racist

caricatures of, 53, 57–58, 59*fig.*, 76; restoration efforts of, 17–18, 28, 33–35, 48, 55, 58, 62, 77, 190n12; sovereignty claims of, 10, 48. *See also* Hawaiian Kingdom
Linnekin, Jocelyn, 177n42
Love, Eric T. L., 33, 150
Lozano, Henry Knight, 210n15
Lyons, Laura E., 168

Machado, Carlos Cirilo, 101
Māhele (1848), 14, 137, 140, 179n60, 211n21
makaʻāinana, 12–14
Manifest Destiny, 151–52
Marin, Francisco de Paula, 145
McKinley, William, 106, 126, 164
McKinley Tariff of 1891, 17, 33, 113, 178n54
Meiji empire, 8, 21, 31, 119–20; annexation, objections to, 127, 129; citizenship and, 40–41, 166; colonization of Hokkaido, 40, 107, 181n7; emigration and, 10; expansionism of, 112; Hawaiian coup, response to, 199n22; informal colonization practice, 110, 124, 128; international law, appeals to, 110–11, 115, 120–21, 123–24, 204n6; Issei and, 27; modernity and, 40, 110, 120, 186n53; state-based sovereignty of, 111; suffrage and, 70, 181n6
migration: Asian, 67; Chinese, 205n15; Japanese, 21, 27, 105, 185n49, 186n56; Portuguese, 21, 198n134
Minamikawa, Fuminori, 206n27
modernity: Hawaiʻi and, 29; Meiji state and, 40, 110, 120, 186n53; Western, 128–29
Montalbo, Josephine, 160

Morant Bay Rebellion, 97, 202n54
Morgan, John Tyler, 163
Morgan Report, 42, 60
Murdock, David, 168–70
Mutsu, Munemitsu, 45, 113, 188n74, 188n77

Nagasawa, Betten, 41
Nahaolelua, Paul, 168
Naniwa (ship), 39*fig.*, 180n2; in *Shinshu Maru* affair, 124–27. *See also* Imada incident
National American Woman Suffrage Association, 73
nationalism: ethnic, 206n27; in Hawaiʻi, 23; race-based, 18, 20, 105, 108; *Shinshu Maru* affair and, 118
nation-building: as empire building, 6
nationhood: Japanese, 120; Kānaka Maoli concept of, 11–12, 165; Western, 35
nation-state: capitalism and, 5–6, 165; definitions of, 173n11; empire and, 5–6, 8–9; as narrative, 170; race and, 10, 132, 165; settler colonialism and, 6–7, 164; sovereignty and, 10, 164; violence of, 167; white supremacy and, 165
Native Hawaiians: federal definition of, 175n24. *See also* Kānaka Maoli (Native Hawaiians)
naturalization: of Asians, 66–71, 132; of Chinese, 66, 69; Issei, 205n11; in Republic of Hawaiʻi, 195n57
naturalization, US: 1790 Naturalization Act, 132
Nāwahī, Emma ʻAʻima Aʻii, 28, 181n9
Nāwahī, Joseph Kahoʻoluhi, 28, 91, 181n9, 200n32
Neumann, Paul, 33, 86, 95, 199n20

Ngai, Mae, 12
Norwood, Thomas, 52–53
Nouchi, Liiko, 160, 219n112
Nowlein, Samuel, 91–92

Oceania, 9, 23
Okihiro, Gary, 161
Ōkuma, Shigenobu, 21–22, 111, 123–24, 127–28, 207n41
Osorio, Jonathan Kay Kamakawiwoʻole, 12, 174n24, 175n27

Pacific, the, 3, 7
Pacific Commercial Advertiser (PCA): annexation, advocacy for, 99; anti-Japanese sentiment in, 46–47, 98–100; *Naniwa* incident reporting, 37–38
Pasternak, Shiri, 49
patriarchy, 72
Paulet, George, 192n27
Pele and Hiʻiaka moʻolelo, 35–36, 185n36
Perkins, Mark ʻUmi, 177n42
Pettigrew, Richard, 81, 179n57
Pilipō, George Washington, 215n56
pineapple industry, 145–48, 214n53, 215n54–55; annexation and, 148; canning, 145–46, 147–48, 158–59, 159fig., 215n56–57; labor camps, 159–60; labor needs, 155–61; settler colonialism and, 136, 146; in Wahiawā, 22–23; in Wahiawa Colony, 146–48, 155–61
Planters' Labor and Supply Company (PL&S), 86–87, 89, 199n23
poʻe aloha ʻāina, 6; appeals to international law, 28, 35–36; constitutional convention protests, 72; independence efforts of, 63–64, 76–77; nation-state making, 164–65; sovereignty claims of, 10, 28
pono, 12, 175n27
Portuguese: citizenship of, 199n17; contract labor, 85; emigration of, 2–3, 83–86, 88, 96–97, 100, 105, 198n15, 206n19; enfranchisement of, 20; labor, 81–82, 84, 89, 96, 114, 206n19; loyalty oath and, 64; migration of, 21, 198n13; racialization of, 20–21, 80–82, 84, 104, 133; suffrage of, 85; whiteness and, 20–21, 80–82, 84, 99, 104–5, 133, 179n58

Quarantine Island (Kamokuʻākulikuli), 25, 106, 109fig., 115, 117, 130fig., 180n1

race, 132; annexation of Hawaiʻi and, 31–32, 65–66, 79, 113, 132–33; Bayonet Constitution and, 16–17, 178n49, 196n67; capitalism and, 7, 111, 165; citizenship and, 26, 43; 1887 Constitution and, 16–17; empire and, 82; nationalism and, 20; nation-state and, 10, 132, 165; as social fact, 82; suffrage and, 43, 47
racialization: Asian, 119; Asian American, 135; of Portuguese, 20–21, 80–82, 84, 104, 133
racism: anti-Asian, 51, 58, 133, 183n17; annexation and, 53; anti-Black, 51–53, 57–58, 133, 191n16; anti-Japanese, 30, 37–38, 124–25; blackening of Liliʻuokalani, 53, 57–58, 59fig., 76; colonialism and, 133; 1875 Reciprocity Treaty and, 51–53; Republic of Hawaiʻi and, 65; Yellow Peril, 108, 204n2
Reciprocity Treaty (1875), 39, 178n54, 182n15, 189n3; racism in, 51–53

242 INDEX

Reis, Eugenia Keohookalani Pilipo, 94*fig.*, 94–95, 104
Reis, Manuel (Manoel Gil dos Reis), 2, 93–97, 94*fig.*, 166, 169; financial success of, 93–94, 103–4, 201n42; indemnity case, 2, 4, 5, 21, 83, 95–97, 101–5, 172n6, 202n50
Renshaw, John B., 135
Republic of Hawai'i, 1–2, 18; citizenship in, 64, 66–71, 195n57, 212n33; constitutional convention, 54, 62–78, 169, 193n40; declaration of, 19–20; democracy, appearance of, 62–63, 65–66, 68, 76; demographics of, 80, 197n1; 1895 counterrevolution, 1–2, 21, 184n26; Issei suffrage and, 48; land seizure, 179n60; loyalty oath, 64; naturalization qualifications, 195n57; racism and, 65; recognition of, 78, 86; suffrage under, 71, 78, 187n66; voter registration, 64–65, 193n40; white supremacy and, 67–68, 109, 111
Rhodes, Cecil, 88
Robinson, James, 141
Roosevelt, Theodore, 126
Royal Hawaiian Band, 36, 185n37
Russ, William, Jr., 71–72

Sai, David Keanu, 177n42, 196n67
Saranillio, Dean Itsuji, 8
Schurz, Carl, 151–52, 217n82
Second Anglo-Boer War, 102, 203n68
Seikyōsha (Association of Politics and Education), 30, 41, 182n12
settler colonialism: Asian, 162; Chinese, 162, 177n44; erasure and, 162; in Hawai'i, 4–5, 19, 23, 26; imperialism and, 4; Issei claims of, 109–10; nation-state and, 6–7, 164; pineapple cultivation and, 22; pineapple industry and, 136, 146; whiteness and, 198n9; white supremacy and, 82, 134, 168–70
settler colonialism, Japanese, 6, 40–43, 118, 162
Shaffer, George Anton, 179n57
Sheridan, Sol N., 153
Sherman, John, 207n41
Shimamura, Hisashi, 119, 123–25, 207n41
Shinshu Maru affair, 106–12, 111–19, 166, 204n1; annexation and, 122; inter-imperial dynamics of, 120; Issei response to, 116–19; nationalism and, 118
Silva, Noenoe K., 57, 76, 164, 200n33
Smith, W. O., 62, 92, 193n32
sovereignty: countersovereignty, 3, 55, 62, 69, 76, 78, 110–11, 172n7; of coup government, 60; ea, 12–13; freedom and, 6; Hawaiian, 4–5; jurisdiction and, 49; Kānaka Maoli claims to, 21–22, 27, 30, 35, 41, 44, 48–50, 111; land and, 176n35; nation-state and, 10, 164; settler sovereignty, 54–55, 172n7; state-based, 18, 21–23, 27, 30, 35, 41, 48–50, 111, 129, 164–65
Stauffer, Robert H., 177n42
Stevens, John L.: Americanization of Hawai'i, 138; coup participation of, 17, 55, 60, 191n23; support for annexation, 31–32, 36–37, 39, 178n55
suffrage: of Asians, 16; under Bayonet Constitution, 96, 196n67; Chinese, 68, 74, 187n66; citizenship and, 66–67; Hawaiian, 14, 17, 26; under Hawaiian Kingdom, 17, 196n67; Issei, 19, 26, 30,

suffrage (continued)
41–45, 47–48, 187n65; Japanese, 74, 166; land ownership and, 12; Meiji government and, 70, 181n6; Portuguese, 74, 85; race and, 43, 47, 74; Republic of Hawai'i and, 71, 78, 187n66

suffrage, women's, 53–54, 72–75; gender and, 72–73; in Hawai'i, 196n74; in Republic of Hawai'i, 72; white supremacy and, 72

sugar industry, 51, 168; 1875 Reciprocity Treaty, 51; immigration policy and, 137; labor needs, 155–56, 157; land policy and, 137–38; McKinley Tariff, 17, 33, 113, 178n54; in US, 52, 189n3

Taniguchi, Yone, 158, 219n105
Tengan, Ty, 177n42
Teves, Stephanie Nohelani, 58
Thomas, Richard, 192n27
Thomas, W. B., 150, 214n46
Thurston, Lorrin A., 20–21, 61–63, 125, 127; advocacy for annexation, 32–34, 80, 183n20; Committee of Thirteen membership, 178n53; coup participation, 16, 197n2; labor recruiting of, 79–81, 86–91, 98, 100, 104–5; Mississippi Plan, 70; Portuguese, racialization of, 133
Tōgō, Heihachirō, 180n2
Tracy, B. F., 32
transpacific order, 10–11, 84, 111, 123, 165, 174n23; US-led, 16
transpacific studies: oceanic turn, 9–10
Treaty of Amity and Commerce, 21, 43, 110, 123
Treaty of Shimonoseki, 107

Tropic Fruit Company, 147, 216n61
Tsugawara, Tsutau, 42

Uchida, Jun, 119
Uniao Portugueza, 98–100

Van Dyke, Jon, 85
violence: anti-Chinese, 194n46; of nation-state, 167; state, 23, 134, 137; structural, 7
Vivas, J. M., 70–71, 193n41

Wahiawā, 133–34, 209n9; pineapple cultivation in, 22–23
Wahiawa Colony, 22–23, 133–36, 140, 169–70, 210n10–12; founding of, 142–45; pineapple cultivation in, 22–23, 146–48; as "pioneers," 134, 141, 149–50, 160–62; promotion of, 149–50; white racial limitations and, 150–53; as white settlement, 152–54; white supremacy and, 162
Wahiawa Settlement Association, 143, 214n45, 216n61; citizenship and, 154; race restrictions, 153–54
Warren, Joyce Pualani, 191n16
Warrior, Robert Allen, 6, 174n13
whiteness, 82, 119; Americanness and, 136; imperialism and, 150–53; Kānaka Maoli and, 80; of Portuguese, 20–21, 80–82, 84, 99, 104–5, 133, 179n58; settler colonialism and, 198n9
white supremacy: coup government and, 2; 1875 Reciprocity Treaty and, 52; empire and, 21, 84; nation-state and, 165; Republic of Hawai'i and, 67–68, 109, 111; settler colonialism and, 82; US

imperialism and, 11; Wahiawa Colony and, 162; women's suffrage and, 72
Wilcox, George N., 178n53
Wilcox, Robert William Kalanihiapo, 1, 91–92, 171n1–2
Wilhelm II, 204n2
Wilkes, Charles, 145
Willis, Albert, 55, 77, 190n12

Wodehouse, James, 37, 61
Women's Christian Temperance Union (WCTU), 74, 196n68
Wood, Edgar, 214n46

Yellow Peril, 108, 112, 204n2; annexation and, 125; contract labor and, 125
Young, Lucien, 42

AMERICAN CROSSROADS

Edited by Earl Lewis, George Lipsitz, George Sánchez, Dana Takagi, Laura Briggs, and Nikhil Pal Singh

1. *Border Matters: Remapping American Cultural Studies,* by José David Saldívar
2. *The White Scourge: Mexicans, Blacks, and Poor Whites in Texas Cotton Culture,* by Neil Foley
3. *Indians in the Making: Ethnic Relations and Indian Identities around Puget Sound,* by Alexandra Harmon
4. *Aztlán and Viet Nam: Chicano and Chicana Experiences of the War,* edited by George Mariscal
5. *Immigration and the Political Economy of Home: West Indian Brooklyn and American Indian Minneapolis, 1945–1992,* by Rachel Buff
6. *Epic Encounters: Culture, Media, and U.S. Interests in the Middle East since 1945,* by Melani McAlister
7. *Contagious Divides: Epidemics and Race in San Francisco's Chinatown,* by Nayan Shah
8. *Japanese American Celebration and Conflict: A History of Ethnic Identity and Festival, 1934–1990,* by Lon Kurashige
9. *American Sensations: Class, Empire, and the Production of Popular Culture,* by Shelley Streeby
10. *Colored White: Transcending the Racial Past,* by David R. Roediger
11. *Reproducing Empire: Race, Sex, Science, and U.S. Imperialism in Puerto Rico,* by Laura Briggs
12. *meXicana Encounters: The Making of Social Identities on the Borderlands,* by Rosa Linda Fregoso
13. *Popular Culture in the Age of White Flight: Fear and Fantasy in Suburban Los Angeles,* by Eric Avila
14. *Ties That Bind: The Story of an Afro-Cherokee Family in Slavery and Freedom,* by Tiya Miles
15. *Cultural Moves: African Americans and the Politics of Representation,* by Herman S. Gray
16. *Emancipation Betrayed: The Hidden History of Black Organizing and White Violence in Florida from Reconstruction to the Bloody Election of 1920,* by Paul Ortiz
17. *Eugenic Nation: Faults and Frontiers of Better Breeding in Modern America,* by Alexandra Stern
18. *Audiotopia: Music, Race, and America,* by Josh Kun

19. *Black, Brown, Yellow, and Left: Radical Activism in Los Angeles,* by Laura Pulido
20. *Fit to Be Citizens? Public Health and Race in Los Angeles, 1879–1939,* by Natalia Molina
21. *Golden Gulag: Prisons, Surplus, Crisis, and Opposition in Globalizing California,* by Ruth Wilson Gilmore
22. *Proud to Be an Okie: Cultural Politics, Country Music, and Migration to Southern California,* by Peter La Chapelle
23. *Playing America's Game: Baseball, Latinos, and the Color Line,* by Adrian Burgos, Jr.
24. *The Power of the Zoot: Youth Culture and Resistance during World War II,* by Luis Alvarez
25. *Guantánamo: A Working-Class History between Empire and Revolution,* by Jana K. Lipman
26. *Between Arab and White: Race and Ethnicity in the Early Syrian-American Diaspora,* by Sarah M. A. Gualtieri
27. *Mean Streets: Chicago Youths and the Everyday Struggle for Empowerment in the Multiracial City, 1908–1969,* by Andrew J. Diamond
28. *In Sight of America: Photography and the Development of U.S. Immigration Policy,* by Anna Pegler-Gordon
29. *Migra! A History of the U.S. Border Patrol,* by Kelly Lytle Hernández
30. *Racial Propositions: Ballot Initiatives and the Making of Postwar California,* by Daniel Martinez HoSang
31. *Stranger Intimacy: Contesting Race, Sexuality, and the Law in the North American West,* by Nayan Shah
32. *The Nicest Kids in Town: American Bandstand, Rock 'n' Roll, and the Struggle for Civil Rights in 1950s Philadelphia,* by Matthew F. Delmont
33. *Jack Johnson, Rebel Sojourner: Boxing in the Shadow of the Global Color Line,* by Theresa Rundstedler
34. *Pacific Connections: The Making of the US-Canadian Borderlands,* by Kornel Chang
35. *States of Delinquency: Race and Science in the Making of California's Juvenile Justice System,* by Miroslava Chávez-García
36. *Spaces of Conflict, Sounds of Solidarity: Music, Race, and Spatial Entitlement in Los Angeles,* by Gaye Theresa Johnson
37. *Covert Capital: Landscapes of Denial and the Making of U.S. Empire in the Suburbs of Northern Virginia,* by Andrew Friedman
38. *How Race Is Made in America: Immigration, Citizenship, and the Historical Power of Racial Scripts,* by Natalia Molina

39. *We Sell Drugs: The Alchemy of US Empire,* by Suzanna Reiss
40. *Abrazando el Espíritu: Bracero Families Confront the US-Mexico Border,* by Ana Elizabeth Rosas
41. *Houston Bound: Culture and Color in a Jim Crow City,* by Tyina L. Steptoe
42. *Why Busing Failed: Race, Media, and the National Resistance to School Desegregation,* by Matthew F. Delmont
43. *Incarcerating the Crisis: Freedom Struggles and the Rise of the Neoliberal State,* by Jordan T. Camp
44. *Lavender and Red: Liberation and Solidarity in the Gay and Lesbian Left,* by Emily K. Hobson
45. *Flavors of Empire: Food and the Making of Thai America,* by Mark Padoongpatt
46. *The Life of Paper: Letters and a Poetics of Living Beyond Captivity,* by Sharon Luk
47. *Strategies of Segregation: Race, Residence, and the Struggle for Educational Equality,* by David G. García
48. *Soldiering through Empire: Race and the Making of the Decolonizing Pacific,* by Simeon Man
49. *An American Language: The History of Spanish in the United States,* by Rosina Lozano
50. *The Color Line and the Assembly Line: Managing Race in the Ford Empire,* by Elizabeth D. Esch
51. *Confessions of a Radical Chicano Doo-Wop Singer,* by Rubén Funkahuatl Guevara
52. *Empire's Tracks: Indigenous Peoples, Racial Aliens, and the Transcontinental Railroad,* by Manu Karuka
53. *Collisions at the Crossroads: How Place and Mobility Make Race,* by Genevieve Carpio
54. *Charros: How Mexican Cowboys are Remapping Race and American Identity,* by Laura R. Barraclough
55. *Louder and Faster: Pain, Joy, and the Body Politic in Asian American Taiko,* by Deborah Wong
56. *Badges without Borders: How Global Counterinsurgency Transformed American Policing,* by Stuart Schrader
57. *Colonial Migrants at the Heart of Empire: Puerto Rican Workers on U.S. Farms,* by Ismael García Colón
58. *Assimilation: An Alternative History,* by Catherine S. Ramírez

59. *Boyle Heights: How a Los Angeles Neighborhood Became the Future of American Democracy,* by George J. Sánchez
60. *Not Yo' Butterfly: My Long Song of Relocation, Race, Love, and Revolution,* by Nobuko Miyamoto
61. *The Deportation Express: A History of America through Mass Removal,* by Ethan Blue
62. *An Archive of Skin, An Archive of Kin: Disability and Life-Making during Medical Incarceration,* by Adria L. Imada
63. *Menace to Empire: Anticolonial Solidarities and the Transpacific Origins of the US Security State,* by Moon-Ho Jung
64. *Suburban Empire: Cold War Militarization in the US Pacific,* by Lauren Hirshberg
65. *Archipelago of Resettlement: Vietnamese Refugee Settlers across Guam and Israel-Palestine,* by Evyn Lê Espiritu Gandhi
66. *Arise! Global Radicalism in the Era of the Mexican Revolution,* by Christina Heatherton
67. *Resisting Change in Suburbia: Asian Immigrants and Frontier Nostalgia in L.A.,* by James Zarsadiaz
68. *Racial Uncertainties: Mexican Americans, School Desegregation, and the Making of Race in Post–Civil Rights America,* by Danielle R. Olden
69. *Pacific Confluence: Fighting over the Nation in Nineteenth-Century Hawai'i,* by Christen T. Sasaki

Founded in 1893,
UNIVERSITY OF CALIFORNIA PRESS
publishes bold, progressive books and journals
on topics in the arts, humanities, social sciences,
and natural sciences—with a focus on social
justice issues—that inspire thought and action
among readers worldwide.

The UC PRESS FOUNDATION
raises funds to uphold the press's vital role
as an independent, nonprofit publisher, and
receives philanthropic support from a wide
range of individuals and institutions—and from
committed readers like you. To learn more, visit
ucpress.edu/supportus.

www.ingramcontent.com/pod-product-compliance
Lightning Source LLC
Chambersburg PA
CBHW021343230426
43666CB00006B/391